### THE ANATOMY OF THE ALMIGHTY

# what a GOD!

Psalm 18:30

## An Invitation to Divine Intimacy

# RUTH LAWRENCE

*What A God! The Anatomy of the Almighty*
Copyright ©2015
by Ruth Lawrence
All rights reserved

Published by Flock Care Publishers

Printed in the United States of America

No part of this publication may be reproduced, stored in a retrieval system, or transmitted in any form or by any means for commercial purposes—for example, electronic, photocopy, recording—without the prior written permission of the publisher. The only exception is brief quotations in printed reviews.

Churches and other noncommercial interests may reproduce portions of this book without the express written permission of the publisher, provided that the text does not exceed 500 words or 5 percent of the entire book, whichever is less, and that the text is not material quoted from another publisher. When reproducing text from this book, include the following credit line: "From What A God! The Anatomy of the Almighty, published by Flock Care Publishers. Used by permission."

ISBN: 978-976-8260-22-2
         978-976-8260-23-9 (eBook)

Unless otherwise indicated, Scripture quotations are taken from the Holy Bible, New International Version ®, NIV ® Copyright © 1973, 1978, 1984, 2011 by Biblica, Inc. ™ Used by permission of Zondervan. All rights reserved worldwide. www.zondervan.com"

"The "NIV" and "New International Version" are trademarks registered in the United States Patent and Trademark Offices by Biblical, Inc. ™"

Scripture quotations marked (TLB) are taken from The Living Bible copyright © 1971. Used by permission of Tyndale House Publishers, Inc., Carol Stream, Illinois 60188. All rights reserved.

Scripture quotations marked (KJV) are taken from the King James Version of the Bible.

Cover design—Christophe Pierre, DesignbySPIRIT
Editor—Pearl D. Griffith, PDG Publications
Interior design—D.E. West, DustJacket Press

# DEDICATION

Dedicated to Yeshua and to those who crave
a deeper and more intimate walk with Him,
the Lover of our souls.

# CONTENTS

**Foreword** .................................................................................. ix
**Preface** .................................................................................... xv
**Acknowledgments** ................................................................. xvii
**Introduction** ........................................................................... xix
**The Anatomy of God**
    Psalm 18 ............................................................................ xxv

**Chapter 1**
    The Hand of God—Elohim, the Sovereign, Mighty Creator
    "You give me your shield of victory and your right hand
    sustains me…" Psalm 18:35 ................................................. 1

**Chapter 2**
    The Voice of God
    "The LORD thundered from heaven; the voice of the Most
    High resounded." Psalm 18:13 ........................................... 21

**Chapter 3**
    The Eye of God—Jehovah Gmolah—The LORD Who Rewards
    "The LORD has rewarded me according to my
    righteousness according to the cleanness of my hands in His
    sight." Psalm 18:24 ............................................................ 39

**Chapter 4**
    The Heart of God
    "…He rescued me because He delighted in me."
    Psalm 18:19 ........................................................................ 53

**Chapter 5**
    The Face of God—Jehovah Rohi, The LORD My Shepherd
    "…I will sing praises to your name." Psalm 18:49 ................. 73

**Chapter 6**
    The Feet of God
    "He parted the heavens and came down; dark clouds were
    under His feet." Psalm 18:9 ............................................... 85

**Chapter 7**
    The Mind of God
    "As for God, His way is perfect..." Psalm 18:30 ........................ 95

**Chapter 8**
    The Breath of God
    "The valleys of the sea were exposed and the foundations of the earth laid bare at your rebuke, O LORD, at the blast of breath from your nostrils." Psalm 18:15 ................................... 107

**Chapter 9**
    The Ear of God
    "...I cried to my God for help. From His temple He heard my voice; my cry came before Him, into His ears." Psalm 18:6 ............................................................................. 119

**Chapter 10**
    The Fist of God—Your Possession of the Promised Land (Victory) is a Shout Away
    "With your help I can advance against a troop; with my God I can scale a wall...He trains my hands for battle..." Psalm 18:29 & 34 ................................................................... 131

**Chapter 11**
    The Back of God—The Afterglow of His Presence
    "Out of the brightness of His presence clouds advanced..." Psalm 18:12 ............................................................................ 145

**Chapter 12**
    The Arm of God—God is your Jehovah Nissi, Your Banner of Victory
    "...my God is my rock in who I take refuge..." Psalm 18:2 .............................................................................. 157

**Chapter 13**
    The Teeth of God—Trust EvEn in The Heat
    "...my God turns my darkness into light." Psalm 18:28 ............................................................................ 169

**Chapter 14**
    The Side of God—If You Believe You Will Receive
    "He is…the horn of my salvation…" Psalm 18:2 ...................... 179

**Chapter 15**
    The Finger of God—God is in the Details
    "It is God who…makes my way perfect."
    Psalm 18:32 .............................................................................. 187

**Chapter 16**
    The Mouth of God—Jehovah Makkeh, The LORD
    Who Molds Me With His Word
    "…consuming fire came from His mouth…"
    Psalm 18:8 ................................................................................ 211

**Chapter 17**
    The Waist of God—Jehovah Tsidkenu, The LORD
    My Righteousness
    "To the faithful you show yourself faithful…He brought
    me out into a spacious place;…" Psalm 18:25 & 19 ................ 233

**Chapter 18**
    The Hair of God—Jehovah M'Kaddesh, The LORD
    My Sanctifier
    "…to the pure you show yourself pure…"
    Psalm 18:26 .............................................................................. 243

**Chapter 19**
    The Head of God
    "…God is alive…Praise Him…From His temple He
    heard my voice…"
    Psalm 18:6b .............................................................................. 255

**Chapter 20**
    The Forehead of God
    "You save the humble but bring low those whose eyes
    are haughty." Psalm 18:27 ....................................................... 263

**Chapter 21**
    The Thigh of God—El Elyon, God Most High, King of kings, LORD of lords
    "…the God above all gods.."
    Psalm 18:13 ................................................................................ 271

**Summary of the Anatomy** ............................................................ 289
**Anatomy Worship Companion** ..................................................... 301
**Scripture Index** ............................................................................. 323

# FOREWORD

The author of this book is Rev. Ruth Lawrence. She is an ordained minister of the international CHURCH OF THE NAZARENE. My acquaintance with her goes back thirty-one years to 1984 when she was in her early teens. I was the first West Indian to serve as the Caribbean Superintendent of our denomination, then the Pilgrim Holiness Church. Part of my duties was to be chairman of the various district conferences. Ruth Watson, as she was then, was among bright, capable high school students who were specially chosen to be tellers at the Jamaica District Conference. I heard that she and some of her cousins, who later qualified, passionately proposed to become medical doctors. Some years later, I learned that she sensed the *voice* of God calling her to the Christian Ministry; and the *hand* of God resting upon her to be His ministerial servant. My appreciation of her grew when I was informed that instead of pursuing her earlier passion to be a medical doctor, she resolutely accepted God's ministerial selection of her. This commitment established in my mind her deep, Christian integrity. She is a fitting author of this book.

It has been inspiring to observe the *finger* of God in "the details" of her life. She studied at the highly accredited Jamaica Theological Seminary (JTS) for the B. A. in Theology; and was listed in the National Dean's Award, USA. She served as Administrative Assistant to the President of JTS & CGST (Caribbean Graduate School of Theology--Jamaica). She met her Nazarene husband-to-be, who also studied at CGST. They married and were assigned to the Trinidad & Tobago District of the Church of the Nazarene. He began service as the Senior Pastor of the Cumuto Church of the Nazarene; and she, as the Administrative Pastor. Since August 1993 she and her husband have added to their Cumuto pastoral duties serving at the Caribbean Nazarene College (CNC), Trinidad. He is a Professor in the Department of Theology. She has served in various offices: as Registrar, as Director of Admissions & Promotions, as Reservations Coordinator, Work & Witness Coordinator, Office Manager and as Executive Secretary to the President. She is currently serving as the Dean of Student Services Development.

Throughout her life, I have observed that she has been ardent as a student at the *feet* of God and as a seeker of the *face* of God. Through this relationship she was led to study and to share, with a group at her local church, truth concerning the anatomy of God, and to writing this book on this vital subject.

In twenty-one chapters, the book deals with twenty-one components of the anatomy of God. It is perhaps the most extensive presentation of what appears to be limited books on this subject. The author gives a compelling reason why God, Who is Spirit, reveals Himself "in anatomical/anthropomorphical terms." She adds: "It is that we can 'understand' Him even more fully and make intimate connect -ions with Him in worship, in witness and in our walk with Him." The author provides a Summary of the Anatomy of God that is invaluable. Readers will take note of her abundant and helpful use of relevant scriptural references. They must also look out for the arresting personal application provided by the author in relation to each particular part of the anatomy of God. Also invaluable is what the author calls "Anatomy Worship Companion." It suggests appropriate songs and exercises to enhance adoring of God and answers from God. The book contains pithy statements such as "The heart of the matter is the matter of the heart"; and to those who say: "I will obey but conditionally, on my terms," the author reminds that "partial obedience is the half-brother of disobedience."

Through the years, it has been my privilege to have kept in close touch with Rev. Lawrence. I have received the family's "Lawrence Letters" regularly. Knowing of my deep interest in and commitment to holiness, and of my preparing a manuscript to seek to have published a book on *Heartbeats of Holiness: Learning, Living, and Loving the Lofty Life*, she invited me to be one of the speakers at a recent Holiness Summit organized and directed by the Trinidad & Tobago District of the Nazarene Church and CNC. Now a General Superintendent Emeritus of The Wesleyan Holiness Church, the new name of the Pilgrim Holiness Church following merger, I am honoured that she has requested me to prepare the Foreword to her book on the anatomy of God.

Casual readers who skim the book can hardly escape benefits. This book, however, is primarily for serious teachers and their students who will study this exhaustive and enlightening presentation to discover or deepen intimacy with God. To all such, everywhere, I not only heartily commend it. I highly recommend it.

*A. Wingrove Taylor, ThB; AB (GBS); MA in Ministerial Education (IWU); DD (Houghton College, SWU, CGST, and GBS); 2630 Paramount Circle, Carmel, IN 46074; 2013*

"This is what we speak, not in words taught by human wisdom but in words taught by the Spirit, explaining spiritual realities with Spirit-taught words. The person without the Spirit does not accept the things that come from the Spirit of God, but considers them foolishness, and cannot understand them, because they are discerned only through the Spirit."

*– I Corinthians 2:13-14*

# PREFACE

In December 2010, the LORD prompted me to study His "anatomy" to teach in our monthly prayer and fasting sessions for 2011 at the Cumuto Church of the Nazarene. In each session, after we examined an aspect of the anatomy of God, we would then go into a time of worship with songs dealing specifically with that part.

We started in January 2011 with the *hand* of God and in February 2011 we looked at the *voice* of God, continuing throughout the remainder of the year exploring the anatomy of God. As a part of the session in February, the LORD directed me to do two exercises. The first was to instruct that each person should listen to the *voice* of God for themselves. Secondly, each person was to listen to the voice of God for someone else and then share with that individual what the LORD told them.

After our session that morning, Minister Samuel George approached me and hesitantly said: "I am not sure how you will receive this but the voice of God told me that you should put this material together so that our people can get this teaching". Rev. Alicia Baptiste happened to be standing beside us at the time and animatedly confirmed that the LORD had told her the same thing. Receiving it as from the LORD, I pondered it in my heart.

It was an exciting journey for us because we never knew which aspect of His anatomy He wanted us to look at next until we completed each monthly session.

In my preparation of this material I discovered two biblical characters, David and Job, who both displayed unusual revelation and understanding about the anatomy of God. However, it was the Psalmist David, whom God described as a man after His own heart, whose material has covered every part of the anatomy in this study. Interestingly enough, the LORD revealed to me that Psalm 18 has every aspect of the anatomy covered in this study.

As you study God's anatomy, my prayer is that your spiritual journey, but more specifically, your prayer life, will be rejuvenated and grow to greater heights.

*Ruth Lawrence*

# ACKNOWLEDGMENTS

I want to express my deepest gratitude to the team that helped to make this book a reality:

- Adonai, my LORD and Master for His Hand directing me to study this aspect of Him so that His people can experience deeper intimacy with Him;

- Ministers Samuel George and Alicia Baptiste who listened to the Voice of God and relayed to me that the LORD wanted me to put this material in book form so that His people could benefit from the information that was being shared;

- Cumuto Church of the Nazarene's Intercessory Prayer Group (2011-2012) whose interest in the study encouraged me to keep studying;

- My family, Mark, Matthew and Rachel who supported me during the preparation and presentation of this material;

- My editor, Pearl D. Griffith for allowing the Finger of God to take care of the details; for asking the Breath of God to breathe on this work and those who will read it, and for relying on the Arm of God that undergirded her and gave her finishing strength. Thank you Sis. Pearl for your partnership in this divine assignment;

- Dr. Wingrove Taylor, a spiritual mentor, for his foreword and blessing of this study;

- My wonderful parents, Rudolph and Eslin Watson, whose assistance made this project possible…thank you Daddy & Mummy.

# INTRODUCTION

"Anthropomorphism is the use of human characteristics to describe something or someone else e.g. the tree raises its arms to the sky. When we speak of God's hands or His feet we are describing God with anthropomorphic language" (*Knowing God Better* Woodrow Kroll pg. 15). Why then does God express Himself in anatomical/anthropomorphic terms? Why does He say in Exodus 33:20-23 "…then I will remove my hand and you shall see my back but not my face…"It is that we can "understand" Him even more fully and make intimate connections with Him in worship, in witness, and in our walk with Him.

God is a Spirit and they that worship Him must worship Him in spirit and in truth. We are made in God's image according to Genesis 1:26, therefore, we can speak of God's anatomy just as truthfully as we can speak of our own. In fact, even though we know that God is Spirit (John 4:24), we also have God's permission to think and speak of Him in physical terms. This doesn't mean that God is a giant person in terms of size. Rather, it means that every human component reflects a characteristic of God. God isn't like us; we have the privilege of being like Him. We are made in His image.

Additionally, this study will help us to make more intelligent petitions to the appropriate aspects of God that address our specific needs. For example, if you are not feeling well you will go to a doctor in order to receive a correct diagnosis. If you have a toothache, a general practitioner may probably prescribe something for the pain but not deal specifically with your problem. If you have a toothache, it would be wise to go to a dentist who specializes in that specific area of your concern. Or, if you are suffering from back pain, a visit to a chiropractor or a specialist in the nature of such a problem, can be helpful. So too with the LORD, to Whom we pray generally about ALL of our needs.

There are some aspects of His anatomy, however, that the LORD has revealed about Himself that address specific needs in our lives. For example, when we examine in our study the *breath* of God, we will learn that God breathes on political situations like a whirlwind; against unjust situations like a flood, and against difficult situations like a Category 10 hurricane. So, when faced with situations such as those mentioned, don't merely ask God to intervene. Instead, ask Him to breathe on them. It makes a big difference! Specifically address the *breath* of God to deal with that situation!!! And deal with it, He will! **What a God! (Psalm 18:30 TLB)**

This is in stark contrast to what we see in Psalm 115:4-8:

> *4 But their idols are silver and gold made by human hands.*
> *5 They have mouths, but cannot speak,*
> *eyes, but they cannot see;*
> *6 they have ears, but cannot hear,*
> *noses, but they cannot smell;*
> *7 they have hands, but cannot feel,*
> *feet, but they cannot walk;*
> *nor can they utter a sound with their throats.*
> *8 Those who make them will be like them*
> *and so will all who trust in them.*

So when do we engage in prayer the *finger* of God? Or, when do we employ in prayer the *feet* of God? And when do we petition in prayer the *arm* of God? This book will address all this and more.

The order in which each part of the anatomy is presented in this book is the order in which each member of the anatomy was revealed to the author. I asked the LORD why He had revealed the different parts of His anatomy in the order that He did, and this was His response:

1. The *hand* of God, which is the first aspect of God's anatomy to be addressed, is the only member of the anatomy that deals specifically with a call to salvation. So, as you read that first chapter, if you are not a Christian, embrace the opportunity to surrender your life to God before engaging the other powerful aspects of God's anatomy. It would be a great thing to have a personal relationship with the One whose anatomy you are going to study. This will make the study much more engaging and spiritually dynamic.

2. The second aspect that we will study is the *voice* of God. When we come into the understanding and appreciation of listening to and obeying the voice of God, we then position ourselves to receive and embrace the revelation regarding the other aspects of His anatomy.

3. The last aspect of God's anatomy that we will study is the *thigh* of God, which looks at God as El Elyon—the God Most High. As we come to the end of the study, we conclude that our God is still triumphant, still victorious, still awesome, still incomparable, the indisputable Champion because He remains El Elyon, the KING of kings, GOD of gods, and LORD of lords!!! There is none like Him, and none can compare!

For each part of this study of the anatomy of God there is a personal application, and, for every believer, a personal benefit to be derived from each component studied.

I have also included a helpful *Anatomy Worship Companion* at the end which provides a suggested format for studying the components of the Anatomy of God.

Finally, to prayerfully approach every chapter of this study, will make an eternal difference to you.

## PRAYER

**LORD, I pray that your teaching will fall like rain
And your words descend like dew,
like showers on new grass;
like abundant rain on tender plants.**
*Deuteronomy 32:2*

# THE ANATOMY OF GOD

References to every part of the anatomy of God are dealt with in this study beginning with the title "What a God He is!" found in Psalm 18:30 (TLB).

Psalm 18 is a song of deliverance which David sang to the LORD when the LORD delivered him from the hand of all his enemies and from the hand of Saul. This song of David is also preserved with minor variations in II Samuel 22. Apart from the introduction, a prelude of praise (verses 1-3) and the conclusion (verses 46-50), in its structure, the song itself is composed of three major divisions:

1. **The LORD's deliverance of David from his mortal enemies** (verses 4-19): The LORD came to the aid of His servant—depicted as a fearful theophany (divine manifestation) of the heavenly Warrior descending in wrathful attack upon David's enemies.

2. **The moral grounds for the LORD's saving help** (verses 20-29): David's righteousness is rewarded. David's assertion of his righteousness (like that of Samuel, Hezekiah and Job) is not a pretentious boast of sinless perfection. Rather, it is a claim that, in contrast to his enemies, he has devoted himself - his heart and life - to the service of the LORD, and that his godliness has been with integrity—the fruit that attests to God's gracious

working in his heart. This authentic righteousness characterizes persons alive in Christ by the Spirit.

3. **The LORD's help recounted** (verses 30-45): With God's help David has crushed all his foes. God has made David the head of nations. He, who had been, it seemed, on the brink of death, sinking into the depths, by God's interventions and blessings in David's behalf have shown him to be the living God. (NIV Text Note)

The whole song is to be understood in the context of David's official capacity and the LORD's covenant with him. What David claims in this grand conclusion—as indeed, in the whole psalm—has been and is being fulfilled in Jesus Christ, David's great descendant.

# PSALM 18

*(Introduction)*

**For the director of music.
Of David the servant of the L<small>ORD</small>.
He sang to the L<small>ORD</small> the words of this song
when the L<small>ORD</small> delivered
him from the hand of all his enemies
and from the hand of Saul. He said:**

*(A prelude of praise)*

¹ I love you, L<small>ORD</small>, my strength.
² The L<small>ORD</small> is my rock, my fortress and my deliverer;
my God is my rock, in whom I take refuge,
my shield and the horn of my salvation, my stronghold.
³ I called to the L<small>ORD</small>, who is worthy of praise,
and I have been saved from my enemies.

*(The LORD's deliverance of David from his mortal enemies)*

⁴ The cords of death entangled me;
the torrents of destruction overwhelmed me.
⁵ The cords of the grave coiled around me;

    the snares of death confronted me.
 ⁶ In my distress I called to the Lord;
    I cried to my God for help.
 From his temple he heard my voice;
    my cry came before him, into his ears.
 ⁷ The earth trembled and quaked,
 and the foundations of the mountains shook;
    they trembled because he was angry.
 ⁸ Smoke rose from his nostrils;
    consuming fire came from his mouth,
    burning coals blazed out of it.
 ⁹ He parted the heavens and came down;
    dark clouds were under his feet.
 ¹⁰ He mounted the cherubim and flew;
    he soared on the wings of the wind.
 ¹¹ He made darkness his covering, his canopy around him—
    the dark rain clouds of the sky.

 ¹² Out of the brightness of his presence clouds advanced,
    with hailstones and bolts of lightning.
 ¹³ The Lord thundered from heaven;
    the voice of the Most High resounded.
 ¹⁴ He shot his arrows and scattered the enemy,
    with great bolts of lightning he routed them.
 ¹⁵ The valleys of the sea were exposed
 and the foundations of the earth laid bare
    at your rebuke, Lord,
    at the blast of breath from your nostrils.

 ¹⁶ He reached down from on high and took hold of me;
    he drew me out of deep waters.
 ¹⁷ He rescued me from my powerful enemy,

    from my foes, who were too strong for me.
<sup>18</sup> They confronted me in the day of my disaster,
    but the LORD was my support.
<sup>19</sup> He brought me out into a spacious place;
    he rescued me because he delighted in me.

*(The moral grounds for the LORD's saving help)*

<sup>20</sup> The LORD has dealt with me according to my righteousness;
    according to the cleanness of my hands he has rewarded me.
<sup>21</sup> For I have kept the ways of the LORD;
    I am not guilty of turning from my God.
<sup>22</sup> All his laws are before me;
    I have not turned away from his decrees.
<sup>23</sup> I have been blameless before him
    and have kept myself from sin.
<sup>24</sup> The LORD has rewarded me according to my righteousness,
    according to the cleanness of my hands in his sight.

<sup>25</sup> To the faithful you show yourself faithful,
    to the blameless you show yourself blameless,
<sup>26</sup> to the pure you show yourself pure,
    but to the devious you show yourself shrewd.
<sup>27</sup> You save the humble
    but bring low those whose eyes are haughty.
<sup>28</sup> You, LORD, keep my lamp burning;
    my God turns my darkness into light.
<sup>29</sup> With your help I can advance against a troop;
    with my God I can scale a wall.

*(The LORD's help recounted)*

³⁰ As for God, his way is perfect:
The Lord's word is flawless;
he shields all who take refuge in him.
³¹ For who is God besides the Lord?
And who is the Rock except our God?
³² It is God who arms me with strength
and keeps my way secure.
³³ He makes my feet like the feet of a deer;
he causes me to stand on the heights.
³⁴ He trains my hands for battle;
my arms can bend a bow of bronze.
³⁵ You make your saving help my shield,
and your right hand sustains me;
your help has made me great.
³⁶ You provide a broad path for my feet,
so that my ankles do not give way.

³⁷ I pursued my enemies and overtook them;
I did not turn back till they were destroyed.
³⁸ I crushed them so that they could not rise;
they fell beneath my feet.
³⁹ You armed me with strength for battle;
you humbled my adversaries before me.
⁴⁰ You made my enemies turn their backs in flight,
and I destroyed my foes.
⁴¹ They cried for help, but there was no one to save them—
to the Lord, but he did not answer.
⁴² I beat them as fine as windblown dust;
I trampled them like mud in the streets.
⁴³ You have delivered me from the attacks of the people;
you have made me the head of nations.
People I did not know now serve me,

⁴⁴ foreigners cower before me;
as soon as they hear of me, they obey me.
⁴⁵ They all lose heart;
they come trembling from their strongholds.

*(Conclusion)*

⁴⁶ The Lord lives! Praise be to my Rock!
Exalted be God my Savior!
⁴⁷ He is the God who avenges me,
who subdues nations under me,
⁴⁸ who saves me from my enemies.
You exalted me above my foes;
from a violent man you rescued me.
⁴⁹ Therefore I will praise you, Lord, among the nations;
I will sing the praises of your name.

⁵⁰ He gives his king great victories;
he shows unfailing love to his anointed,
to David and to his descendants forever.

CHAPTER 1

# THE HAND OF GOD
Elohim, the Sovereign, Mighty Creator

*"You give me your shield of victory and your right hand sustains me..."*
*Psalm 18:35*

Shouts of joy and victory
resound in the tents of the righteous:
"The Lord's right hand has done mighty things!
[16] The Lord's right hand is lifted high;
the Lord's right hand has done mighty things!"
*Psalm 118:15-16*

### A. THE HAND OF GOD REFLECTS HIS POWER...

**Joshua 4:21-24** [21] He said to the Israelites, "In the future when your descendants ask their parents, 'What do these stones mean?' [22] tell them, 'Israel crossed the Jordan on dry ground.' ²³ For the Lord your God dried up the Jordan before you until you had crossed over. The Lord your God did to the Jordan what he had done to the Red Sea when he dried it up before us until we had crossed over. ²⁴ He did this so that all the peoples of the earth might know that the hand of the Lord is powerful and so that you might always fear the Lord your God."

**I Kings 8:42**

"…for they will hear of your mighty hand…" i.e. of God's great power demonstrated by His interventions in the history of His people."

**Job 36:26,32 (TLB)**

"God is so great that we cannot begin to know Him…See how He spreads the lightning around Him…He fills His hands with lightning bolts. He hurls each at its target…" God works with equal effectiveness with either hand.

**Psalm 21:8**

Your hand will lay hold on all your enemies; your right hand will seize your foes.

**Psalm 89:13 (TLB)**

"Strong is your arm! Strong is your hand! Your right hand is lifted high in glorious strength.

**Isaiah 26:11**

"…your hand is lifted high but they do not see it." This is a sign of power.

**Daniel 8:25 (TLB)**

He will be a master of deception, defeating many by catching them off guard as they bask in false security. Without warning he will destroy them. So great will he fancy himself to be that he will even take on the Prince of Princes in battle; but in so doing he will seal his own doom, for he shall be broken by the hand of God, though no human means could overpower him.

## Habakkuk 3:4 (TLB)

From His hands flash rays of brilliant light. He rejoices in His awesome power.

## Revelation 1:16

In His right hand He held seven stars...

### 1. TO SAVE

## Exodus 13:3

"The LORD brought you out of it with a mighty hand."

Exodus 15 is a hymn celebrating God's spectacular victory over Pharaoh and his army. The focus of the song is God Himself:

- He has hurled into the sea (v.1,4)
- The LORD is my strength and my defense (v.2)
- The LORD is a warrior (v.3)
- Your right hand, O LORD was majestic in power (v.6)
- Your right hand, O LORD, shattered the enemy (v.6)
- You threw down those who opposed you (v.7)
- You stretch out your right hand and the earth swallows your enemies (v.12)

## Job 10:7

"...no one can rescue me from your hand."

Paul also understood how to appropriate the hand of God in his life. In what situations would you appeal to the hand of God?

## II Corinthians 1:8-10 (TLB)

"I think you ought to know, dear brothers, about the hard time we went through in Asia. We were really crushed and overwhelmed, and feared we would never live through it. We felt we were doomed to die and saw how powerless we were to help ourselves; but that was good, for then we put everything into the hands of God, who alone could save us from a terrible death."

## 2. TO CREATE & SUSTAIN

Two facets of God make up the word Elohim:
- total power, might, complete sovereignty, and
- complete creativity.

In using the name Elohim, Genesis 1:1 makes the statement that tremendous, unimaginable power is involved in the force of God's creativity. ***(Hickey)***

**Job 10:8-9**

Your hands shaped me and made me…you molded me like clay…

**Job 12:10**

In His hand is the life of every creature and the breath of all mankind.

**Job 34:19**

"…who shows no partiality to princes and does not favour the rich over the poor for they are all the work of His hands"

**Psalm 19:1**

The heavens declare the glory of God the skies proclaim the work of his hands.

**Psalm 74:17 (TLB)**

"…all nature is within your hands…"

**Psalm 95:4-5**

"In His hand are the depths of the earth and the mountain peaks belong to Him. 5 The sea is His for He made it and His hands formed the dry land…"

**Proverbs 30:4 (TLB)**

"…who has gathered up the wind in the hollow of His hands…"

**Isaiah 40:12**

"…who has measured the waters in the hollow of His hand…"

**Isaiah 48:13 (TLB)**

"…It was my hand that laid the foundations of the earth, and the palm of my right hand spread out the heavens above."

## Isaiah 64:8
Yet, O LORD, you are our Potter. We are the clay and you are the Potter; we are all formed byyour hand.

## Isaiah 66:2
"My hand has made both earth and skies.

## Acts 7:49-50
"Heaven is my throne, and the earth is my footstool. What kind of house will you build for me?" says the LORD. "Or where will my resting place be? Has not my hand made all these things?"

### 3. TO HEAL

## Exodus 16:3
If only we had died by the LORD's hand in Egypt.

## Job 5:18 (TLB)
"…He injures but His hands also heal."

## Luke 4:40
"…the people brought to Jesus all who had various kinds of sickness, and laying His hands on each one, He healed them.

## Luke 7:16 (TLB)
The story of Jesus raising a widow's son from the dead "A great fear swept the crowd, and they exclaimed with praises to God, "…we have seen the hand of God at work today."

## Acts 4:30
Stretch out your hand to heal and perform signs and wonders through the name of your holy servant Jesus.

## B. THE HAND OF GOD REFLECTS HIS PROTECTION…

### 1. FROM YOUR ENEMIES

## Ezra 8:22-23 & 31
I was ashamed to ask the king for soldiers and horsemen to protect us from enemies on the road, because we had told the king,

"The gracious hand of our God is on everyone who looks to him, but his great anger is against all who forsake him." ²³ So we fasted and petitioned our God about this, and he answered our prayer… On the twelfth day of the first month we set out from the Ahava Canal to go to Jerusalem. The hand of our God was on us, and he protected us from enemies and bandits along the way.

**Psalm 17:7**

"…you who save by your right hand, those who take refuge in you from their foes…"

**Psalm 81:11-14 (TLB)**

"But no, my people won't listen. Israel doesn't want me around. So I am letting them go their blind and stubborn way, living according to their own desires…oh that my people would listen to me…How quickly then I would subdue her enemies! How soon my hands would be upon her foes."

**Psalm 121:6-7 (TLB)**

Jehovah protects you day and night. He keeps you from all evil and preserves your life.

**Psalm 125:2 (TLB)**

Just as the mountains surround and protect Jerusalem so the Lord surrounds and protects His people.

**Isaiah 49:2 (TLB)**

"…in the shadow of His hand He hid me…"

As spirit beings we have diplomatic immunity like the earthly diplomats who sometimes seek refuge at their embassies. David understood this concept of diplomatic immunity when in Psalm 18:2 he said, "The LORD is my fort where I can enter and be safe, no one can follow me in or slay me."

**Isaiah 51:16**

"…I have put words in your mouth and covered you with the shadow of my hand…"

David knew exactly which characteristic of God to appeal to when faced with particular situations. When he was under attack by ungodly foes in the accounts of I Samuel 21-24 David appealed to the LORD as judge in Psalm 17:14 "O LORD, by your hand save me from such people."

**Psalm 31:20 (TLB)**

"Hide your loved ones in the shelter of your presence, safe beneath your hand, safe from all conspiring men."

**Psalm 138:7**

"...you stretch out your hand against the anger of my foes, with your right hand you save me."

### 2. FROM HIS GLORY

**Exodus 33:22-23**

"When my glory passes by, I will put you in a cleft in the rock and cover you with my hand until I have passed by. Then I will remove my hand and you will see my back."

### 3. FROM UNJUST SITUATIONS

**I Peter 2:23 (TLB)**

"...when He (Christ) suffered He did not threaten to get even; He left His case in the hands of God who always judges fairly."

## C. THE HAND OF GOD REFLECTS HIS PROVISION

### 1. OF OUR POSSESSIONS/BLESSINGS

Whatever you can think of that you possess has come because of the hand of God.

**I Chronicles 29:14**

Everything comes from you, and we have given you only what comes from your hand.

**I Chronicles 29:16**

"…as for all this abundance…it comes from your hand, and all of it belongs to you.."

**Psalm 44:2-3**

"With your hand you drove out the nations and planted our ancestors; you crushed the peoples and made our ancestors flourish. It was not by their sword that they won the land, nor did their arm bring them victory; it was your right hand, your arm, and the light of your face, for you loved them."

**Psalm 104:28 (TLB)**

"…you open wide your hand to feed them and they are satisfied with all your bountiful provision."

**Psalm 145:16**

"…you open your hand and satisfy the desires of every living thing."

**Ecclesiastes 2:24-26 (TLB)**

"So I decided that there was nothing better for a man to do than to enjoy his food and drink and his job. Then I realized that even this pleasure is from the hand of God. For who can eat or enjoy apart from Him.

## 2. OF HIS FAVOUR

**Ezra 7:6**

The king had granted him everything he asked for the hand of the Lord His God was on him.

**Ezra 7:9**

"…he arrived in Jerusalem on the first day of the 5th month for the gracious hand of His God was on him."

**Ezra 8:18**

Because the gracious hand of our God was on us they brought us…a capable man…

**Ezra 7:27-28**

Praise be to the LORD, the God of our ancestors, who has put it into the king's heart to bring honour to the house of the Lord in Jerusalem in this way and who has extended His good favour to me before the king and his advisors…because the hand of the LORD my God was on me, I took courage and gathered leaders from Israel to go with me.

**Proverbs 21:1 (TLB)** confirms that the king's heart is in the hand of the LORD; He directs it like a watercourse wherever He pleases.

**Nehemiah 2:7-8**

If it pleases the king, may I have letters to the governors…and may I have a letter to Asaph…And because the gracious hand of my God was upon me, the king granted my requests.

**Nehemiah 2:18**

I also told them about the gracious hand of my God upon me…

### 3. OF HIS PROMISES

**II Chronicles 6:15**

You have kept your promise to your servant David my father; with your mouth you have promised and with your hand you have fulfilled it.

**Ezekiel 47:14 (TLB)**

"I promised with hand raised in oath of truth…"

### 4. OF HIS STRENGTH

**Psalm 63:8**

"…your right hand upholds me…"

**Psalm 16:8 (TLB)**

"… Because He is at my right hand, I will not be shaken…"

**Psalm 18:35 (TLB)**

"…you give me your shield of victory and your right hand sustains me…"

**Isaiah 41:10**

"So do not fear for I am with you; do not be dismayed, for I am your God. I will strengthen you and help you; I will uphold you with my righteous right hand."

## 5. OF GUIDANCE

**Psalm 139:9-10 (TLB)**

"If I ride the morning winds to the farthest oceans, even there your hand will guide me…"

**Ezekiel 40:1**

"…on that very day the hand of the LORD was upon me…"

## 6. OF DIVINE REVELATION

"…the hand of the LORD was strong upon me…" A phrase repeated 6 times in Ezekiel 3:14, 22, 8:1, 33:22, 37:1; 40:1 indicating an overpowering experience of divine revelation from the hand of God.

a. 3:22 "…I was helpless in the hand of God…"
b. 8:1 "…the hand of the Sovereign LORD came upon me there…"
c. 33:22 "…now the hand of the LORD had been upon me the previous evening and he had healed me so that I could speak again…"
d. 37:1 "The hand of the LORD was upon me and He brought me out by the Spirit of the LORD and set me in the middle of a valley…"

**Jeremiah 1:9**

Then the LORD reached out His hand and touched my mouth and said, "Now I have put my words in your mouth…"

### 7. TO ANIMALS

**Isaiah 34:17**

Desert creatures will meet with hyenas, and wild goats will bleat to each other; there the night creatures will also lie down. [15] The owl will nest there and lay eggs, she will hatch them, and care for her young under the shadow of her wings; there also the falcons will gather, each with its mate. He allots their portions; His hand distributes them by measure.

## D. THE HAND OF GOD REFLECTS HIS PERSONAL CARE

**Zechariah 10:12**

"The Lord says, I will make my people strong with power from me! They will go wherever they wish and wherever they go, they will be under my personal care."

**Deuteronomy 33:3** reminds us "surely it is you who love the people, all the holy ones are in your hand." We are the LORD's treasured possession.

### 1. OF YOUR SOUL...

**Job 12:10 (TLB)**

"For the soul of every living thing is in the hand of God."

### 2. OF YOUR SECURITY...

**Psalm 1:9-11**

"...Therefore my heart is glad and my tongue rejoices; my body also will rest secure, [10] because you will not abandon me to the realm of the dead, nor will you let your Faithful One see decay. [11] You make known to me the path of life; you will fill me with joy in your presence, with eternal pleasures at your right hand. You fill me with joy in your presence with eternal pleasures at your right hand..." David speaks here of the life he now enjoys by the gracious provision and care of God.

### 3. OF YOUR LIFE…

**Psalm 31:15**

"My times are in your hands…" All the events and circumstances of life are in the hands of the LORD. David understood this and could say in 31:5 Into your hands I commit my spirit. This is the climactic expression of trust in the LORD, thus entrusting to God's care, his very life.

### 4. OF YOUR STEPS…

**Psalm 37:23-24 (TLB)**

"If the LORD delights in a man's way He makes his steps firm; though he stumble, he will not fall, for the LORD upholds him with His hand."

### 5. OF HIS CHILDREN…

**Psalm 48:10 (TLB)**

"…your right hand is filled with righteous acts."

### 6. OF HIS BRIDE…

**Isaiah 62:3**

You will be a crown of splendor in the LORD's hand, a royal diadem in the hand of your God.

### 7. OF YOUR FUTURE…

**Luke 1:66 (TLB)**

And everyone who heard about it thought long thoughts and asked, "I wonder what this child will turn out to be? For the hand of the LORD is surely upon him in some special way."

## 8. OF YOU...

**Isaiah 49:15-16**

I will not forget you! See, I have engraved you on the palms of my hands.

## PERSONAL APPLICATION

That last verse encompasses our personal application for the hand of God. When we need to write a number or some important information that we don't want to forget, when we have no paper handy, what do we do? We write it in the palm of our hands so that we can retrieve the important information later on when needed (i.e. provided we have not washed it off). He has it engraved, not written in ink.

In Psalm 77 the Psalmist David faced a time of great personal distress, and anguished bewilderment. He thought about the former days, the years of long ago:

> ⁶ I remembered my songs in the night.
> My heart meditated and my spirit asked:⁷
> "Will the LORD reject forever?
> Will he never show his favor again?
> ⁸ Has his unfailing love vanished forever?
> Has his promise failed for all time?
> ⁹ Has God forgotten to be merciful?
> Has he in anger withheld his compassion?"

As David in his distress continued to remember the former days, in verses 11-20, he said:

> I will remember the deeds of the LORD;
> YES, I WILL REMEMBER YOUR MIRACLES OF LONG AGO.
> ¹² I will consider all your works
> and meditate on all your mighty deeds.

> ¹³ Your ways, O God, are holy.
> What god is as great as our God?
> ¹⁴ You are the God who performs miracles;
> you display your power among the peoples.
> ¹⁵ With your mighty arm you redeemed your people.

With this comforting recollection, David pulls himself out of his distress, and says, "To this I will appeal: the years of the right hand of the Most High."

You have read about the hand of God and now you know all that, as a believer, you have access to in the hand of God. At those low points in your walk with God, like the Psalmist David, remember all that the hand of God has done for you and appeal to the years of the right hand of the Most High. When we pray, let us thank the LORD for His Hand in our lives as evidenced by His power, His protection, His provision and His personal care.

You have learnt that the hand of God reflects His power, His protection, His provision, and His personal care. I want to challenge you further to the real issue at hand. That issue is not our awareness of all that the hand of God reflects but it is rather that we do not seek the power, protection, provision and personal care from HIS hand. Sometimes we look for covering from the wrong sources.

**Isaiah 30:1-4 (TLB)**

"Woe to the obstinate children, declares the LORD, you ask advice from everyone but me and decide to do what I don't want you to do. You yoke yourselves with unbelievers (form alliances but not by my Spirit NIV) thus piling up your sins. For without consulting me you have gone down to Egypt to find aid and have put your trust in Pharaoh for his protection. But in trusting Pharaoh you will be disappointed, humiliated and disgraced, for he can't deliver on his promises to save you. For though his power extends to Zoan and Hanes yet it will all turn out to your shame—he won't help one little bit!"

### Isaiah 31:1-2,4 (NIV)

Woe to those who go down to Egypt for help who rely on horses who trust in the multitude of their chariots and in the great strength of their horsemen but do not look to the Holy One of Israel or seek help from the LORD…But the Egyptians are mere mortals and not God; their horses are flesh and not spirit. When the LORD stretches out His hand, those who help will stumble, those who are helped will fall, both will perish together.

The proof of this is seen in II Kings 24:1a, II Chronicles 36:6 and II Kings 24:7

After the Egyptian defeat at Carchemish (Jeremiah 46:2) in 605 B.C., Jehoiakim transferred allegiance to Nebuchadnezzar of Babylon. When Jehoiakim later rebelled, he again allied himself with Egypt. During Jehoiakim's reign Nebuchadnezzar King of Babylon invaded Judah, attacked Jehoiakim and bound him with bronze shackles to take him to Babylon. The king of Egypt did not march out from his own country again (to assist Jehoiakim) because the king of Babylon had taken all his territory (NIV Text Note).

## E. THE HAND OF GOD REFLECTS HIS POURING OUT OF JUDGMENT

### Deuteronomy 2:14-15 (TLB)

" So it took us 38 years to finally get across Zered Brook from Kadesh! For the LORD had decreed that this could not happen until all the men, who 38 years earlier were old enough to bear arms, had died. Yes, the hand of the LORD was against them until finally all were dead."

### Job 4:8-9 (TLB)

"Experience teaches that it is those who sow sin and trouble who harvest the same. They die beneath the hand of God."

**Job 27:13-23 (TLB)**

"This is the fate awaiting the wicked from the hand of the Almighty…"

**Psalm 39:10-11 (TLB)**

"LORD, don't hit me anymore—I am exhausted beneath your hand. When you punish a man for his sins, he is destroyed…"

**Psalm 75:8**

"…in the hand of the LORD is a cup full of foaming wine mixed with spices, He pours it out and all the wicked of the earth drink it down to its very dregs." The spices used increased the intoxicating effect. It is drunk down because God pours it out Himself. They have no choice.

**Isaiah 5:25**

Therefore the LORD's anger burns against His people; His hand is raised and He strikes them down. The mountains shake and the dead bodies are like refuse in the streets. Yet for all this, His anger is not turned away; His hand is still upraised.

**Isaiah 14:26-27**

This is the plan determined for the whole world; this is the hand stretched out over all nations. For the LORD Almighty has purposed and who can thwart Him? His hand is stretched out and who can turn it back?

**Isaiah 19:16**

In that day the Egyptians will become weaklings. They will shudder with fear at the uplifted hand that the LORD Almighty raises against them.

**Isaiah 31:2b-3 (TLB)**

He will rise up against the house of the wicked, against those who help evildoers. But the Egyptians are men and not God; their horses are flesh and not spirit. When the LORD stretches out His hand, he who helps will stumble, he who is helped will fall; both will perish together.

**Isaiah 43:13**

"...no one can deliver out of my hand. When I act, who can reverse it?"

**Isaiah 51:17**

Awake...you who have drunk from the hand of God." Experiencing God's judgment is often compared to becoming drunk on strong wine. It is the fate of wicked nations in particular.

**Jeremiah 25:12-17**

But when the seventy years are fulfilled, I will punish the king of Babylon and his nation, the land of the Babylonians for their guilt," declares the LORD, "and will make it desolate forever. [13] I will bring upon that land all the things I have spoken against it, all that are written in this book and prophesied by Jeremiah against all the nations. [14] They themselves will be enslaved by many nations and great kings; I will repay them according to their deeds and the work of their hands."[15] This is what the LORD, the God of Israel, said to me: "Take from my hand this cup filled with the wine of my wrath and make all the nations to whom I send you drink it. [16] When they drink it, they will stagger and go mad because of the sword I will send among them."[17] So I took the cup from the LORD's hand and made all the nations to whom he sent me drink it.

**Ezekiel 44:12 (TLB)**

Because they have encouraged the people to worship other gods...I have raised my hand and taken oath that they must be punished.

**Habakkuk 2:16**

The cup from the LORD's right hand is coming around to you and disgrace will cover your glory.

**Zephaniah 3:14-15 (TLB)**

Sing...shout...be glad and rejoice...for the LORD will remove His hand of judgment and disperse the armies of your enemy.

**Acts 13:9-11 (TLB)**

"God has laid His hand of punishment upon you (Elymas the sorcerer) and you will be stricken awhile with blindness."

**Hebrews 10:30-31**

The LORD will judge His people. It is a dreadful thing to fall into the hands of the Living God.

## F. THE HAND OF GOD REFLECTS HIS PIERCED HANDS

Luke 24 tells of two disciples who left Jerusalem to go to their home in the village of Emmaus. As they walked, they talked about recent events. A lot had happened in one week. Seven days before, Jesus had arrived triumphantly in the city of David. Before the week ended, He had been arrested, tried, crucified and put in a tomb. That very morning, rumors of Jesus' resurrection had spread like wildfire.

Trudging along, they didn't notice this fellow traveler until He asked them about their conversation and their obvious grief. One of them, Cleopas, couldn't believe someone who had been in Jerusalem would be unaware of the events that had occurred. Upon hearing their account of what had happened, their new companion then proceeded to amaze them with His ability to explain the Scriptures and how they related to the Christ. The trip flew by, and the two convinced the stranger to join them for the night.

At supper, the stranger, in a very familiar way, gave thanks for the meal and began to break the bread. At that moment, they finally noticed His hands—freshly scarred. Then they knew who He was. Those pierced hands had given Him away. As he said to Thomas "Put your finger here; see my hands…"

Like those disciples, the last thing we notice about God—His pierced hands—represents His deepest expression of love for us. He was wounded for us, that our wounds might be healed. He suffered in our place that our sins might be truly forgiven. God's pierced hands demonstrate His personal, intimate involvement in your life.

Let our prayer today be, "LORD, please help me to never lose awareness of Your pierced hands." If you have not accepted this wonderful, awesome Jesus as the LORD and Saviour of your life, you are not only missing out on the blessings that come with the hand of God, but you are making a choice to keep yourself in an uncomfortable state.

Listen to the Psalmist David:

> *Psalm 32:3-5 (TLB) "There was a time when I wouldn't admit what a sinner I was. But my dishonesty made me miserable and filled my days with frustration. All day and all night your hand was heavy on me. My strength evaporated like water on a sunny day until I finally admitted all my sins to you and stopped trying to hide them. I said to myself, "I will confess them to the LORD." And you forgave me! All my guilt is gone."*

> *Psalm 32:1-2 (TLB) "What happiness for those whose guilt has been forgiven! What joys when sins are covered over! What relief for those who have confessed their sins and God has cleared their record!"*

In order to get into a relationship with the LORD as Saviour of your life, do this:

**A**ccept what He is saying to your heart right now;
**B**elieve Him by faith and;
**C**onfess by repeating the following prayer:

> **I am a sinner who needs you Jesus. You died on the cross to deliver me from sin and the power of the devil. Please forgive me of all my sins. I acknowledge you. I accept you as my LORD and Saviour. Fill me with the power of the Holy Spirit.**

**Help me to live righteously until I see you face to face. I declare that I am a child of God. I declare that I am a Christian. Thank you Lord for forgiving me! Thank you LORD for cleansing me with your precious blood that flowed from Calvary! Now I know I am forgiven! Now I know that I am cleansed! I am your child. Amen!**

If you have said that prayer and opened your heart to the LORD, tell someone about it right now. Your next step will be to find a church in your community that helps with your spiritual growth.

*Today is in God's hands and so are you.*

*His hands are strong and will uphold you;*
*His hands are great and will enfold you;*
*His hands are gentle and will embrace you;*
*His hands are protective and will cover you;*
*His hands are reassuring and will quiet you;*
*His hands are powerful and will defend you;*
*His hands are parental and will train you;*
*His hands are masterful and will conform you;*
*His hands are compassionate and will care for you;*
*His hands are healing and will renew you;*
*His hands are calming and will comfort you;*
*His hands are giving and will bless you.*

*The hands that hold you will never let you down.*

*Roy Lessin, DaySpring*

CHAPTER 2

# THE VOICE OF GOD
Elohim, the Sovereign, Mighty Creator

*"The Lord thundered from heaven;
the voice of the Most High resounded."*
*Psalm 18:13*

**Psalm 29:1-9**

Praise the LORD, you angels of His; praise His glory and His strength.

Praise Him for His majestic glory, the glory of His name. Come before Him clothed in sacred garments.

The voice of the LORD echoes from the clouds. The God of glory thunders through the skies.

So powerful is His voice; so full of majesty.

It breaks down the cedars

It splits the giant trees of Lebanon. It shakes Mount Lebanon and Mount Sirion....

The voice of the LORD thunders through the lightning.

It resounds through the deserts and shakes the wilderness of Kadesh.

The voice of the LORD spins and topples the mighty oaks. It strips the forest bare. They whirl and sway beneath the blast..."

## A. THE VOICE OF GOD IS LIKENED TO/ASSOCIATED WITH THUNDER/POWER

**Job 37:2-5**

Listen! Listen to the roar of His voice (rain was falling); to the rumbling that comes from His mouth. He unleashes His lightning beneath the whole heaven and sends it to the ends of the earth. After that comes the sound of His roar; He thunders with His majestic voice. When His voice resounds, He holds nothing back. God's voice thunders in marvelous ways..."

**Job 40:9**

Do you have an arm like God's, and can your voice thunder like His?

**Psalm 46:6 (TLB)**

The nations rant and rave in anger but when God speaks the earth melts in submission and kingdoms totter into ruin.

**Psalm 68:33**

To him that rideth upon the heavens of heavens, which were of old; lo, He doth send out His voice, and that a mighty voice. (KJV)

**Psalm 77:18**

"The voice of thy thunder was in the heaven: the lightnings lightened the world..." (KJV)

**Isaiah 30:30-31**

The LORD will cause men to hear His majestic voice...the voice of the Lord will shatter Assyria.

**Jeremiah 10:3 (TLB)**

It is His voice that echoes in the thunder of the storm clouds.

**Ezekiel 1:24 (TLB)**
"…their wings roared like waves against the shore, or like the voice of God, or like the shouting of a mighty army."
**Daniel 10:6**
"…His voice like the sound of a multitude…"
**Revelation 1:15**
"…His voice was like the sound of rushing waters."

## B. THE VOICE OF GOD CAN BE HEARD/LISTENED TO

**Deuteronomy 5:23-27**
"When you heard the voice out of the darkness, while the mountain was ablaze with fire, all the leaders of your tribes and your elders came to me. ²⁴ And you said, "The Lord our God has shown us his glory and his majesty, and we have heard his voice from the fire. Today we have seen that a person can live even if God speaks with them.²⁵ But now, why should we die? This great fire will consume us, and we will die if we hear the voice of the Lord our God any longer. ²⁶ For what mortal has ever heard the voice of the living God speaking out of fire, as we have, and survived? ²⁷ Go near and listen to all that the Lord our God says. Then tell us whatever the Lord our God tells you. We will listen and obey."

The offer of life versus death and destruction:
**Deuteronomy 30:19-20**
"Now choose life so that you and your children may live and that you may love the LORD your God, listen to His voice and hold fast to Him."
**Song of Solomon 2:14 (TLB)**
"…call to me and let me hear your lovely voice."
**Isaiah 66:6**
"What is all the commotion in the city? What is that terrible noise from the Temple? It is the voice of the LORD taking vengeance on His enemies."

**Zephaniah 3:17 (TLB)**

"Is that a joyous choir I hear? No, it is the LORD Himself exulting (rejoicing) over you in happy song."

**Matthew 3:17**

"And a voice from heaven said, 'This is my Son, whom I love, with Him I am well pleased.'"

**John 5:25,28-29**

"Very truly I tell you, a time is coming and has now come when the dead will hear the voice of the Son of God and those who hear will live…Do not be amazed at this, for a time is coming, when all who are in their graves will hear His voice and come out…those who have done what is good will rise to live, and those who have done what is evil will rise to be condemned."

This is a reference not only to the future resurrection but also to the fact that Christ gives life now. The spiritually dead who hear Him receive life from Him.

**John 10:3 (TLB)**

The gatekeeper opens the gate for him (the Shepherd) and the sheep hear his voice and come to Him; and he calls his own sheep by name and leads them out…they follow him for they recognize his voice. They won't follow a stranger but will run from him, for they don't recognize his voice.

The sheep recognized the voice of their own shepherd and responded only to him. The shepherd did not call sheep randomly, but only those that belonged to him.

**Acts 7:31-32(TLB)**

When he (Moses) saw this, he was amazed at the sight. As he went over to look more closely, he heard the LORD's voice: "I am the God of your fathers, the God of Abraham, Isaac and Jacob…"

The above references show stark contrast to the other voices that cannot be heard!

**Psalm 115:4-6**

But their idols are silver and gold, made by human hands. They have mouths, but cannot speak, eyes, but they cannot see, they have ears, but cannot hear, noses but they cannot smell; they have hands, but cannot feel,..nor can they utter a sound with their throats. Those who make them will be like them and so will all who trust in them.

**Psalm 135:15-17 (TLB)**

The heathen worship idols of gold and silver, made by men - idols with speechless mouths, sightless eyes and ears that cannot hear; they cannot even breathe.

**Isaiah 44:6-20 (TLB)**

The LORD, the King of Israel, says—yes, it is Israel's Redeemer, the LORD Almighty, who says it—I am the First and Last; there is no other God. Who else can tell you what is going to happen in the days ahead? Let them tell you if they can, and prove their power. Let them do as I have done since ancient time. Don't, don't be afraid. Haven't I proclaimed from ages past (that I would save you)? You are my witnesses—is there any other God? No! None that I know about! There is no other Rock! What fools they are who manufacture idols for their gods. Their hopes remain unanswered. They themselves are witnesses that this is so, for their idols neither see nor know. No wonder those who worship them are so ashamed. Who but a fool would make his own god—an idol that can help him not one whit! All that worship these will stand before the Lord in shame, along with all these carpenters—mere men—who claim that they have made a god. Together they will stand in terror.

> "[12]The metalsmith stands at his forge to make an axe, pounding on it with all his might. He grows hungry and thirsty, weak and faint. [13]Then the woodcarver takes the axe and uses it to make an idol. He measures and marks out a block of wood and carves the figure of a man. Now he has a wonderful idol that

cannot so much as move from where it is placed. ¹⁴ He cuts down cedars, he selects the cypress and the oak, he plants the ash in the forest to be nourished by the rain. ¹⁵ And after his care, he uses part of the wood to make a fire to warm himself and bake his bread, and then—he really does—he takes the rest of it and makes himself a god—a god for men to worship! An idol to fall down before and praise! ¹⁶ Part of the tree he burns to roast his meat and to keep him warm and fed and well content, ¹⁷ and with what's left he makes his god: a carved idol! He falls down before it and worships it and prays to it. "Deliver me," he says. "You are my god!"

¹⁸ Such stupidity and ignorance! God has shut their eyes so that they cannot see, and closed their minds from understanding. ¹⁹ The man never stops to think or figure out, "Why, it's just a block of wood! I've burned it for heat and used it to bake my bread and roast my meat. How can the rest of it be a god? Should I fall down before a chunk of wood? ²⁰ The poor, deluded fool feeds on ashes; he is trusting what can never give him any help at all. Yet he cannot bring himself to ask, "Is this thing, this idol that I'm holding in my hand, a lie?"

## C. THE VOICE OF GOD MUST BE OBEYED

**I Samuel 15:22**

"…Does the LORD delight in burnt offerings and sacrifices as much as in obeying the voice of the LORD? To obey is better than sacrifice, and to heed is better than the fat of rams."

### 1. TRUTH #1:

If you are not in the practice of listening then you are not obeying the voice of God e.g. My vehicle was parked in a mall car park and when I returned to it I found under the windshield wipers an invitation to a carnival activity. Because there was no garbage receptacle close by I just tossed it in the car with the intention of discarding it when I got home. I live on the campus of a Christian tertiary-level institution. As I approached my home the voice of the LORD prompted me to discard the invitation before I arrived home. I acknowledged the voice of God and indicated that when I locate a bin along the way I would discard the invitation. However, as the journey progressed and I got closer to my home, I forgot to keep looking for a bin and He gave me a very strong reminder. I immediately made a greater effort to locate a bin and discarded that invitation. We must never doubt what the voice of God tells us to do.

### 2. TRUTH #2:

Your sacrifices to God of time, money, resources, etc. are only acceptable when brought with an attitude of obedience to God.

## D. WHY DO YOU NEED TO HEAR FROM GOD?
*(Jon Walker, March 2011)*

1. It proves that you are in God's family…it confirms your relationship because God talks to His children.
   **John 10:27**
   My sheep recognize my voice and follow me. (NLT)

2. It protects you from mistakes.
   **Proverbs 3:6**
   Listen for God's voice in everything you do and everywhere you go; He's the one who will keep you on track. (MSG)
3. It produces success in life
4. It helps you to test things people tell you God told them. **Numbers 24:11**

## E. WHAT HAPPENS WHEN YOU HEAR HIS VOICE & OBEY?

### 1. YOU WILL BE THE RECIPIENT OF GOD'S BLESSING AND PROTECTION

**Exodus 9:20**

People who did not even belong to God (Egyptians) or claim Him as their God were protected because of their obedience to His warnings.

**Exodus 15:26 (TLB)**

He (Moses) said, "If you will listen to the voice of the LORD your God, and obey it, and do what is right, then I will not make you suffer the diseases I sent on the Egyptians, for I am the Lord, who heals you."

### 2. YOU AND YOUR CHILDREN WILL BE SUCCESSFUL IN FUTURE ENDEAVOURS

**Deuteronomy 5:23-29 (TLB)**

23 But when you heard the loud voice from the darkness, and saw the terrible fire at the top of the mountain, all your tribal leaders came to me 24 and pleaded, "Today the LORD our God has shown us His glory and greatness; we have even heard His voice from the heart of the fire. Now we know that a man may speak to God and not die; 25

but we will surely die if He speaks to us again. This awesome fire will consume us. 26-27 What man can hear, as we have, the voice of the living God speaking from the heart of the fire, and live? You go and listen to all that God says, then come and tell us, and we will listen and obey. 28 And the LORD agreed to your request, and said to me, "I have heard what the people have said to you, and I agree. 29 Oh, that they would always have such a heart for me, wanting to obey my commandments. Then all would go well with them in the future, and with their children throughout all generations!

### 3. YOU WILL DEVELOP A DEEPER LEVEL OF RELATIONSHIP/INTIMACY WITH GOD

**Revelation 3:20**

"…if anyone hears my voice and opens the door I will come in and eat with that person and they with me…"

### 4. YOU WILL STAND FIRM/BE SOLID

**Luke 6:47-48 (TLB)**

But all those who listen and obey me are like a man who builds a house on a strong foundation laid upon the underlying rock. When the floodwaters rise and break against the house, it stands firm for it is strongly built.

## F. WHAT HAPPENS WHEN YOU HEAR HIS VOICE AND DON'T OBEY?

### 1. YOU COURT DESTRUCTION

**Exodus 10:7 (TLB)**

The court officials (Egyptians who had been in support of Pharaoh) now came to Pharaoh and asked him, "Are you going to destroy us completely? Don't you know even yet that all Egypt lies in ruins? Let the men go and serve Jehovah **their** God!"

**Daniel 9:11-13 (TLB)**

All Israel has disobeyed; we have turned away from you and haven't listened to your voice. And so the awesome curse of God has crushed us…but even so we still refuse…

### 2. YOU PROVOKE GOD

**Psalm 95:7-9 (TLB)**

Oh that you would hear Him calling you today and come to Him! 8 Don't harden your hearts as Israel did in the wilderness at Meribah and Massah. 9 For there your fathers doubted me, though they had seen so many of my miracles before. My patience was severely tried by their complaints.

### 3. YOU MOVE FROM UNDER THE COVERING OF GOD'S PROTECTION PLAN

**Luke 6:49 (TLB)**

But those who listen and don't obey are like a man who builds a house without a foundation. When the floods sweep down against that house, it crumbles into a heap.

A Christian sister shared these two examples with me:

1. Early one morning, shortly after 6:00 a.m. as she was going down a main street in the city and the road was very clear; with hardly any cars in sight; the voice of God told her to move away from the left lane and go over to the right. She reasoned that there was no need to do that as the road was very clear. Moments later a car came out of nowhere and hit her car on the left side.

2. She had some business to attend to in the capital city and parked her vehicle on the street. The voice of God told her to move the car from where she had parked it and park it elsewhere. She was about to heed the voice of God when the rain started to drizzle so she abandoned the plan. When she returned from doing her business, her car was missing…it had been stolen!

### 4. YOU MISS OPPORTUNITIES TO BE USED BY HIM

I was preparing to speak at a Women's Retreat. While packing my suitcase, the LORD told me to put a pack of matches in it. I made a mental note but in the process of leaving I forgot and left it behind. While being driven to the venue for the Retreat, we saw a church bus parked on the side of the road. People were outside the bus and they were intently focusing on getting something done. The driver pulled up to see if she could offer any assistance to them. When we got closer a gentleman approached our vehicle and asked us if we had any matches; they were trying to burn something but had no matches!!! Needless to say I was disappointed that I had not been more diligent about putting the matches in my suitcase because clearly I missed an opportunity to be used by Him and for Him to get the glory.

## G. THE LORD SELECTS THOSE WHO HEAR HIS VOICE

**Exodus 19:19** "…
Moses spoke and the voice of God answered him.."
**Deuteronomy 4:33-36**
Has any other people heard the voice of God speaking out of fire, as you have, and lived? An entire nation heard the voice of God

speaking to it from fire…He let you hear His voice instructing you from heaven…you even heard His words from the centre of the fire. (TLB)

**I Samuel 3:4**

Then the LORD called Samuel…

**John 10:16**

(My) other sheep will listen to my voice.

## H. EXAMPLES OF WHAT GOD SPEAKS

### 1. TURN TO HIM

**Psalm 95:7 (TLB)**

Today if you hear His voice do not harden your hearts.

**Isaiah 30:21**

Whether you turn to the right or to the left your ears will hear a voice behind you saying, "This is the way; walk in it."

### 2. SEARCHES FOR YOU

**Genesis 3:9**

Where are you? This was a rhetorical question to Adam. God graciously seeks those who attempt to hide from Him in their sin and shame.

### 3. WARNINGS (THROUGH PEOPLE)

Hurricane Gilbert hit Jamaica September 12, 1988. It was a Category 5 hurricane with a 40-mile wide eye that covered the entire island, left many without electricity and killed more than 200 people. The LORD gave warnings but some heeded them while others did not. Even up to the day before the hurricane hit, there were not many persons in the supermarkets purchasing items. The common belief was that the hurricane would not hit Jamaica.

There is a report of a gentleman who went to Germany to warn the Jews about the coming holocaust and only 6,000 persons left Germany with him. The rest remained and millions died. Before any tragedy God always sends a warning.

Exodus 9:20—People who did not even belong to God (Egyptians) or claim Him as their God were protected because of their obedience to His warnings.

September 11, 2001 which in hindsight is today referred to as "9/11"

-- An evangelist had a dream months before the actual event and the LORD instructed him to fast concerning this impending disaster. While sharing it with us ministers, he expressed sadness that he did not pray about it.

## 4. WITNESS THAT JESUS IS TRULY THE SON OF GOD

**I John 5:6-8 (TLB)**

And we know He is, because God said so, with a voice from heaven when Jesus was baptized, and again as He faced death. Yes, not only at Jesus' baptism but also as He faced death. And the Holy Spirit, forever truthful, says it too. So we have these three witnesses: the voice of the Holy Spirit in our hearts, the voice from heaven at Christ's baptism, and the voice before He died. And they all say the same thing: that Jesus Christ is the Son of God.

## I. WHAT HINDERS US FROM HEARING THE VOICE OF GOD?

### 1. PRIDE

**Zephaniah 3:2**

In her pride she won't listen even to the voice of God. Pride says we don't need God's help.

### 2. FEAR

We are afraid of what God might say to us.

### 3. BITTERNESS

We hold on to hurts and choose not to forgive, our hearts grow hard. We become defensive and resist God's love, His Word and His voice. *(Rick Warren, 2011)*

## J. HOW CAN I HEAR GOD'S VOICE? / WAYS IN WHICH GOD'S VOICE CAN BE HEARD

1. When you pray don't do all the talking. Communication is a two-way street.
2. Be silent before Him. Practice meditation.
3. He will impress you while you read His Word;
4. He will impress you while you pray to Him;
5. He will give you dreams and visions. There are over 50 dreams in the Bible.

**Job 33:14-19 (TLB)**

For God does speak—now one way, now another—though man may not perceive it. In a dream, in a vision of the night, when deep sleep falls on men as they slumber in their beds, He may speak in their ears and terrify them with warnings to turn man from wrongdoing

and keep him from pride to preserve his soul from the pit, his life from perishing by the sword.
**Acts 2:17**
In the last days, God says, I will pour out my Spirit on all people… Your young men will see visions, your old men will dream dreams.

6. He will impress your thoughts
7. Tune in to Him; respond to His nudges

When you see someone who really resembles someone that you know…pray for that individual.

When you call someone's name in error don't say " Sis. P is calling my name!" …Pray for that individual.

When someone comes forcefully to your mind…pray for that person.

## K. HOW DO I KNOW IT IS THE VOICE OF GOD?

1. Is what you hear consistent with Scripture? Does it agree with the Bible?

God will never contradict His written Word:
**Luke 21:33**
Heaven and earth will pass away but my words will never pass away.
**Galatians 1:8-9(TLB)**
Let God's curses fall on anyone, including myself, who preaches any other way to be saved than the one we told you about; yes, if an angel comes from heaven and preaches any other message, let him be forever cursed. I will say it again: if anyone preaches any other Gospel than the one you welcomed, let God's curse fall upon him.
**I John 4:1 (TLB)**
Dearly loved friends, don't always believe everything you hear just because someone says it is a message from God: test it first to see if it really is.

2. Is there confirmation in the mouth of 2 or 3 witnesses (Pharaoh's officials Exodus 10:7) e.g. mature believers:

**Ephesians 3:10**

God's intent is that through the church, the manifold wisdom of God should be made known.

3. Is there an inner witness of the Spirit? Do I sense God's peace about it?

4. Is it convicting or condemning? Conviction is from God to correct you, nudge you; condemnation is from Satan to make you feel guilty in a vague way. *(Rick Warren, Purpose Driven Connection, 2011)*

**Romans 8:1**

There is no condemnation to those who belong to Christ Jesus

## PERSONAL APPLICATION

### GOD VOICES TO US WHAT WE NEED TO HEAR

**I Kings 19:9**

And the word of the LORD came to him: "What are you doing here, Elijah?"

Context:

1. Post Mount Carmel—channel of God's power
2. I Kings 18:29 (TLB)
   They raved all afternoon until the time of the evening sacrifice but there was no reply, **no voice**, no answer.
3. Elijah ran ahead of a chariot and reached the destination before the chariot. This was a display of God's presence in His life. However shortly after Elijah received a threat (19:2) He realized that he was not in the favour of the powers that be of the land, not in favour with authority. He received the threat because God, through Elijah, was a threat to the enemy. The enemy is not going to threaten or direct his attack at God but at His worthy representatives.

4. Elijah became afraid.
5. Elijah became depressed, downcast, suicidal "I have had enough" Yes I know that I am being used by you, yes I am faithful, yes I am committed but…kill me! Elijah concluded that his work was fruitless and consequently that life was not worth living. He was filled with self-doubt and requested that he die, perhaps so another could continue the struggle against Jezebel and Baal. Let someone else take up this fight; but it was not his fight…the battle is the Lord's.
6. God, in His mercy, provided sustenance and rest for His discouraged servant.
7. God is asking you the question today "What are you doing here? Why are you in this place in your spiritual journey? This is a place of self-pity! A place of hiding! A place of discouragement! A place of aloneness! We get to this place as leaders. God is asking "What are you doing here?" God wants you to articulate your thoughts and your feelings to him. God is waiting on you to pour your heart to Him. He is saying to you right now, "Speak to me, my son! Speak to me, my daughter!"
Elijah let it all out "I have worked very hard for you but the people that you have given me have broken their covenant with you and torn down your altars and killed your prophets, and only I am left; and now they are trying to kill me too."
8. The LORD responded: He passed by and there was a mighty windstorm… an earthquake… a fire… and then a whisper. Then a voice said to him, "Why are you here Elijah?" He gave the same answer.
9. Then the LORD told him:
    a. Go back
    b. Anoint two kings and your successor.
10. The LORD has need of you.

We need to listen to the voice of God in order to speak to the voice of God.

Do our voices reflect the voice of God? Youth leaders, we need to teach our young people how to hear the voice of God. We need to teach our children how to hear the voice of God. Samuel, at 12 years of age, was taught by his mentor, Eli, how to hear the voice of God.

**I Samuel 3:8-10:**

⁸ A third time the Lord called, "Samuel!" And Samuel got up and went to Eli and said, "Here I am: you called me." Then Eli realized that the Lord was calling the boy. ⁹ So Eli told Samuel, "Go and lie down, and if he calls you, say, 'Speak, Lord, for your servant is listening.'" So Samuel went and lay down in his place. ¹⁰ The Lord came and stood there, calling as at the other times, "Samuel! Samuel!" Then Samuel said, "Speak, for your servant is listening."

Samuel became a powerful intercessor for the nation of Israel; He learned how to listen to the voice of God.

CHAPTER 3

# THE EYE OF GOD
Jehovah Gmolah – The Lord Who Rewards

*"The LORD has rewarded me according to
my righteousness according to
the cleanness of my hands in His sight."
Psalm 18:24*

The eye of the LORD is not like our eyes. We look at our faces in a mirror and after looking at ourselves, we go away and immediately forget what we look like. James 1:24

References to the eye of God suggest:

**1. HIS PENETRATING INSIGHT**

**Revelation 19:12; 1:14; 2:18 (TLB)**
"His eyes were like flames…of fire…whose eyes penetrate like flames of fire.

## 2. HIS ALL-SEEING NATURE

Ezekiel 1:18 "…full of eyes all around…"

## A. THE EYE OF THE LORD:

### 1. SEES…

**Job 11:11**
For He knows perfectly all the faults and sins of mankind; He sees all sin without searching.

**Jeremiah 16:17**
My eyes are on all their ways; they are not hidden from me, nor is their sin concealed from my eyes.

**Hebrews 4:13**
Nothing in all creation is hidden from God's sight. Everything is uncovered and laid bare before the eyes of Him to who we must give account.

There is a marked difference in the behavior of people whenever authority is present:

- Motorists are circumspect on the road whenever there is a police presence.
- Students are respectful whenever the principal is present.
- Employees are on the ball whenever the boss is around, but when he is gone on vacation….pressure.
- Some children behave appropriately when their fathers are around.

What would our churches be like if persons acted like God could see everything that they did? What would the Kingdom of God throughout our country be like? What would our nation be like? In my younger years as a child, there was a healthy fear of God and of the things of God. One did not get into wrong doing because we knew that God could see us.

Technology and satellite imagery enable us to see persons in real time. Google Earth is amazing technology! Without the aid of those devices, though, God can see everyone **at the same time!** We are like a reality show in which all of our actions are observed by an audience of One—God.

**Zechariah 3:9**

"See the stone I have set in front of Joshua! There are seven eyes on that one stone…" This was symbolic of infinite intelligence (omniscience) and divine care. 7=fullness; completeness, perfection.

**Zechariah 4:10**

"These seven are the eyes of the LORD which range throughout the earth."

**Revelation 5:6**

"Then I saw a Lamb…he had seven horns and seven eyes…" The term "seven horns" symbolizes full strength.

### SEES IN THE DARK

**Job 34:21-25 (TLB)**

For God carefully watches the goings on of all mankind; He see them all. 22 No darkness is thick enough to hide evil men from His eyes 23 So there is no need to wait for some great crime before a man is called before God in judgment…He watches what they do and in a single night He overturns them, destroying them.

**Psalm 139:11-12 (TLB)**

"If I try to hide in the darkness, the night becomes light around me. For even darkness cannot hide from God; to you the night shines as bright as day. Darkness and light are both alike to you."

**Daniel 2:22**

He knows what lies in darkness.

We are also impressed when watching the movies and see that the night time is not an obstacle when a search is taking place. Searchers put on their night-vision glasses to see what is happening around them. God can do that too.

## YOU CANNOT HIDE FROM HIM

**Exodus 3:7-9**

⁷ The Lord said, "I have indeed seen the misery of my people in Egypt. I have heard them crying out because of their slave drivers, and I am concerned about their suffering. ⁸ So I have come down to rescue them from the hand of the Egyptians and to bring them up out of that land into a good and spacious land, a land flowing with milk and honey—the home of the Canaanites, Hittites, Amorites, Perizzites, Hivites and Jebusites. ⁹ And now the cry of the Israelites has reached me, and I have seen the way the Egyptians are oppressing them.

**Jeremiah 16:17**

For I am closely watching you and I see every sin. You cannot hope to hide from me. (TLB)// My eyes are on all their ways they are not hidden from me nor is their sin concealed from my eyes. (NIV)

**Jeremiah 23:24**

Who can hide in secret places so that I cannot see him? declares the LORD.

**Amos 9:3-4**

Though they hide themselves on the top of Carmel…though they hide from my eyes at the bottom of the sea…I will keep my eyes on them for harm and not for good.

The wicked fleeth when no man pursueth. For some people, the fact that God watches us so closely is an uncomfortable feeling because we are aware that we are not living the way we should, or we might be engaging in activities that we know are not pleasing to God. For others, the fact that God is watching us so closely brings us a feeling of warmth because we are in an up-to-date relationship with Him. In such a case it is comforting to us that God's eyes are on us. Listen to David:

**Psalm 139:7-11 (TLB)**

"I can never be lost to your Spirit!! I can never get away from my God! If I go up to heaven, you are there; if I go down to the place of the dead, you are there. If I ride the morning winds to the farthest oceans, even there your hand will guide me, your strength will support me."

If you wanted to hide from God, where would you hide? Or, if you wanted to indulge in a wrongful activity, where would you do it so that God would not see?

**Genesis 3:8**

"…(Adam & Eve) heard and they hid from the LORD God among the trees of the garden…" This was not a very good hiding place even from humans much more the All-seeing God!!! Sin alienates us from God; allows us to have the perception that we will not be found out.

Where are you? God graciously seeks those who attempt to hide from Him in their sin and shame.

What He sees in our lives causes Him to hide His eyes from us:

**Isaiah 1:15-17:**

When you spread out your hands in prayer, I will hide my eyes from you; even when you offer many prayers, I am not listening. Your hands are full of blood; wash and make yourselves clean. Take your evil deeds out of my sight! Stop doing wrong, learn to do right! Seek justice, defend the oppressed. Take up the cause of the fatherless, plead the case of the widow.

### SEES, RECORDS AND STORES

**Job 11:11 (TLB)**

"…When He sees evil does He not take note?"

**Jeremiah 29:23**

For they have done outrageous things in Israel; they have committed adultery with their neighbors' wives, and in my name they have uttered lies which I did not authorize. I know it and am a **witness** to it," declares the LORD."

So many times I have watched the news and have seen someone videotape an individual being brutalized by the police. Then when the case gets to court it is thrown out because of some technicality. God's video recording will not be thrown out. Judgment Day will be a movie of our secret lives for all to see.

### 2. WATCHES OVER THE LAND & NATIONS

**Exodus 3:16**

"Go, assemble the elders of Israel and say to them, 'the Lord, the God of your fathers—the God of Abraham, Isaac and Jacob—appeared to me and said: I have watched over you and have seen what has been done to you in Egypt.'"

**Deuteronomy 11:12**

It is a land the LORD your God cares for; the eyes of the LORD your God are continually on it from the beginning of the year to its end.// day after day throughout the year (TLB)

**Psalm 66:7**

He rules forever by His power; His eyes watch the nations, let not the rebellious rise up against Him.

**Amos 9:8 (TLB)**

The eyes of the LORD are watching Israel, that sinful nation and I will root her up and scatter her…

### 3. WATCHES OVER THE WICKED

**Job 24:23 (TLB)**

He may let them rest in a feeling of security but His eyes are on their ways.

**Proverbs 15:3**

The eyes of the LORD are ***everywhere*** keeping watch on the wicked and the good.

Sometimes it seems to the wicked and those looking on that they get away with their evil deed, murder. However, scripture teaches us that wickedness and injustice have to become ripe for God's punishment.

**Genesis 15:16 (TLB)**

"...the wickedness of the Amorite nations will not be ready for punishment."

**Exodus 2:25 (TLB)**

Looking down upon them, He knew that the time had come for their rescue.

**Hosea 13:12 (TLB)**

Ephraim's sins are harvested and stored away for punishment.

**Revelation 14:18 (TLB)**

Just then the angel who has power to destroy the world with fire, shouted to the angel with the sickle, "Use your sickle now to cut off the clusters of grapes from the vines of the earth, for they are fully ripe for judgment."

## 4. TAKES CAREFUL NOTE OF WHAT YOU DO AND THE CONDITION OF YOUR LIFE

**Deuteronomy 12:25 (TLB)**

"...you will be doing what is right in the eyes of the LORD."

**Deuteronomy 6:16 (TLB)**

You must actively obey Him in everything He commands. Only then will you be doing what is right and good in the LORD's eyes.

**Job 7:17-20**

What is mankind that you make so much of them, that you give them so much attention, that you examine them every morning and test them every moment? Will you never look away from me, or let me alone even for an instant? If I have sinned, what have I done to you, you who see everything we do?

**Jeremiah 14:17 (TLB)**

Night and day my eyes shall overflow with tears; I cannot stop crying for my people have been run through with a sword and lie mortally wounded.

**Daniel 9:18**

"…open your eyes and see the desolation of the city that bears your name…"

## B. WHY DOES THE LORD WATCH US SO CLOSELY?

### 1. TO REINFORCE US

**II Chronicles 16:9**

For the eyes of the LORD range throughout the earth to strengthen those whose hearts are committed to Him. He does this through the network of His family, prayer and encouraging words.

### IN OUR MINISTRY

**Zechariah 4:10 (TLB)**

Do not despise this small beginning, for the eyes of the LORD rejoice to see the work begin (on the temple) to see the plumbline in the hand of Zerubbabel.

### 2. TO REMIND US OF HIS LOVE FOR US

**Psalm 33:13-18**

From heaven the Lord looks down and sees all mankind;[14] from His dwelling place He watches all who live on earth—[15] He who forms the hearts of all, who considers everything they do.[16] No king is saved by the size of his army; no warrior escapes by his great strength.¹⁷ A horse is a vain hope for deliverance; despite all its great strength it cannot save. ¹⁸ But the eyes of the Lord are on those who fear Him, on those whose hope is in His unfailing love, to deliver us from death and keep them alive in famine…

**I Peter 3:12**

For the eyes of the LORD are on the righteous and his ears are attentive to their prayer.

"When we understand that God looks at us through eyes of love it will help us to look at others with their failings, shortcomings, weaknesses and faults, through God's eyes of love. We will no longer use the circumstances or sins of others to define who they are. We will see them through the eyes of Jesus.

   a. When others saw a woman caught in adultery, Jesus saw a woman who would sin no more;
   b. When others saw a blind man, Jesus saw a man who was able to see;
   c. When others saw wasted perfume, Jesus saw a woman of willing sacrifice;
   d. When others saw an impulsive, impetuous disciple named Peter, Jesus saw a stable rock for building the church;
   e. When others saw evil men pounding nails into a cross, Jesus saw men who did not know what they were doing."
   *(Jon Walker, August 4, 2012)*

### 3. TO REGARD OUR PATHS

**Psalm 11:4**

The LORD is in His holy temple, the Lord is on His heavenly throne. He observes everyone on earth, His eyes examine them. The LORD examines the righteous.

**Psalm 25:4-10**

4 Show me the path where I should go, O LORD; point out the right road for me to walk. 5 Lead me; teach me; for you are the God who gives me salvation. I have not hope except in you. 6,7 Overlook my youthful sins, O LORD! Look at me instead through eyes of mercy and forgiveness, through eyes of everlasting love and kindness. 8 The LORD is good and glad to teach the proper path to all who go astray; 9 He will teach the ways that are right and best to those who humbly turn to Him. 10 And when we obey Him, every path He guides us on is fragrant with His lovingkindness and His truth.

**Psalm 34:15**

The eyes of the LORD are on the righteous.

**Psalm 80:14**

"…look down from heaven and see! Watch over this vine."

**Jeremiah 23:23 (TLB)**

For a man's ways are in full view of the LORD and he examines all his paths

This shatters the distance theory. There is a concept that God created the universe, wound it up like clockwork and is not involved in the affairs of man. The song popularizing this concept was "God is watching us from a distance…"

### 4. TO REWARD US

**Jeremiah 32:19**

"…your eyes are open to the ways of all mankind; you reward each person according to their conduct and as their deeds deserve."

**Psalm 37:18 (TLB)**

Day by day the LORD observes the good deeds done by godly men and gives them eternal rewards. He rewards each one of us according to what our works deserve.

**Psalm 62:12**

And with you, LORD, is unfailing love; and you reward everyone according to what they have done.

Rick Warren, in his book "Purpose Driven Life," states that life is a test. God tests us in various ways in our response to problems, success, conflict, illness, disappointment, and even the weather.

**Amos 4:6** confirms this:

"I sent you hunger," says the LORD, "but it did no good; you still would not return to me." The passage highlights that crops were ruined, rain held back for three months, blight and mildew on farms, locusts ate figs and olive trees, plagues were sent, young men were killed in war, but they would not return to God.

As we have looked at the hand of God, there is a personal application there for us: we are engraved on the palm of His hand.

And when we looked at the voice of God there was a personal application there as well: God speaks to us exactly what we need, and when we need it, in that still, small voice.

## PERSONAL APPLICATION:

**Zechariah 2:8 (TLB)**

The LORD of Glory has sent me against the nations that oppressed you; for he who harms you sticks his finger in Jehovah's eye/the apple of His eye. This is the unique, uncommon favour that the LORD has for His people.

**Deuteronomy 32:10**

"…He shielded him and cared for him; He guarded him as the apple of His eye."

The apple of His eye literally means "little man of His eye" referring to the pupil, a delicate part of the eye that is essential for vision and therefore must be protected at all costs. We know how sensitive our eyes are; they pick up things easily and quickly.

- Scents—when an onion is being cut up, it burns your eyes;
- When something blows into our eyes while we are walking on a windy day or driving…it is painful to our eyes;
- When we are frying something at the stove and we hear "pop," our eyes will instantly shut in order to protect our eyes;
- Any hint of danger to our bodies and our hands defensively go up to protect our face/our eyes. I have a badly stitched injury on my thumb to prove it.

Our pupil is precious; we guard it at all costs. God treats us like the pupil of His eye: that is what we are to Him. Any hint of danger, and we are shielded. Any fiery onslaught, and we are also shielded.

Star Wars…at any hint of danger the Commander instructs that the shields go up and be locked.

So, with this in mind, let us look at this verse again…the LORD of Glory has sent me against the nations that oppressed you; for he who harms you sticks his finger in Jehovah's eye/the apple of His eye!! Ouch!

David was so cognizant of this covering that he asked God, in Psalm 17:8, "Keep me as the apple of your eye/Protect me as you would the pupil of Your eye."

If you are enjoying this kind of coverage, well, God is also saying to you "…guard my teaching as the pupil of your eye."

## WHAT IS THE DANGER OF NOT SEEING THE LORD?

### 1. LIKE BALAAM WE WILL COME CLOSE TO OPPOSING THE LORD.

**Numbers 22:21-31**

[21] Balaam got up in the morning, saddled his donkey and went with the Moabite officials. [22] But God was very angry when he went, and the angel of the Lord stood in the road to oppose him. Balaam was

riding on his donkey, and his two servants were with him. ²³ When the donkey saw the angel of the Lord standing in the road with a drawn sword in his hand, it turned off the road into a field. Balaam beat it to get it back on the road.

²⁴ Then the angel of the Lord stood in a narrow path through the vineyards, with walls on both sides. ²⁵ When the donkey saw the angel of the Lord, it pressed close to the wall, crushing Balaam's foot against it. So he beat the donkey again.

²⁶ Then the angel of the Lord moved on ahead and stood in a narrow place where there was no room to turn, either to the right or to the left. ²⁷ When the donkey saw the angel of the Lord, it lay down under Balaam, and he was angry and beat it with his staff. ²⁸ Then the Lord opened the donkey's mouth, and it said to Balaam, "What have I done to you to make you beat me these three times?"

²⁹ Balaam answered the donkey, "You have made a fool of me! If only I had a sword in my hand, I would kill you right now."

³⁰ The donkey said to Balaam, "Am I not your own donkey, which you have always ridden, to this day? Have I been in the habit of doing this to you?"

"No," he said.

"Then the Lord opened Balaam's eyes, and he saw the angel of the Lord standing in the road with his sword drawn. SO HE BOWED LOW AND FELL FACE DOWN. (WORSHIP)"

## 2. WE CAN MISS THE TRUE PICTURE OF WHO WE REALLY ARE AS WE STAND IN HIS PRESENCE

### Isaiah 6:1-5

"Woe to me! I cried. I am ruined! For I am a man of unclean lips and I live among a people of unclean lips and my eyes have seen the King, the Lord Almighty."

Our prayer today is that we want to see the LORD; He sees us and we want to see Him. How do we get a glimpse of the LORD? He comes in on the wings of our worship. Until we get such a revelation of the LORD we will not be able to really worship the LORD as we ought to. We really need to come to the place where we fervently ask God to open our eyes so that we can see. Then, and only then will we access the very throne room of God.

CHAPTER 4

# THE HEART OF GOD

*"...He rescued me because He delighted in me."*
*Psalm 18:19*

Unlike previous topics in this study, not very many verses make reference to the heart of God, although there are many which deal with the heart of man. Our study of this part of the anatomy of God will take a different approach.

## A. WHAT DO WE KNOW ABOUT THE HEART OF GOD?

**Proverbs 27:19** tells us that a man's heart reflects the man, and so we know that God's heart reflects who He is.

### 1. HIS GENTLENESS/HUMILITY

**Matthew 11:29**
Take my yoke upon you and learn from me, for I am gentle and **humble in heart.**

### 2. HIS COMPASSION

**Luke 7:13 (TLB)**

When the LORD saw her (widow of Nain) His **heart overflowed with sympathy** "Don't cry." Psalm 145:8-9 The LORD is gracious and compassionate, slow to anger and rich in love. The LORD is good to all; He has compassion on all He has made.

### 3. HIS TENDER CARE/PROTECTIVE OF HIS OWN

**Isaiah 40:11**

He tends His flock like a shepherd. He gathers the lambs in His arms and carries them **close to His heart** = Deuteronomy 26:19 If you do, He will make you greater than any other nation, allowing you to receive praise, honor and renown; but to attain this honor and renown you must be a holy people to the LORD your God, as He requires.

### 4. HIS DESIRE TO MENTOR HIS LEADERS

**Jeremiah 3:15**

I will give you **shepherds after my own heart** who will lead you with knowledge and understanding

**Ezekiel 34** gives an account of shepherds who are not after God's own heart.

> *The word of the Lord came to me:* [2] *"Son of man, prophesy against the shepherds of Israel; prophesy and say to them: 'This is what the Sovereign Lord says: Woe to the shepherds of Israel who only take care of themselves! Should not shepherds take care of the flock?* [3] *You eat the curds, clothe yourselves with the wool and slaughter the choice animals, but you*

*do not take care of the flock. ⁴ You have not strengthened the weak or healed the sick or bound up the injured. You have not brought back the strays or searched for the lost. You have ruled them harshly and brutally. ⁵ So they were scattered because there was no shepherd, and when they were scattered they became food for all the wild animals. ⁶ My sheep wandered over all the mountains and on every high hill. They were scattered over the whole earth, and no one searched or looked for them.*

*⁷ "'Therefore, you shepherds, hear the word of the Lord: ⁸ As surely as I live, declares the Sovereign Lord, because my flock lacks a shepherd and so has been plundered and has become food for all the wild animals, and because my shepherds did not search for my flock but cared for themselves rather than for my flock, ⁹ therefore, O shepherds, hear the word of the Lord: ¹⁰ This is what the Sovereign Lord says: I am against the shepherds and will hold them accountable for my flock. I will remove them from tending the flock so that the shepherds can no longer feed themselves. I will rescue my flock from their mouths, and it will no longer be food for them.*

*¹¹ "'For this is what the Sovereign Lord says: I myself will search for my sheep and look after them. ¹² As a shepherd looks after his scattered flock when he is with them, so will I look after my sheep. I will rescue them from all the places where they were scattered on a day of clouds and darkness. ¹³ I will bring them out from the nations and gather them from the countries, and I will bring them into their own land. I will pasture them on the mountains of Israel, in the ravines and in all the settlements in the land. ¹⁴ I will tend them in a good pasture, and the mountain heights of Israel will be their grazing land. There they will lie down in good grazing land, and there they will feed in a rich pasture on the mountains of Israel. ¹⁵ I myself will tend my sheep and have them lie down, declares the Sovereign Lord. ¹⁶ I will search for the lost and bring back the strays. I will bind up the injured and strengthen the weak, but the sleek and the strong I will destroy. I will shepherd the flock with justice.*

*¹⁷ "'As for you, my flock, this is what the Sovereign Lord says: I will judge between one sheep and another, and between rams and goats. ¹⁸ Is it not enough for you to feed on the good pasture? Must you also trample the rest of your pasture with your feet? Is it not enough for you to drink clear water? Must you also muddy the rest with your feet? ¹⁹ Must my flock feed on what you have trampled and drink what you have muddied with your feet?*

*²⁰ "'Therefore this is what the Sovereign Lord says to them: See, I myself will judge between the fat sheep and the lean sheep. ²¹ Because you shove with flank and shoulder, butting all the weak sheep with your horns until you have driven them away, ²² I will save my flock, and they will no longer be plundered. I will judge between one sheep and another. ²³ I will place over them one shepherd, my servant David, and he will tend them; he will tend them and be their shepherd. ²⁴ I the Lord will be their God, and my servant David will be prince among them. I the Lord have spoken.*

**Psalm 23** gives an account of the LORD as our Shepherd:

> *The Lord is my shepherd, I shall not be in want.*
> *² He makes me lie down in green pastures,*
> *he leads me beside quiet waters,*
> *³ he restores my soul.*
> *He guides me in paths of righteousness*
> *for his name's sake.*
> *⁴ Even though I walk*
> *through the valley of the shadow of death*
> *I will fear no evil,*
> *for you are with me;*
> *your rod and your staff,*
> *they comfort me.*
> *⁵ You prepare a table before me*
> *in the presence of my enemies.*
> *You anoint my head with oil;*
> *my cup overflows.*
> *⁶ Surely goodness and love will follow me*
> *all the days of my life,*
> *and I will dwell in the house of the*
> *Lord forever.*

## 5. HIS DESIRE TO COMMUNE WITH US

**II Chronicles 7:16 (TLB)**

For I have chosen this Temple and sanctified it to be my home forever; my eyes and my heart shall always be here.

**v.15 (TLB)**

So He will listen, wide awake, to every prayer made in this place.

**v.12 (TLB)**

This is the place where God wanted His people to sacrifice to Him.

## 6. HIS PLANS AND PURPOSES

**Psalm 33:11**

But the plans of the LORD stand firm forever, the purposes of His heart through all generations. "The idea of God's heart carries a powerful message of comfort and hope to us. God's Word uses the term to let us know about God's "softer" side Has anyone ever received a greater compliment than Samuel's description of David as a "man after God's heart" (I Sam.13:14)? We must remember that God's heart is not sentimental. It is true. God isn't confused or fickle about His feelings toward us. Unlike our hearts, "this people draw nigh unto me with their mouth and honoureth me with their lips but their heart is far from me", His heart is pure. And God delights in those who devote their lives to pursue "after His own heart". (Knowing God Better Woodrow Kroll Pg. 15)

**Jeremiah 23:20 & 30:24**

The anger of the LORD will not turn back until He fully accomplishes the purposes of His heart.

## REFERENCES TO THE KIND OF HEART WE MUST HAVE:

We are encouraged not to have a heart that is fearful, hard, stiff-necked or evil. What do the Scriptures say about the kind of heart we must have?

**I Kings 3:12**
"…give you a **wise and discerning** heart…"
**I Kings 9:4**
"…walk before me in **integrity** of heart…"
**I Kings 9:4**
"…heart was fully **devoted to God**."
**II Kings 22:19**
"…because your heart was **responsive**…"
**Psalm 51:17**
"…a **broken and a contrite** heart…"
**Psalm 73.1**
How good God is to Israel to those who are **pure** in heart//Psalm24 "…clean hands and a pure heart…"
**Psalm 86:11**
"…an **undivided** heart…"
**Psalm 90:12**
"…heart of **wisdom**…"
**Psalm 108:1**
"…my heart is **steadfast**…"
**Psalm 125:4**
"those who are **upright** in heart…"
**Jeremiah 32:39**
"…**singleness** of heart…"
**Ezekiel 18:31**
"… a **new** heart…"
**Ephesians 1:18**
"…the eyes of your heart may be **enlightened**…"
**Ephesians 5:19**
"…make **music in your heart** to the Lord…"

## WHAT WAS IT THAT COMMENDED DAVID TO GOD?

David lived his life in passionate pursuit of God's heart.

**Psalm 89:15-17** gives us a synopsis of one who pleases God:

- They know how to praise God in tough times and in good times; they rejoice all day.
- They know how to walk before God blamelessly;
- They find their righteousness in God's righteousness;
- They find their glory in God's strength and not their own;
- They revel in the favour of God not the praise of men. They find everything they need in God and return everything to God.

Many aspects in the life of David give us a reflection of God's heart. For example:

- He had a wise heart in the selection of his friends and handled success.
- He had a heart that understood the principle of service.
- He knew how to behave himself wisely in the presence of his enemies.

Let us focus on this aspect of David's life: his intimate moments:

David, the MAN after God's own heart, as a worshipper, he transformed Israel's ritualistic worship to a personal, expressive, adoration of God. He was able to transform the worship of Israel because he introduced them to the kind of worship one brings out of relationship; the kind of worship David experienced firsthand. He was a true worshipper.

As worship leaders, when we lead in worship, we take persons on a spiritual journey into the very throne room of God; into the Holy of Holies, where we have already been throughout the week. Among other things, we should know:

- how to get there;
- what can easily distract us from getting there;
- what we see when we get there; and
- how to worship when we get there.

A true worshipper (and we are all worshippers, not only the worship leaders) knows the conditions for entry:

**In Psalm 24**, David shares with us, "Who may climb the mountain of the LORD and enter where He lives? Who may stand before the LORD? Only those with pure hands and hearts, who do not practice dishonesty and lying. These are the ones who are allowed to stand before the LORD and worship the God of Jacob."

This psalm was a processional liturgy composed either for the occasion when David brought the ark to Jerusalem or for a festival commemorating the event. We are going to take a look at the events that caused David to pen these lines.

Let us begin with II Samuel 6:1-11. The Ark of the Covenant was being moved to Jerusalem. The Ark of the Covenant was a sacred portable chest, which, along with its two related items, the Mercy Seat (the golden lid which was a slab of pure gold) and Cherubim, was the most important sacred object of the Israelites during the wilderness period. It was also known as the Ark of the LORD/God/Testimony. The Ark contained the Ten Commandments, golden pot of manna and Aaron's rod which had budded.

The Ark symbolized the throne of the LORD, the great king who chose to dwell among His people. The atonement cover stood between the Testimony in the Ark and the cherubim over which God was enthroned. It revealed how by grace God provides a way for sinful humans to be in covenant with Himself, the holy God.

The Ark was carried by the sons of Levi during the wilderness wandering (Deuteronomy 31:9). It was carried into the Jordan River by the priests, and the Ark caused the waters to part so Israel could cross on dry ground (Joshua 3:6-4:18). During the conquest of the land of Canaan, the ark was carried at the fall of Jericho (Joshua 6:4-11); and later, it was deposited at Shiloh, which had become the home of the tabernacle (Joshua 18:1).

Trusting the "magic power" of the ark rather than God, the Israelites took the ark into battle against the Philistines and suffered a crushing defeat (I Samuel 4:1-11). The Philistines captured the ark, only to send it back when disaster struck their camp (I Samuel 5-6). It remained at Kirjath Jearim during Saul's reign until David brought it to Jerusalem (I Chronicles 13:3-14; 15:1-28). David recognized the great significance of the ark as the earthly throne of Israel's God. As a true theocratic king he wished to acknowledge the LORD's kingship and rule over both himself and the people by restoring the ark to a place of prominence in the nation.

The persons who did not know God had a holy fear of and respect for God's presence I Samuel 4:5. The Philistines heard the Ark of the LORD was in the camp and they were afraid.

David, in preparing to receive the Ark makes a new cart and brought it from the house of Abinadab; it was being guided; David and the whole house of Israel were worshipping, celebrating with all their might before the LORD, with songs and harps, lyres, tambourines, sistrums and cymbals, waving branches of juniper trees. The oxen stumbled and Uzzah puts out his hand to steady the Ark. The anger of the LORD flared out against him and he killed him for doing this, so that Uzzah died there beside the Ark, struck down for his irreverent act. Why, do you ask, when he was only trying to help!

Verse 8 tells us that David was angry at what the LORD had done. His initial reaction was resentment that his attempt to honour the LORD had resulted in a display of God's wrath. David's anger was accompanied by fear—not the wholesome fear of proper honour and respect for the LORD but an anxiety arising from the acute sense of his own guilt.

Let us turn to I Chronicles 15:1-2,12, 15 "David now built…a new Tabernacle to house the Ark of God, and issued these instructions: When we transfer the Ark to its new home, no one except the Levites may carry it, for God has chosen them for this purpose; they are to minister to him forever…Now sanctify yourselves with all your brothers so that you may bring the Ark of Jehovah, the God of Israel, to the place I have prepared for it. The LORD destroyed us before because we handled the matter improperly---you were not carrying it. Then the Levites carried the Ark on their shoulders with its carrying poles, just as the LORD had instructed Moses."

Now we get a better picture of why the LORD acted so swiftly and decisively at Uzzah's actions. Although Uzzah's intent may have been good, he violated the clear instructions the LORD had given for handling the Ark. At this important new beginning in Israel's life with the LORD, the LORD gives a shocking and vivid reminder to David and Israel that those who claim to serve Him must acknowledge His rule with absolute seriousness.

**WHEN SOMETHING NEW IS BEING SET UP OR ESTABLISHED NOTHING LESS THAN GOD'S STANDARD MUST BE TOLERATED.**

### Leviticus 10:1-3 (TLB)

Nadab and Abihu offered unauthorized fire; fire came out from the presence of the LORD and consumed them—a new era was being established. "I will show myself holy among those who approach me and I will be glorified before all the people."

**Joshua 7:12-13**

With Achan's disloyalty to the LORD, resulting in his execution, a new community had to be made aware that it existed for God and not vice versa; I will not be with you any more unless you destroy whatever among you is devoted to destruction…You cannot stand against your enemies until you remove it.

**Acts 5:1-22**

A new community of faith  It was important to set the course properly at the outset in order to leave no doubt that God will not tolerate hypocrisy and deceit. David copied the wrong deed of those who were doing the same thing but for different reasons. The Philistines in their effort to return the Ark to Israel, made a new cart. David, in spite of the instructions he had received, followed their example. The Philistines had no prior instructions to carry out their plan and they had no relationship with the God of Israel.

It is against this backdrop that David writes Psalm 24 realizing that he had been presumptuous, and had taken for granted God's goodness, and His friendship. To say, "I am a friend of God, He calls me friend"; indeed, but don't forget who we are dealing with: the earth is the LORD'S and everything in it.  It is not about me or you. It has nothing to do with us. It is all about God.

## WHO THEN MAY ASCEND?
## AND, WHO MAY APPROACH?
## AND, WHO MAY STAND IN HIS PRESENCE?

Well, I want to share some of the lessons I have learnt about who is a true worshipper:

As true worshippers who want God to respond to our worship, we would want to ensure that everything is in order when we come into His presence. There must be a connection with God in worship…that is why we come to worship Him. In some churches, the congregation is ready to worship at the start, with no prompting, no winding up, no encouragement.

David says in **Psalm 65:4,**

"Blessed are those you choose and bring near to live in your courts."

## B. WHO IS A TRUE WORSHIPPER?

### 1. A TRUE WORSHIPPER HAS CLEAN HANDS —GUILTLESS ACTIONS.

**II Samuel 22:21**

"The LORD has dealt with me according to my righteousness, according to the cleanness of my hands He has rewarded me."

It was David's desire to please the Lord in his service as the Lord's anointed and his recognition that the Lord rewards those who faithfully seek Him. God responds to man in kind…to the blameless, you show yourself blameless (v.26)

What do your hands do throughout the week? In the evenings when you are alone with the opposite sex? What do they type on the computer? On the internet? On messenger? On Facebook? Or, when you text? As a Christian, what kinds of actions do you engage in?

What about your thought life? And, what about your conversation?

**Ephesians 4:28-9**

Do not let any unwholesome talk come out of your mouths, but only what is helpful for building others up according to their needs, that it may benefit those who listen.

### 2. A TRUE WORSHIPPER HAS A PURE HEART.

**Psalm 73:1**

Surely God is good to those who are pure in heart, those who love and serve God with undivided loyalties/undivided heart. Know that

God demands purity I Chronicles 15:12 consecrate yourselves. The holiness of God demands the purity of God's people engaged in the service or worship of God.

A pure heart has to do with right attitudes and motives. This is yet another expression of David's repeated emphasis on authentic godliness as involving inner and outer holiness. Jesus said, "the pure in heart will see God." It is only those who present themselves before God choosing daily to walk blamelessly before Him in humility who will be used of God. Not only will they be used, but they will be saved from judgment.

## 3. A TRUE WORSHIPPER DOES NOT LIFT UP HIS SOUL TO AN IDOL

A true worshipper does not worship or put his trust in man or anything else for that matter. It is only those who refuse to compromise the standards that God has set out for them (who hath not lifted up his soul unto vanity).

**Psalm 25:1 (TLB)**

To you O LORD, I lift up my soul, in you I trust O my God. The LORD is the ONLY ONE to whom our reverence should be directed.

Know that God is a God of order I Chronicles 15:12 There is a place for carrying out instructions as given. Worship personnel and properties must reflect the holiness of God and therefore be treated appropriately. Even with David, a man after God's own heart, amidst the throng and the festive atmosphere, the sacredness of God as seen in the Ark must not be lost. That which has been consecrated to God must remain distinct from the profane realm of the world.

David to Solomon I Chronicles 28:9 (TLB)

"Solomon my son, get to know the God of your fathers. Worship… Him with a clean heart and a willing mind, for the LORD sees every heart and understands and knows every thought."

True worshippers immediately take care of issues that affect intimacy. They repent easily when they realize that they were wrong. Cain like David, got angry when his act of worship was rejected! But Cain's response differed from David's. David dealt with it and moved on; but Cain did not deal with it and by his response/attitude he allowed the enemy who was crouching at the door to enter. If we have the wrong motives when we enter God's presence sin crouches at our door waiting to enter when we open the door with the wrong response. You can master sin with correct attitudes to and motives in worship. Mastering sin begins with correct attitudes to worship in God's presence. If you don't address issues that affect your intimacy with the lover of your soul, they will affect your relationship.

### 4. A TRUE WORSHIPPER DOES NOT SWEAR BY WHAT IS FALSE

…who does not practice dishonesty and lying.

### 5. A TRUE WORSHIPPER WORSHIPS THE FATHER IN SPIRIT AND IN TRUTH.

True worshippers are the kind the Father seeks. God is spirit and His worshippers must worship Him in spirit. It is not *where* we worship that counts but *how* we worship. Is our worship spiritual and real? Do we have the Holy Spirit's help? For God is spirit and we must have His spirit.

### 6. A TRUE WORSHIPPER HERALDS THE APPROACH OF THE KING OF GLORY.

**Psalm 24:7-8 (TLB)**
"Open up you ancient gates and let the King of Glory in. Who

is this King of glory? The LORD strong and mighty, the LORD mighty in battle."

The LORD who has triumphed over all my enemies, and all my fears. This great and awesome and powerful God; God who has been faithful to us; provided for us in ways we never dreamed; the Lord is approaching; lift up your heads in jubilant reception of the victorious King of glory. After you have taken care of your hands, heart, mind and lips, you can deal with your confidence before the King. Lift up your head to receive the king.

Then David said something that really stuck with me. In verse 6, he said, "This is the generation of them that seek Him, that seek thy face, O Jacob." Here is a comparison between the wrestling experience of Jacob with God and the level of seeking that is required in order that the King of Glory shall come in.

**II Samuel 6:12 (TLB)**

"After the men who were carrying the Ark had gone 6 paces, they stopped and waited so that David could sacrifice…and David danced before the LORD with all his might…King David was leaping and dancing before the LORD. David was wearing priest's clothing. After 6 paces David realized that they had gotten it right this time and this was cause for celebration…Look what the LORD hath done…You don't understand what I went through to be at this point and I just need to give my God the praise. Sometimes people will look at your worship and despise you but they don't know how it felt when the LORD healed you; when the LORD provided that scholarship; when the LORD showered down His blessings upon your life…I don't know what you came to do, but I came to praise the LORD! When the Spirit of the LORD comes upon my heart I will dance like David danced!

Michal, David's wife, daughter of Saul, watched David from a window and she despised him in her heart…How the King of Israel has distinguished himself today, disrobing in the sights of the slave girls of his servants as any vulgar fellow would. My father, King Saul, did not behave in such a manner; he did not worship like that! He was circumspect! My God what will people think?!! He kept his bearing and people knew he was the King. Michal was correct because Saul, however, did not have the kind of relationship with the LORD that David had.

People around you, like David's wife Michal, have no appreciation for the significance of what God is doing in your life and deeply resent your public display. David told her "It was before the LORD, who chose me rather than your father Saul, or anyone from his house when he appointed me ruler over the LORD's people Israel…I will celebrate before the LORD, sing unto the LORD, I will sing to Him a new song… Hallelujah, hallelujah…I will sing to Him a new song. I will become even more undignified than this, and I will be humiliated in my own eyes. I am willing to act like a fool in order to show my joy in the LORD. Yes, and I am willing to look even more foolish than this, but I will be respected by the girls of whom you spoke.

David was a worshipper first and then a king. David knew that who he worshipped was the one who had made him king. David knew the mighty power of God. David was a man who made many blunders but he was known as a man after God's own heart…a worshipper… ."As the deer panteth for the water so my soul longeth after you…"

**Psalm 139:23 (TLB)**

"Search me O God, and know my heart; test my thoughts…"

**Jeremiah 17:10**

"I the LORD search the heart and examine the mind…"

If the LORD searches your heart today will He find a heart that is just like His? How can you know if your heart is like God's heart? Do a spiritual EEG. Let the Word of God look deep into your heart. Read the Bible. Keep God's word close to your heart.

Closet worship cannot be contained. You may claim to possess a quiet disposition and are therefore a quiet worshipper—okay. Well, if you remain quiet when your favourite athlete wins the 100 m dash at the Olympics; or if you are quiet at a concert; or when your preferred political party has just won the general elections; or when your favourite team has won the series with a nail-biting finish…then you are a quiet person.

David, as a true worshipper, has given us tips on how to truly prepare the way to have God reward us with His presence in worship. It is a waste of time, a mere religious exercise to come and set aside time to meet with God and not be successful.

Let us put *first things* first! To derive the full benefit of your worship experience, you may want to prepare yourself with the following exercise. If so, **please stand**:

## C. HOW DO WE PREPARE TO BE A TRUE WORSHIPPER?

**1. Clean hands—With both hands outstretched up in the air, your palms facing up, make the following declaration:**

Elohim, here are my hands that you created, wash them, cleanse them with your blood, break the chains that bind my hands to do evil. I dedicate them to you in the name of the Father, Son and Holy Spirit, they are yours. I consecrate them for your use now. Your word tells me that you are holding me by my right hand, and saying to me, "Don't be afraid. I am here to help you." Help me to keep my hands clean. Help them not to be idle. Keep them from wrong doing, and help me lift them to praise You. Amen!

**2. Pure heart—With your right hand outstretched in front of you; palm turned up, left hand on your heart, make the following declaration:**

El Elyon, examine my heart. Create in me a new, clean heart filled with clean thoughts and right desires. God, I give my heart to you. Give me an undivided heart that I may serve you without competing loyalties. Help me to seek you with all of my heart; help me to hide your

Word in my heart so that I will not sin against you. Fix my thoughts on what is true and good and right. Help me to think about things that are pure and lovely and dwell on the fine, good things in others. Amen!

**3. Allegiance only to El Shaddai—right hand outstretched in front of you; palm turned up, left hand on your forehead and make the following declaration:**

I pledge allegiance to you, El Shaddai. Examine my mind. I give you permission to continuously transform my mind. Take my heart and form it; take my mind transform it; take my will conform it to yours, O LORD. Amen!

**4. Clean lips—place the fingers of both hands on your lips and make the following declaration:**

LORD, take the coal, cleanse my lips. Forgive me for lying lips, a deceptive tongue and a mouth filled with slander and filthy language. May my spoken words and unspoken thoughts be pleasing to you El Shaddai (Psalm 19:14). Set a guard over my mouth O LORD, keep watch over the door of my lips (Psalm141:3) May my lips overflow with praise to you every day (Psalm 119:171) I want to be known as a wo/man after God's own heart. Amen!

When we looked at the hand of God, the personal application there for us was: we are engraved in the palm of His hand.

When we looked at the voice of God, the personal application there for us as well was: God speaks to us exactly what we need, and when we need it, in that still, small voice.

When we looked at the eye of God, the personal application there for us was: listen.

**Zechariah 2:8**

The LORD of Glory has sent me against the nations that oppressed you; for he who harms you sticks his finger in Jehovah's eye/the apple of His eye. This is the unique favour that the LORD has for His people.

**Deuteronomy 32:10**

"…He shielded him and cared for him; He guarded him as the apple of His eye.

## PERSONAL APPLICATION:

**Deuteronomy 5:29**

"O that they would always have such a heart for me, **wanting to obey my commandments**. A man after God's own heart must be obedient to what God tells him to do and therefore must be able to hear His voice. God's wants us to have hearts like His. We are going to examine briefly the life of one who was known to be a "man after God's own heart." If this man's heart reflected God's heart then it means that this is what will give us a glimpse into God's heart."

**Acts 13:22**

"…I have found David…a man after my own heart; **he will do everything I want him to**."

**I Samuel 13:14**

"But now your (Saul's) kingdom will not endure; the LORD has sought out a man after His own heart and **appointed him ruler of His people**…"

**I Samuel 16:7**

"…Do not consider his appearance or his height for I have rejected him. The LORD does not look at the things people look at. People look at the outward appearance but the LORD looks at the heart."

David had nothing to give to God but his heart. God does not care about appearance, personality, ability, superior intelligence. What matters to Him is your heart. If your heart is right, God will use you. The heart of the matter is the matter of the heart.

## CHAPTER 5

# THE FACE OF GOD
Jehovah Rohi, The Lord My Shepherd

*"...I will sing praises to your name."*
***Psalm 18:49***

### A. RESPONSES TO THE FACE OF GOD:

There are varying responses to seeing the face of God. There is one thing that determined why these responses were different, but we will look at that after the responses:

### 1. FEAR OF DEATH

To see God's face was believed to bring death. This is confirmed by God's statement in Exodus 33:20 But…you cannot see my face, for no one may see me and live…I will put you in a cleft in the rock and cover you with my hand until I have passed by. Then I will remove my hand and you will see my back; but my face must not be seen.

**Genesis 32:30**

Jacob named the place Peniel (The Face of God") for he said It is because I saw God face to face and yet my life was spared. This statement indicates the prevailing thought that to see God's face would bring death. Hosea 12:4 also confirms that Jacob met God face to face "He met God there at Bethel face to face. God spoke to him…"

**Genesis 16:13 (TLB)**

Thereafter Hagar spoke of Jehovah—for it was He who appeared to her—as "the God who looked upon me," for she thought, "I saw God and lived to tell it." That is why the well was called Beer Lahai Roi—well of the Living One who sees me.

**Judges 13:22 (TLB)**

"We will die!" Manoah cried out to his wife, "for we have seen God."

### 2. FRIEND WITH FRIEND

**Exodus 33:11 (TLB)**

The LORD would speak to Moses face to face as a man speaks with his friend.

**Numbers 12:8**

"With him I speak face to face…" To Moses God spoke with special clarity as though face to face. Face to face is the most direct contact with God

**Numbers 14:14 (TLB)**

"And they will tell the inhabitants of this land about it. They have already heard that you, O LORD, are with these people and that you, O LORD, have been seen face to face…"

**Deuteronomy 5:4**

"The LORD spoke to you face to face out of the fire on the mountain…"

**Deuteronomy 34:10**

Since then no prophet has risen in Israel like Moses whom the LORD knew face to face.

**Job 19:26-27 (TLB)**
"...this body shall see God...Yes I shall see Him, not as a stranger but as a friend!"

**Hebrews 1:1 (TLB)**
Long ago God spoke in many different ways to our fathers through the prophets (in visions, dreams and even face to face), telling them little by little about His plans.

### 3. FANTASTIC

**Matthew 17:1-3 (TLB)**
"...Jesus took Peter, James, and his brother John to the top of a high and lonely hill, and as they watched, His appearance changed so that His face shone like the sun...Peter blurted out, "Sir, it's wonderful that we can be here! If you want me to, I'll make three shelters..."

### 4. FOR I AM A MAN OF UNCLEAN LIPS

...my eyes have seen the King, the LORD Almighty
**Isaiah 6:1-5**
Isaiah acknowledges that his outward conduct expresses a profound moral uncleanness within his inner being. In the presence of God's absolute moral perfection, he recognizes the lack of holiness in his own life. His humble confession constitutes a prayer for personal sanctification.

A similar response is found in Luke 5:8 when in the face of God's miraculous deed, Peter responds by saying, "Go away from me, LORD, I am a sinful man."

Relationship is what made the foregoing responses so different.

# B. LET US NOW EXAMINE THE FACE OF GOD USING THE LETTERS F.A.C.E. IN REVERSE ORDER I.E. E.C.A.F. THE PERSONAL APPLICATION IS AT THE END.

### 1. EMBODIMENT/ ESSENCE

Concrete expression of something; a tangible or visible expression of an idea of quality; the act or process by which something is made tangible or visible. The face of Jesus (His presence) is mentioned in conjunction with the name of Jesus.

**Numbers 6:25 (TLB)**

Read the verse that follows the Aaronic blessing, "…May His face shine upon you…so they will put my name on the Israelites and I will bless them."

**Psalm 89:15-16**

"Blessed are those who…walk in the light of your presence O LORD. They rejoice in your name all day long…"

**Hosea 12:4 (TLB)**

He met God there at Bethel face to face…Jehovah is His name.

**Revelation 22:3-4 (TLB)**

The throne of God and of the Lamb will be in the city and His servants will serve Him. They will see His face and His name will be on their foreheads.

The name of God evokes the face of God…the very presence of God. At the name of Jesus every knee will bow and every tongue confess in His presence. Jesus is as near as the mention of His name.

### 2. CONCEALMENT

Why does God conceal His face from us? The following verses outline not only why God hides His face from us but will also show the consequences involved when God conceals His face from us.

In the Scripture, the majority of cases mentioned, in which God turned His face away, was because of:

a. Our wickedness in turning to other gods
b. A breach in our relationship with Him

**Deuteronomy 31:17**

On that day I will become angry with them and forsake them; I will hide my face from them and they will be destroyed…and I will certainly hide my face on that day because of all their wickedness in turning to other gods.

**Deuteronomy 32:20**

I will hide my face from them and see what their end will be. Why? Vs. 15-19 "He abandoned the God who made him and rejected the Rock His Saviour. They made Him jealous with their foreign gods and angered Him with their detestable idols. They sacrificed to demons, which are not God—gods they had not known…You deserted the Rock, who fathered you; you forgot the God who gave you birth. The LORD saw this and rejected them because He was angered by His sons and daughters." If you reject God, He will reject you. If you don't acknowledge Him here on earth, He will not acknowledge you before His father in heaven. If your forget God, He will forget you.

**Ezra 9:6**

O my God I am too ashamed and disgraced to lift up my face to you, my God because our sins are higher than our heads.

**Job 34:29**

If He hides His face who can see Him?

**Psalm 13:1**

How long will you hide your face? (ignore). For use in combination with "forget." In moments of need the Psalmist frequently asks God why He hides His face (88:14), or plead with Him not to do so (27:9, 69:17; 102:2; 143:7).

When He does hide His face, those who depend on Him can only despair.

**Psalm 30:7**

O LORD when you favoured me, you made my mountain stand firm; but when you hid your face, I was dismayed.

**Psalm 34:16**

The face of the LORD is against those who do evil to cut off the memory of them from the earth.

**Psalm 44:24**

Why do you hide your face and forget our misery and oppression.

**Psalm 51:9**

"Hide your face from my sins.."

**Psalm 102:2**

Do not hide your face from me when I am in distress.

**Psalm 104:29**

When you hide your face they are terrified.

**Psalm 143:7**

Do not hide your face from me or I will be like those who go down to the pit.

**Isaiah 54:8**

In a surge of anger I hid my face from you for a moment. (Isaiah 1—context=meaningless offerings, evil assemblies…when you spread out your hands in prayer I will hide my eyes from you.

God hid His face from Israel and urged them to stop doing wrong, learn to do right, seek justice, encourage the oppressed. Come now let us reason together…let us meet face to face.

**Isaiah 57:17**

I was enraged by his sinful greed, I punished him and hid my face in anger yet he kept on in his willful ways.

**Isaiah 59:2 (TLB)**

But the trouble is that your sins have cut you off from God. Because of sin he has turned his face away from you and will not listen anymore.

**Isaiah 64:7**

No one calls on your name or strives to lay hold of you, for you have hidden your face from us and have given us over to our sins.

**Jeremiah 18:17**

I will show them my back and not my face. This was God's response to Judah in the stubbornness of their evil hearts they turned their backs to God and he was going to do the same to them.

**Ezekiel 15:7-8**

I will set my face against them. Although they have come out of the fire, the fire will yet consume them. And when I set my face against them you will know that I am the LORD.

**Ezekiel 39:23 (TLB)**

And the nations will know why Israel was sent away to exile, it was punishment for sin…therefore I turned my face away from them and let their enemies destroy them. 24 I turned my face away and punished them in proportion to the vileness of their sins.

**Micah 3:4**

Then they will cry out to the LORD but He will not answer them. At that time He will hide His face from them because of the evil they have done. Disobedience leads to separation from God.

**I Peter 3:12**

For the eyes of the LORD are on the righteous and His ears are attentive to their prayer but the face of the LORD is against those who do evil.

### 3. ACCESS

**Matthew 18:10**

See that you do not look down on one of these little ones. For I tell you that their angels in heaven always see the face of my Father in heaven.//for I tell you that in heaven their angels have constant access to my Father (TLB)

These guardian angels have constant access to your Father in heaven. So there is a warning that God's children should not be looked down upon. What former aspect of our study that we have already looked at, does this remind you of? We are the apple of God's eye. Anyone who troubles you sticks their finger in the eye of God.

### 4. FAVOUR/ BLESSING

When God shines His face on a person, blessing, deliverance and victory become evidence of His love for us.

**Numbers 6:25 (TLB)**

May the LORD bless you and keep you; May His face be radiant with joy because of you. May He be gracious to you; grant you His favour and give you His peace. Known as the Aaronic Benediction/ Blessing, a priestly blessing. This is how Aaron and his sons shall call down my blessings upon the people of Israel; and **I myself** will personally bless them."

**Psalm 4:6 (TLB)**

Who can show us any good? Let the light of your face shine upon us. In the face of widespread uncertainty David prays for the LORD to bless…a common expression for favour.

**Psalm 30:7**

O LORD when you favoured me you made my royal mountain stand firm, but when you hid your face I was dismayed.

**Psalm 31:16**

Let your face shine on your servant; save me in your unfailing love.

**Psalm 44:3**

It was not by their sword that they won the land nor did their arm bring them victory; it was your right hand, your arm and the light of your face, for you loved them. Psalm 89:15-16 Blessed are those who have learned to acclaim you, who walk in the light of your presence O LORD. They rejoice in your name all day long.

**Psalm 67:1 (TLB)**

May God be gracious to us and bless us and make His face shine upon us. Why? 67:2…that your ways may be known on earth." May

God's favour to His people be so obvious that all the world takes notice.

**Psalm 80:3, 7, 19 (TLB)**

Restore us O God/O God Almighty/O LORD God Almighty, make your face shine upon us that we may be saved.

**Psalm 119:135**

Make your face shine upon your servant and teach me your decrees.

**Daniel 9:17**

For your sake, O LORD, look with favour on your desolate sanctuary (NIV)

Let your face shine again with peace and joy upon your desolate sanctuary (TLB)

## PERSONAL APPLICATION

What then should be our appropriate response to the face of God? We are encouraged to:

### 1. SEEK HIS FACE

**II Chronicles 7:14**

"...humble themselves and pray and seek my face

**I Chronicles 16:11 (TLB) /Psalm 105:4**

Look to the LORD and His strength; seek His face always

**Psalm 24:6**

Such is the generation of those who seek Him, who seek your face O God of Jacob. What is such? The generation who seeks and finds the face of God will receive blessing from the LORD and vindication from God His Saviour (i.e. fruits of vindication such as righteous treatment from a faithful God.

**Psalm 27:8**

My heart says of you "Seek His face! Your face LORD I will seek. Do not hide your face from me.

**Psalm 105:4**

Look to the LORD and His strength seek His face always.

**Psalm 119:58**

I have **sought** your face with *all my heart*... (Deut. 4:29 assures us that if you **seek** the LORD your God you will **find** Him if you look for Him with *all your heart* and with all your soul.)

### 2. SHOW AGAIN HIS FACE/REFLECT HIS FACE

**Exodus 34:29**

When Moses came down from Mount Sinai with the two tablets of the covenant law in his hands, he was not aware that his face was radiant because he had spoken with the LORD. His face glowed from being in the presence of God. Because of this radiance upon his face, Aaron and the people of Israel were afraid to come near him (pretty much the same response to seeing the face of God). When Moses had finished speaking with them, he put a veil over his face but whenever he went into the Tabernacle to speak with the LORD, he removed the veil until he came out again then he would pass on to the people whatever instructions God had given him and the people would see his face aglow. Afterwards he would put the veil on again until he returned to speak with God.

He who had asked to see God's glory, now quite unawares, reflects the divine glory.

Today, however:

**II Corinthians 3:12-18**

We are not like Moses who would put a veil over his face to keep the Israelites from gazing at it while the radiance was fading away... we all who with unveiled face contemplate the LORD's glory are being transformed into his image with ever-increasing glory, which comes from the LORD who is the Spirit.

We who believe are made partakers of this glory by being gradually transformed into the likeness of Christ. Let us take the time to gaze upon His face so that we can be true reflectors of what we see. We need to reflect His face to those around us, our sphere of influence, our friends, coworkers.

**II Corinthians 4:6 (TLB)**

For God who said, "Let there be light in the darkness," has made us understand that it is the brightness of His glory that is seen in the face of Jesus Christ." The light that now shines in Paul's heart, qualifying him to be the proclaimer of Christ, is the knowledge of the glory of God as it was displayed in the face of Christ who has come, not just from an earthly tabernacle, but from the glorious presence of God in heaven itself.

### 3. SEE HIS FACE

When you draw close to the heart of God you will see His face

**Song of Solomon 2:14**

My dove in the clefts of the rock, in the hiding places on the mountainside show me your face, let me hear your voice; for your voice is sweet and your face is lovely (into songs)

**Daniel 10:6**

"…His face like lightning…"

**Revelation 1:13-16**

"…I (John) saw someone like the Son of Man…His head and hair were white like wool as white as snow…His face was like the sun shining in all its brilliance.

**I Corinthians 13:12**

In the same way, we can see and understand only a little about God now, as if we were peering at His reflection in a poor mirror; but someday we are going to see Him in his completeness, face to face.

The imagery is of a polished metal (probably bronze) mirror in which one could receive only an imperfect reflection in contrast to seeing the Lord directly and clearly in heaven. The Christian will know the LORD to the fullest extent possible for a finite being, similar to the way the LORD knows the Christian fully and infinitely. This will not be true however, until the LORD returns. In ancient times criminals were banished from the presence of the King. One blessing of eternity will be to see the LORD face to face.

**Isaiah 53:2-5**

He had no beauty or majesty to attract us to Him; in our eyes there was no attractiveness at all, nothing to make us want Him; nothing in His appearance that we should desire Him. We despised Him and rejected Him—a man of sorrows, acquainted with bitterest grief. We turned our backs on Him; we turned our faces away from His face and looked the other way when He went by. He was despised and we didn't care. Yet it was our grief He bore, our sorrows that weighed Him down…He was wounded and bruised for our sins.

**Isaiah 52:14ff (TLB)**

See, my servant will…be raised and lifted up and highly exalted. Just as there were many who were appalled at Him, His appearance was so disfigured beyond that of any man and His form marred beyond human likeness…by His stripes we are healed.

Because of what Christ did for us on Calvary, today we can have relationship with Him and gaze into His loveliness.

CHAPTER 6

# THE FEET OF GOD
Elohim, the Sovereign, Mighty Creator

*"He parted the heavens and came down;
dark clouds were under His feet."*
**Psalm 18:9**

## A. APPEARANCE OF THE FEET OF GOD (JESUS)

**Exodus 24:9-10 (TLB)**
Moses, Aaron and Nadab & Abihu and the 70 elders of Israel went up. And they saw the God of Israel; under His feet there seemed to be a pavement of brilliant sapphire stones as clear as the heavens.

**Revelation 1:15 (TLB)**
"…His feet were like bronze glowing/ like fine brass, as if burned in a furnace. Greek word for brass is chalkolibanon pronounced khal-kol- ib-an-on meaning whiteness or brilliancy.

# B. REFERENCES TO THE FEET OF GOD (JESUS)

## 1. VICTORY OVER ENEMIES

**I Corinthians 15:25**

For He must reign until He has put all His enemies under His feet. The last enemy to be destroyed is death For He "has put everything under his feet." The term "under His feet" is an Old Testament figure for complete conquest. Ancient kings often had themselves portrayed as placing their feet on vanquished enemies.

**Joshua 10:24 (TLB)**

"Come here and put your feet on the necks of these 5 kings. So they came forward and placed their feet on their necks. Joshua said to them, "Do not be afraid: do not be discouraged. Be strong and courageous. This is what the LORD will do to all the enemies you are going to fight." This was public humiliation of the defeated enemy chieftains and this was the usual climax of warfare in the ancient Near East.

**I Kings 5:3**

"You know that because of the wars waged against my father David from all sides, he could not build a temple for the Name of the LORD his God until the LORD put his enemies under his feet…"

**II Chronicles 9:18**

The throne had six steps and a footstool of gold was attached to it… A royal footstool as part of the throne.

**Job 9:13**

God does not restrain His anger, even the cohorts of Rahab (a mythical sea monster Job 26:12) cowered at His feet.

**Psalm 45:5**

Let your sharp arrows pierce the hearts of the king's enemies, let the nations fall beneath your feet.

**Psalm 77:16-19**

(Red Sea account) "…though your footprints were not seen.."

**Psalm 110:1**

The LORD says to my Lord: "Sit at my right hand until I make your enemies a footstool for your feet."

**Nahum 1:2-3**

The LORD is a jealous and avenging God…the LORD takes vengeance on His foes…His way is in the whirlwind and the storm and clouds are the dust of His feet.

**Hebrews 10:12-13**

But when this priest (Christ) had offered for all time one sacrifice for sins, He sat down at the right hand of God. And since that time He waits for His enemies to be made His footstool…"

### 2. RULER OF EVERYTHING

**Eph.1:10**

Christ is the head of everything

**Ephesians 1:22-23**

And God placed all things under His feet and appointed Him to be head over everything for the church which is His body the fullness of Him who fills everything in every way."

## C. RESPONSES TO THE FEET OF GOD (JESUS)

### 1. SIT AT…TO LEARN

*Sitting at the feet of someone embraces the idea of learning from that person.*

**Deuteronomy 33:3**

Sure it is you who love the people…at your feet they all bow down and from you receive instruction…"

In **Acts 22:2**, Paul is given an opportunity to defend himself and he begins his defense like this, "I am a Jew, born in Tarsus…brought up in this city at the feet of Gamaliel, being thoroughly trained according to the law of our fathers…" Gamaliel was the most honored rabbi of the first century; he was the most famous Jewish teacher of his time and traditionally listed among the "heads of schools". So Saul was one of his students.

*Mary was constantly found at the feet of Jesus.*
**Luke 10:38-39**

"…(Mary) sat at Jesus' feet and was listening to His word."

Mary sat at the feet of Jesus to learn. We gather from the text that there was a lot of hustle and bustle around her but Mary was not distracted as she attentively listened to all that Jesus had to say to her. She shut everything else out. She shut out the work that just had to get done; she shut out the one who raised the concern. She realized that in spite of all that was happening around her; in spite of all that she had to be involved in this was the moment; this was what mattered the most…sitting at the feet of Jesus. Mary was receiving here what she would get nowhere else.

The account of the healing of a demon possessed man in Luke 8 also gives an interesting twist. When the demon possessed man saw Jesus (v.28) he cried out and fell at His feet, shouting at the top of his voice, "What do you want with me, Jesus Son of the Most High God? I beg you don't torture me!" After Jesus sent the demons into a herd of pigs (v.33) the villagers found the man from whom the demons had gone out, sitting at Jesus' feet, dressed and in his right mind; and they were afraid…"

## 2. ANOINT…TO SHOW REVERENCE, GRATITUDE AND LOVE

**John 12:3 (TLB)**

"…she anointed the feet of Jesus and wiped His feet with her hair." Mary was in this act expressing to Jesus:

**Reverence**—this was no adoration of an idol. This was her act of worship to God. Her giving was an act of worship. Mary honoured Jesus without saying a word, just by her actions.

**Gratitude**—Jesus had given tokens of His love to her and her family. Jesus had raised her brother, Lazarus, who was reclining at the table, from the dead. She probably pondered how she could show her appreciation. Jesus has given us tokens of His love through His death on the cross. Where is our act of gratitude in the lives we live, in the way we serve, in our response to God while in His presence?

**Love**—Mary loved Jesus, plain and simple, and it was so clearly seen in this act. The use of her hair to wipe His feet was unusual because a respectable woman in those days did not unbind her hair in public. BUT the taboo of the society/day did not prevent her from expressing her love. The use of her hands to wash the feet of Jesus was also an act of humility as it was the work of a servant? No task to God in the Kingdom of God should seem too menial for you to do. It is being done for God and is an expression of love.

A similar account of Jesus is found in Luke 7:36-48 where His feet are anointed by a sinful woman to show love:

> [36] *When one of the Pharisees invited Jesus to have dinner with him, He went to the Pharisee's house and reclined at the table.* [37] *A woman in that town, who had lived a sinful life learned that Jesus was eating at the Pharisee's house, so she came there with an alabaster jar of perfume.* [38] *As she stood behind him at his feet weeping, she began to wet his feet with her tears. Then she wiped them with her hair, kissed them and poured perfume on them.*
>
> [39] *When the Pharisee who had invited him saw this, he said to himself, "If this man were a prophet, he would know who is touching him and what kind of woman she is—that she is a sinner."*

*⁴⁰ Jesus answered him, "Simon, I have something to tell you."*

*"Tell me, teacher," he said.*

*⁴¹ "Two men owed money to a certain moneylender. One owed him five hundred denarii,[a] and the other fifty. ⁴² Neither of them had the money to pay him back, so he canceled the debts of both. Now which of them will love him more?"*

*⁴³ Simon replied, "I suppose the one who had the bigger debt forgiven."*

*"You have judged correctly," Jesus said.*

*⁴⁴ Then he turned toward the woman and said to Simon, "Do you see this woman? I came into your house. You did not give me any water for my feet, but she wet my feet with her tears and wiped them with her hair. ⁴⁵ You did not give me a kiss, but this woman, from the time I entered, has not stopped kissing my feet. ⁴⁶ You did not put oil on my head, but she has poured perfume on my feet. ⁴⁷ Therefore, I tell you, her sins have been forgiven—as her great love has shown. But whoever has been forgiven little loves little."*

*⁴⁸ Then Jesus said to her, "Your sins are forgiven."*

### 3. FALL DOWN...TO WORSHIP

**Job 1:20**

Background...the Sabeans attacked and carried away your oxen, donkeys...he fire of God fell from the sky and burned up the sheep and the servants...the Chaldeans formed 3 raiding parties and swept down on your camels and carried them off and killed your servants...your sons and daughters were feasting at the oldest brother's house when suddenly a mighty wind swept in from the desert and struck the four corners of the house. It collapsed on them and they are dead…" Job fell to the ground in worship. In the midst of tragedy, Job fell to the ground in worship. We need to take the time to build intimacy with God, spend time at His feet.

**Matthew 28:8-10**

"So the women hurried away from the tomb, afraid yet filled with joy, and ran to tell His disciples. Suddenly Jesus met them "Greetings" He said, they came to Him, clasped His feet and worshipped Him…"

**Luke 5:8**

⁸ When Simon Peter saw this, he fell at Jesus' knees and said, "Go away from me, Lord; I am a sinful man!" Peter fell down at the feet of Jesus in awe of the wonder of God…great things He hath done.

**John 11:32**

"She is mourning her brother, Lazarus' death and when she saw Jesus she "…fell down at His feet…" Mary took to His feet her grief. Mary had spent so much time at His feet that in her time of need it was the one place that she was comfortable. She was accustomed to being at His feet and looking/gazing into His face. She was ushered into His presence, went right into the throne room of the Most High God without fanfare, introduction, or 2 choruses to warm her up. Circumstances did not affect her worship. In the midst of the funeral service, while the coffin was present, mourners were mourning, Mary was able to bow down at the feet of Jesus and worship God in the midst of her grieving.

### 4. PIERCED…FOR OUR SALVATION

**Mark 15:24**

"And they crucified Him…"

A Roman means of execution in which the victim was nailed to a cross. Heavy, wrought-iron nails were driven through the wrists and the heel bones. If the life of the victim lingered too long, death was hastened by breaking his legs (John 19:33) First-century authors vividly describe the agony and disgrace of being crucified.

### 5. EXAMINE...TO IDENTIFY

**Luke 24:39-40**

"Look at my hands and my feet. It is I myself! Touch me and see... When He had said this, He showed them His hands and feet…" This indicates that Jesus' feet as well as His hands were nailed to the cross.

## PERSONAL APPLICATION

### 6. WASH...TO SERVE

In **John 13:15**, God's response to our feet is seen, and it shows what He wants us to do.

**John 13 - Jesus Washes His Disciples' Feet**

*¹It was just before the Passover Festival. Jesus knew that the hour had come for him to leave this world and go to the Father. Having loved his own who were in the world, he loved them to the end.*

*²The evening meal was in progress, and the devil had already prompted Judas, the son of Simon Iscariot, to betray Jesus. ³Jesus knew that the Father had put all things under his power (under His feet), and that he had come from God and was returning to God; ⁴so he got up from the meal, took off his outer clothing, and wrapped a towel around his waist. ⁵After that, he poured water into a basin and began to wash his disciples' feet, drying them with the towel that was wrapped around him.*

*⁶He came to Simon Peter, who said to him, "LORD, are you going to wash my feet?"*

*⁷Jesus replied, "You do not realize now what I am doing, but later you will understand."*

*⁸"No," said Peter, "you shall never wash my feet."*

*Jesus answered, "Unless I wash you, you have no part with me."*

## WHAT A GOD!

*⁹"Then, Lord," Simon Peter replied, "not just my feet but my hands and my head as well!"*

*¹⁰Jesus answered, "Those who have had a bath need only to wash their feet; their whole body is clean. And you are clean, though not every one of you." ¹¹For he knew who was going to betray him, and that was why he said not everyone was clean.*

*¹²When he had finished washing their feet, he put on his clothes and returned to his place. "Do you understand what I have done for you?" he asked them. ¹³"You call me 'Teacher' and 'Lord,' and rightly so, for that is what I am. ¹⁴Now that I, your Lord and Teacher, have washed your feet, you also should wash one another's feet. ¹⁵I have set you an example that you should do as I have done for you. ¹⁶Very truly I tell you, no servant is greater than his master, nor is a messenger greater than the one who sent him. ¹⁷Now that you know these things, you will be blessed if you do them.*

This menial task was normally performed by a servant. It was a dirty job because the roads being dusty and muddy, feet were usually dirty. A culturally fitting example would be to have to clean the toilet of your brother who is having a bad case of vomiting and diarrhea.

Another example of a menial task is found in John 1:27 "… whose sandals I am not worthy to untie." This too was a menial task fit only for a slave. Disciples would perform all sorts of service for their rabbis (teachers), but loosing sandals was expressly excluded. On this occasion there was no servant and no one else volunteered. Jesus had His disciples book the upper room but they did not book any servant to wash their feet before they ate. Jesus' action, which occurred during the meal, not upon arrival, was done deliberately to emphasize a point. Nobody was humble enough to take the job. They were too busy fighting for the greatest position in the Kingdom. It was a lesson in humility, which also set forth the principle of selfless service that was so soon to be exemplified in the cross.

Peter objected, through apparently no one else did. His objection was a mixture of humility (he did not want Jesus to perform this lowly service for him) and pride (he tried to dictate to Jesus). "Unless I wash you," …Jesus' reply looks beyond the incident to what it actually symbolized. Peter needed a spiritual cleansing. The external washing was a picture of cleansing from sin, which Christians also sometimes need.

It should bring you to tears when you see how God bent and therefore how low we also should bend in service to each other. Christians should be willing to perform the most menial services for one another. As we fall down in worship at Jesus' feet, recall how he washed the feet of his disciples. Then go and do thou likewise.

# CHAPTER 7
# THE MIND/THOUGHTS OF GOD

*"As for God, His way is perfect…"*
*Psalm 18:30*

The mind is that part of a person responsible for thought, feelings, intention etc. It also refers to an inclination, desire or purpose

## A. REFERENCES TO THE MIND OF GOD

**I Samuel 2:35**
"I will raise up for myself a faithful priest who will do according to what is in My heart and mind."

**Jeremiah 7:31**
"They have built the high places of Topheth in the Valley of Ben Hinnom to burn their sons and daughters in the fire—something I did not command nor did it enter my mind."

With reference to the mind of God, two things are always mentioned:

1. We don't know the mind of God.
2. He does not change His mind.

## 1. WE DO NOT KNOW THE MIND OF GOD

**Job 11:7-8 (TLB)**
"Do you know the mind…of God…His mind is fathomless-what can you know in comparison."
**Isaiah 40:13 (TLB)**
"Who has understood the mind of the LORD?"
**Isaiah 55:8-9**
"For my thoughts are not your thoughts, neither are your ways my ways declares the LORD. As the heavens are higher than the earth, so are my thoughts (higher) than your thoughts."
**Micah 4:12**
"But they do not know the thoughts of the LORD; they do not understand His plan…"
**Romans 11:33-34 (TLB)**
"…How impossible it is for us to understand His decision and His methods! For who among us can know the mind of the LORD?"
**I Corinthians 2:16**
"For who has known the mind of the LORD so as to instruct Him? But we have the mind of Christ."

## 2. GOD DOES NOT CHANGE HIS MIND

**Numbers 23:19 (TLB)**
God is not a man that He should lie, not a son of man that He should change His mind.
**I Samuel 15:29**
He who is the Glory of Israel does not lie or change His mind; for He is not a human being that He should change His mind.

**Job 36:5 (TLB)**

"God is mighty and firm in His purpose." God's power assures the fulfillment of His purpose.

**Psalm 33:11**

But the plans of the Lord stand firm forever, the purposes of His heart through all generations.

**Psalm 34:16 (TLB)**

But the LORD has made up His mind to wipe out even the memory of evil men from the earth.

**Psalm 89:34 (TLB)**

I will not…alter what my lips have uttered.

**Psalm 102:27**

"…but you remain the same…"

**Psalm 110:4**

The LORD has sworn and will not change His mind.

**Isaiah 31:2 (TLB)**

In His wisdom He will send great evil on His people and will not change His mind.

**Jeremiah 15:1**

"Then the LORD said to me, even if Moses and Samuel were to stand before me, my heart would not go out to this people. Send them away from my presence.

## B. DID GOD THEN CHANGE HIS MIND IN THE FOLLOWING EXAMPLES?

### 1. ABRAHAM PLEADS FOR SODOM

**Genesis 18:20-32**

Then the LORD said, "the outcry against Sodom and Gomorrah is so great and their sin so grievous that I will go down and see if what they have done is as bad as the outcry that has reached me…" Will you sweep away the righteous with the wicked? What if there are fifty righteous people in the city? Will you really sweep it away and not spare the place for the sake of the fifty righteous people in it?…Then the LORD said If I find fifty righteous people in the city of Sodom, I will spare the whole place for their sake…forty-five…forty…thirty.. twenty…ten…for the sake of ten I will not destroy it."

Abraham based his plea on the justice and authority of God, confident that God would do what was right for all involved, the innocent as well as the guilty. Abraham's questioning did not arise from a spirit of haggling but of compassion for his relatives and of **wanting to know God's ways.**

## 2. THE GOLDEN CALF

**Exodus 32:10**

"Now leave me alone so that my anger may burn against them and that I may destroy them. Then I will make you (Moses) into a great nation."

**What change brought about God's reaction? Verse 9 , *"I have seen these people, the LORD said to Moses and they are a stiff-necked people."***

**Genesis 12:2**

God had promised Abraham that He would make him into a great nation:

God affirmed this promise to Moses in Exodus 3:6

"I am the God of your father, the God of Abraham, the God of Isaac and the God of Jacob." Moses responds to God verses 11-14 "O LORD why should your anger burn against your people, whom you brought out of Egypt with great power and a mighty hand?…Remember your servants Abraham, Isaac and Israel to whom you swore by your own self "I will make your descendants as numerous as the stars in the sky…Then the LORD relented and did not bring on His people the disaster He had threatened."

Using God's own words Moses appeals to God's special relationship to Israel then to God's need to vindicate His name in the eyes of the Egyptians and finally to the great patriarchal promises. Moses interceded on behalf of the people of Israel.

**Deuteronomy 9:18-29**

Then once again I fell prostrate before the LORD for forty days and forty nights: I ate no bread and drank no water because of all the sin you had committed doing what was evil in the LORD's sight and so arousing His anger. I feared the wrath and anger of the LORD …I prayed to the LORD and said "O Sovereign LORD, do not destroy your people, your own inheritance that you redeemed by your great power…Remember your servants Abraham, Isaac and Jacob; overlook the stubbornness of this people, their wickedness and their sin. Otherwise the country from which you brought us will say, "Because the LORD was not able to take them into the land He had promised them, and because He hated them He brought them out to put them to death in the wilderness."

### 3. DAVID'S CENSUS

**II Samuel 24:10-17**

David was conscience-stricken after he had counted the fighting men and he said to the Lord "I have sinned greatly in what I have done…This is what the LORD says: I am giving you three options… Choose one of them for me to carry out against you…so the Lord sent a plague (3 days) on Israel from that morning until the end of the time designated and 70,000 people died. When the LORD stretched out His hand to destroy Jerusalem, the LORD was grieved because of the calamity and said to the angel who was afflicting the people "Enough! Withdraw your hand."

**What change brought about God's reaction?** *His compassion*

### 4. THE LORD REJECTS SAUL AS KING

**I Samuel 15:10**

Then the word of the LORD came to Samuel "I regret that I have made Saul king, because he has turned away from me and has not carried out my instructions…"

**What change brought about God's reaction?** *Saul's move away from God.*

### 5. NABOTH'S VINEYARD

**I Kings 21:19-29**

Say to him (Ahab king of Israel) This is what the LORD says Have you not murdered a man and seized his property?…This is what the LORD says: "In the place where dogs licked up Naboth's blood, dogs will lick up your blood…" When Ahab heard these words, he tore his clothes, put on sackcloth and fasted. He lay in sackcloth and went around meekly. Then the word of the LORD came to Elijah… Have you noticed how Ahab has humbled himself before me? Because he has humbled himself I will not bring this disaster in his day, but I will bring it on his house in the days of his son." (I Kings 22:38)

Ahab's subsequent repentance occasioned the postponement of certain aspects of this prophecy until the time of his son Joram. Ahab himself was killed in battle and his body brought to Samaria where dogs licked the blood being washed from his chariot. (Partial fulfillment)

### 6. STORY OF JONAH

God tells Jonah to go to the great city of Nineveh and preach against it, because its wickedness has come up before Him. (Nahum later states that Nineveh's sins included plotting evil against the LORD (Nahum 1:11) cruelty and plundering in war (2:12-13; 3:1, 19); prostitution and witchcraft (3:4) and commercial exploitation (3:16). Jonah runs away…great fish sent (1:17) Jonah prayed and the LORD commanded the fish to vomit Jonah onto dry land. Then the word of the LORD came to Jonah a second time (3:1) Go to the great city of Nineveh and proclaim to it the message I give you…forty more days and Nineveh will be overturned. The Ninevites believed God…proclaimed a fast, and all of them from the greatest to the least put on sackcloth… the king…took off his royal robes, covered himself with sackcloth and sat down in the dust.

"Do not let any people or animals, herds or flock taste anything; do not let them eat or drink. But let people and beast be covered with sackcloth. Let everyone call urgently on God. Let them give up their evil ways and their violence. Who knows? God may yet relent and with compassion turn from His fierce anger so that we will not perish."

10 When God saw what they did and how they turned from their evil ways, He relented and did not bring on them the destruction He had threatened. 4:1 But to Jonah this seemed very wrong and he became angry. O LORD is this not what I said when I was still at home? That is what I tried to forestall by fleeing to Tarshish. I knew that you are a gracious and compassionate God, slow to anger and abounding in love, a God who relents from sending calamity.

In His mercy, the LORD responds to human repentance, by forgiveness.

Jeremiah 18:7-10 helps us to merge the two concepts together that God does not change His mind and yet we see where He relents.

If at any time I announce that a nation or kingdom is to be uprooted, torn down and destroyed and if that nation I warned repents of its evil, then I will relent and not inflict on it the disaster I had planned. 9 And if at another time I announce that a nation or kingdom is to be built up and planted, and if it does evil in my sight and does not obey me, then I will reconsider the good I had intended to do for it."

The LORD retains the right to limit His own absolute sovereignty on the basis of human response to His offers of pardon and restoration and His threats of judgment and destruction. If…if…if…if… God's promises and threats are conditioned on man's actions. God, who

Himself does not change nevertheless will change His preannounced response to man, depending on what the latter does. Also see Jeremiah 26:3, 19.

## PERSONAL APPLICATION

**Romans 8:5-6**

"Those who live according to the sinful nature have their minds set on what that nature desires; but those who live in accordance with the Spirit have their minds set on what the Spirit desires…"

Excerpts from "The Battlefield of the Mind: Winning the Battle in your Mind" Joyce Meyer

1. As a person thinks in his heart, so is he//so does he become Proverbs 23:7 Your life, your actions will always be a direct result of your thoughts. If you have a negative mind-set, you will have a negative life. But if you renew your mind according to God's plan for you, you will have an abundant life.

2. Arm yourself for the battle…Satan is coming after you with a carefully crafted plan of attack, one you might not even see coming. In fact one of his best tricks is deception and you might not even believe you are in a war. Arm yourself "For the weapons of our warfare are not physical but they are might before God for the overthrow and destruction of strongholds…we lead every thought and purpose away captive into the obedience of Christ." II Corinthians 10:4-5

    *"When negative thoughts impact us, it is our responsibility, with the help of the Holy Spirit, to capture, and arrest that thought. There must be no further development of that first thought. It must not be allowed to bloom, or grow into anything more. Do not indulge that thought into deeper thoughts. The LORD taught me that our second thought after that first one is a prayer of help to God."* – Ruth Lawrence

3. In the following verse Jesus tells us how we can go inside Satan's head and break free of his grip when he attacks us. "If you abide in My word (hold fast to my teachings and live in accordance with them) you are truly my disciples. And you will know the truth and the truth will set you free." John 8:31-32 We must absorb the knowledge of God's truth into our minds, renewing our minds with the wisdom and power of His Word. God's Word, the Bible is our arsenal, containing all the weapons we need to win the crucial battle for our minds.

   Your thoughts are powerful. They aren't just images and attitudes that lurk in your head; they determine who you are and who you are going to become! Over the next 24 hours, your mind could generate as many as 50,000 thoughts. So a penny for your thoughts can bring you $500.00 a day.

4. You don't have to go hunting for stuff that's bad for your mind; it will come to you. Good and right thoughts take effort. You have to choose to think God's way, then continue to choose right thoughts every day and every night. Be patient with yourself as you try to reprogramme your mind that has been corrupted with all kinds of worldly viruses and worms. Because God is the ultimate IT expert, He can reprogramme your mental hard drive, clean up the viruses and install firewalls to protect you in the future.

   Positive minds produce positive lives. Negative minds produce negative lives. Practice being positive in each situation that arises in your life.

   Mind-binding spirits are like tiny seeds that satan plants in your mind. In time these seeds sprout into weeds of doubt, insecurity, unbelief and cynicism. These pollute and clutter the landscape of your mind.

The Jamaica Reggae artiste Bob Marley sang, "Emancipate yourselves from mental slavery, none but ourselves can free our minds." Some of us are slaves to negative thoughts; unwholesome thoughts and we cannot free ourselves from these things.

**Romans 8:5-6**

*"Those who live according to the sinful nature have their minds set on what the nature desires (so how are they going to free their minds); but those who live in accordance with the Spirit have their minds set on what the Spirit desires."*

I used to picture the possibility that a big screen was over our heads and it displayed to everyone looking at us, every thought that we had. If this was so, we would watch our thought life.

Only the LORD can free our minds. When Satan gives you thoughts—they are temptation. When God gives you thoughts—they are inspiration. (Rick Warren) Which are you going to choose?

**Romans 8:6**

*The mind of sinful man is death, but the mind controlled by the Spirit is life and peace.*

**Philippians 4:6-7**

*Do not be anxious about anything but in every situation, by prayer and petition with thanksgiving present your requests to God. And the peace of God which transcends all understanding will guard your…minds in Christ Jesus.*

As a young Christian in high school, I had a friend who attended the same school and lived very close to me; so we would travel to school and back home together every day. She was a good friend with one problem though: she had a smutty mind. It didn't matter what comment was made, my friend always had a smutty response. I intended to just ignore it and pray that my influence would rub off on her. However, I knew I was in some deep trouble when, one morning in church, while listening to the sermon, the preacher made a comment and my mind automatically had a smutty response. That did it!! I did two things:

firstly, I asked the LORD to intervene and help me out of the situation, and, secondly, I literally committed to memory Philippians 4:8 and recited it daily. Well, the LORD heard my cry and one day my friend informed me that she was unable to travel with me anymore because of some extra-curricular activities that she was now involved with. She had felt rather badly that she had to do that but I told her that I would be fine, and I was! ALL PRAISE TO GOD.

Rick Warren uses the principle of replacement this way i.e. whatever you want to change in your life, replace it. For example, if you are watching television and a show comes on that you know is bad for you to watch, change the channel; replace the friends that pull you away from relationship with Adonai; and replace the music on the cell phone that does not bring glory to God.

**Philippians.4:8**

*Whatever is true, whatever is noble, whatever is right, whatever is pure, whatever is lovely, whatever is admirable—if anything is excellent or praiseworthy—think about such things.*

Paul understood the influence of one's thought life. For example, the way you think will determine the way you feel, and the way you feel will determine the way you act. What a person allows to occupy his mind will sooner or later influence his speech and his actions.

> **"Watch your thoughts, for they become words.**
> **Watch your words, for they become actions.**
> **Watch your actions, for they become habits.**
> **Watch your habits, for they become character.**
> **Watch your character, for it becomes your destiny."**

Paul's exhortation to think about such things is followed by a second exhortation "put it into practice". The combination of virtues listed in v.8-9 is sure to produce a wholesome thought pattern which in turn will result in a life of moral and spiritual excellence. When Satan gives us thoughts—they are temptation. However, when God gives us thoughts—they are inspiration.

**Isaiah 26:3**

He will keep him in perfect peace whose mind is stayed on Him.

**Romans 12:2**

Do not conform any longer to the pattern of this world, but be transformed by the renewing of your mind.

**Philippians 2:5**

Let this mind be in you which was also in Christ Jesus (humility, love, compassion)

"Father, teach me to wage spiritual war in your manner and not according to the world. Guide me to live, to fight, to argue and to enter conflict with weapons of the Spirit and not weapons of the flesh. Be my strength, LORD, when I am up against the wall. Father, bring me to a point where I no longer have any confidence in the flesh but my confidence is only in you. LORD, train me so that when I face conflict, discouragement or temptation; when I collide with any obstacle, I rely on you and your way. The truth says that you have given me the power and authority to demolish arguments and every pretense that sets itself up against the knowledge of you. Show me how to take every thought captive and make it obedient to Christ. Show me how to do that, and show me what to do. I commit to doing what you teach me to do. May this be so, my LORD."

**II Timothy 3:14-15**

"Continue in the things which you have learned and been assured of, knowing from whom you have learned them and that from childhood you have known the Holy Scriptures, which are able to make you wise for salvation through faith which is in Christ Jesus.

"The only trustworthy avenue of insight into the mind of God is His Word"

*(Vessels of Honour, Woodrow Kroll)*

CHAPTER 8

# THE BREATH/NOSTRILS OF GOD

*"The valleys of the sea were exposed
and the foundations of the earth
laid bare at your rebuke, O LORD,
at the blast of breath from your nostrils."*
*Psalm 18:15*

A breath – the intake and expulsion of air during respiration…a slight gust of air.

## A. THE BREATH OF GOD IS ASSOCIATED WITH LIFE, UNDERSTANDING, WIND, HOLY SPIRIT AND DESTRUCTION.

### 1. LIFE

**Genesis 2:7**
The LORD God formed a man from the dust of the ground and breathed into his nostrils the breath of life and the man became a living being. Adam is the only person to have God breath into Him.

**Genesis 1:30**

"And to all the beasts of the earth and all the birds in the sky and all the creatures that move along the ground—everything that has the breath of life in it…" Humans and animals alike have the breath of life in them. (Physically we have an affinity with animals but the difference is that man is made in the image of God.)

**Job 27:3-4**

"As long as I have life within me, the breath of God in my nostrils, my lips will not speak wickedness and my tongue will not utter lies."

**Job 33:4**

"The Spirit of God has made me, the breath of the Almighty gives me life."

**Job 34:14-15**

If God were to withdraw His Spirit all life would disappear and mankind would turn again to dust.

**Ezekiel 37:6**

I will put breath in you and you will come to life. Then you will know that I am the LORD.

### 2. GIVING UNDERSTANDING

**Job 32:8 (NIV)**

"But it is the spirit in a man, the breath of the Almighty that gives him understanding."

**Job 32:8 (TLB)**

"But it is the spirit in a man, the breath of the Almighty that makes him intelligent."

### 3. WIND

**Isaiah 40:6-7**

"…All people are like grass, and all their faithfulness is like the flowers of the field. The grass withers and the flowers fail because the breath of the LORD blows on them."

### Psalm 103:15-16

"The life of mortals is like grass, he flourishes like a flower of the field; the wind blows over it and it is gone and its place remembers it no more.

## 4. THE HOLY SPIRIT

### Job 26:13 (NIV)

By His breath the skies became fair.

### Job 26:13 (TLB)

The heavens are made beautiful by His Spirit.

### John 20:22

And with that He breathed on them and said, "Receive the Holy Spirit."

## 5. DESTRUCTION

**OF THE WICKED**—*God's judgment is fearfully severe*

### Job 4:8-9

"As I have observed, those who plow evil and those who sow trouble reap it. At the breath of God they perish; at the blast of His anger they are no more."

### Job 15:30

"He [the wicked man] will not escape the darkness; a flame will wither his shoots and the breath of God's mouth will carry him away (destroy him-TLB)

### Isaiah 11:4

"…with the breath of His lips He will slay the wicked."

**OF THE LAWLESS ONE**

### II Thessalonians 2:8-10 (TLB)

"Then this wicked one will appear, whom the LORD Jesus will burn up with the breath of His mouth and destroy by His presence when He returns. This man of sin will come as Satan's tool, full of satanic power, and will trick everyone with strange demonstrations, and will do great miracles. He will completely fool those who are on their way to hell because they have said no to the Truth; they have refused to believe it and love it and let it save them."

Despite the impressiveness of the lawless one, he will easily be destroyed by Christ.

## BY FIRE

**Psalm 18:8**

"smoke rose from His nostrils, consuming fire came from His mouth, burning coals blazed out of it."

**Isaiah 30:33 (TLB)**

"Topheth (a region outside Jerusalem where children were sacrificed to Molech…it was a place of burning) has long been prepared; it has been made ready for the king. Its fire pit has been made deep and wide, with an abundance of fire and wood; the breath of the LORD, like a stream of burning sulfur //like fire from a volcano (NIV) sets it ablaze." Genesis 19:24 "…the LORD rained down burning sulfur on Sodom and Gomorrah."

## BY ICE

**Job 37:10-13**

"The breath of God produces ice and the broad waters become frozen." Here is a metaphor for a chilling wind.

[11]He loads the clouds the moisture; he scatters His lightning through them. [12]At His direction they swirl around over the face of the whole earth to do whatever He commands them. [13]He brings the clouds to punish men, or to water His earth and show His love.

Elihu reveals a sophisticated observation of atmospheric conditions and their effects 36:27-28 e.g. the cyclonic behavior of clouds in v.12 above. Such forces originate from God's command and always perform His will for mankind, whether for good or for ill. V.13

**Psalm 147:16-17**

"He spreads the snow like wool and scatters the frost like ashes. 17 He hurls down His hail like pebbles. Who can withstand His icy blast?

### BY WATER—*overwhelm*

**Isaiah 30:28**

"His breath is like a rushing torrent rising up to the neck. He shakes the nations in the sieve of destruction."

### BY WIND

**Psalm 48:7 (TLB)**

For God destroys the mightiest warships with a breath of wind.

**Isaiah 40:23-24 (TLB)**

He dooms the great men of the world and brings them all to naught. 24 They hardly get started, barely take root, when He blows on them and their work withers and the wind carries them off like straw.

## B. THE LORD WANTS TO BREATHE ONTO YOUR SITUATIONS (PERSONAL, FAMILIAL, CHURCH, NATION) TO BRING TO LIFE THINGS THAT ARE DEAD THAT NEED TO BE RESTORED; TO DEAL WITH INJUSTICE; AND TO DEAL WITH THE VERY DIFFICULT SITUATIONS THAT WE FACE.

### 1. GOD WANTS TO BREATHE ON OUR POLITICAL SITUATIONS (LIKE A WHIRLWIND)

**Isaiah 40:23-24**

"He brings princes to naught and reduces the rulers of this world to nothing. No sooner are they sown, no sooner do they take root in the ground than **He blows on them and they wither and a whirlwind sweeps them away like chaff.**

**Isaiah 40:17**

"Before Him all the nations are as nothing; they are regarded by Him as worthless and less than nothing." 2:22  Stop trusting in man who has but a breath in his nostrils NIV //Puny man! Frail as his breath! Don't ever put your trust in him!  God alone is worthy of the esteem that we give to frail leaders.

**II Kings 13:14-19 (Jehoash, Aram/eans)**

Therefore, what magnitude of breath do you want?
Category 5 winds or 10?

> *¹⁴ Now Elisha had been suffering from the illness from which he died. Jehoash king of Israel went down to see him and wept over him. "My father! My father!" he cried. "The chariots and horsemen of Israel!"*
>
> *¹⁵ Elisha said, "Get a bow and some arrows," and he did so. ¹⁶ "Take the bow in your hands," he said to the king of Israel. When he had taken it, Elisha put his hands on the king's hands.*
>
> *¹⁷ "Open the east window," he said, and he opened it. "Shoot!" Elisha said, and he shot. "The Lord's arrow of victory, the arrow of victory over Aram!" Elisha declared. "You will completely destroy the Arameans at Aphek."*
>
> *¹⁸ Then he said, "Take the arrows," and the king took them. Elisha told him, "Strike the ground." He struck it three times and stopped. ¹⁹ The man of God was angry with him and said, "You should have struck the ground five or six times; then you would have defeated Aram and completely destroyed it. But now you will defeat it only three times."*

Therefore, what magnitude of breath do you want God to breathe on our political situations?

Declare the breath of God like a whirlwind over these situations.

## 2. GOD WANTS TO BREATHE AGAINST UNJUST SITUATIONS *(INJUSTICE) (LIKE A FLOOD)*

**Isaiah 59:15-21**

"Truth is nowhere to be found…The LORD looked and was displeased that there was no justice. 16 He saw that there was no one, He was appalled that there was not one to intervene; so His own arm worked salvation for Him, and His own righteousness sustained Him…18 According to what they have done, so will He repay wrath to His enemies and retribution to His foes, He will repay the islands their due. 19 From the west, men will fear the name of the LORD, and from the rising of the sun, they will revere His glory, For He will come like **a pent up flood that the breath of the LORD drives along**. The Redeemer will come to Zion, to those in Jacob who repent of their sins."

**Amos 5:7, 10-15, 21-24**

*There are those who turn justice into bitterness*
*and cast righteousness to the ground.*
*¹⁰ There are those who hate the one who upholds justice in court*
*and detest the one who tells the truth.*
*¹¹ You levy a straw tax on the poor*
*and impose a tax on their grain.*
*Therefore, though you have built stone mansions,*
*you will not live in them;*
*Though you have planted lush vineyards,*
*you will not drink their wine.*
*¹² For I know how many are your offenses*
*and how great your sins.*
*There are those who oppress the innocent and take bribes*
*and deprive the poor of justice in the courts.*
*¹³ Therefore the prudent keep quiet in such times,*
*for the times are evil.*

> *¹⁴ Seek good, not evil,*
> *that you may live.*
> *Then the Lord God Almighty will be with you,*
> *just as you say he is.*
> *¹⁵ Hate evil, love good;*
> *maintain justice in the courts.*
> *Perhaps the Lord God Almighty will have mercy*
> *on the remnant of Joseph.*
>
> *²¹ "I hate, I despise your religious feasts;*
> *I cannot stand your assemblies.*
> *²² Even though you bring me burnt offerings and grain offerings,*
> *I will not accept them.*
> *Though you bring choice fellowship offerings,*
> *I will have no regard for them.*
> *²³ Away with the noise of your songs!*
> *I will not listen to the music of your harps.*
> *²⁴ But let justice roll on like a river,*
> *righteousness like a never-failing stream!*

Therefore, what magnitude of breath do you want God to breathe on unjust situations?

Declare the breath of God like a flood over these situations.

## 3. GOD WANTS TO BREATHE ON OUR DIFFICULT SITUATIONS

The children of Israel experienced the mighty hand of God releasing them from Egypt in a massive exodus. They are now faced with a situation where Pharoah's army is marching after them and the Red Sea is before them. When faced with a difficult situation… between the devil and the deep blue sea, what is our first response?... Why me LORD? I have served you faithfully. I don't deserve this!

**Exodus 14:10-12**

Was it because there were no graves in Egypt that you brought us to the desert to die? What have you done to us…Didn't we say to you in Egypt…Leave us alone…it would have been better for us to serve the Egyptians than to die in the desert."

They vented, and it even seems unfair that they would say these things to such a loving God. But haven't we also been faced with situations that we seemed not to deserve? There was no one really that we could turn to because of how we really felt about the situation, and we vented, cried into our pillows, thought we were over it, and just as we started to think about it, a fresh wave of tears would come.

If we don't see in the physical how it is going to work out, and the situation seems impossible because there is just nowhere to turn, God is saying that He wants to breathe on that situation right now.

What did He do for the children of Israel?

**Exodus 14:21**

"…drove the sea back with a strong east wind…"

**Exodus 15:8**

"By the blast of your nostrils the waters piled up…" The poet praises the LORD and calls the wind "blast of your nostrils."

**Psalm 18:15**

"The valleys of the seas were exposed…at the blast of breath from your nostrils." Psalm 18:7-15 The LORD came to the aid of His servant—depicted as a fearful theophany (divine manifestation) of the heavenly Warrior descending in wrathful attack upon David's enemies. He sweeps down upon them like a fierce thunderstorm.

He parted the waters!! He exposed the valleys of the sea!! He created a way! He made a way where there was no way!

Additionally, God did not only deal with what was before them by making a way through the Red Sea (which would probably have been good enough for them to get away), but He also took care of what was behind them! He guaranteed that their enemies would not chase them again.

**Exodus 15:10**

"But you blew with your breath and the sea covered them."

God wants not only to make a way for you, but whatever He creates to take care of what is before you, will also take care of what is behind you!

Therefore, what magnitude of breath do you want God to breathe on your difficult situations?

Declare a blast from the nostrils of God over your situations.

## PERSONAL APPLICATION

### THE BREATH OF RESTORATION

The breath of God is always with us.

**Isaiah 59:21**

"As for me, this is my covenant with them (those who repent of their sins), says the LORD, "My Spirit, who is on you, will not depart from you, and my words that I have put in your mouth will always be on your lips, on the lips of your children and on the lips of their descendants from this time on and forever," says the LORD."

God wants to breathe His Spirit into what is dead. Is there a situation in your life that no longer lives? Has it died? It is not only dead but it seems also that it is buried in the grave? God is saying to you, "Come, I want to breathe my Spirit into those bones that they may live" …a spirit of Restoration.

We invite the breath of God to breathe into our dead situations and bring wholeness, healing, restoration. Come from the four winds, O breath, and breathe.

**Ezekiel 37:4-10**

"Prophesy to these bones and say to them, 'Dry bones, hear the word of the Lord! 5 This is what the Sovereign Lord says to these bones: I will make breath[a] enter you, and you will come to life. 6 I will attach tendons to you and make flesh come upon you and cover you with skin; I will put breath in you, and you will come to life. Then you will know that I am the Lord.'"

⁷ So I prophesied as I was commanded. And as I was prophesying, there was a noise, a rattling sound, and the bones came together, bone to bone. ⁸ I looked, and tendons and flesh appeared on them and skin covered them, but there was no breath in them.

⁹ Then he said to me, "Prophesy to the breath; prophesy, son of man, and say to it, 'This is what the Sovereign Lord says: Come from the four winds, O breath, and breathe into these slain, that they may live.'" ¹⁰ So I prophesied as he commanded me, and breath entered them; they came to life and stood up on their feet—a vast army.

It was after the prophetic Word that put life into the dead bones was spoken, that the tendons and the flesh were restored. Therefore, whatever action needs to be put in place; whatever process is needed for that marital relationship, dead relationship, or lost opportunity, understand that the breath of God has already breathed life into the dead bones of your situation. In other words, the dry bones have already come together by the breath of God. Be patient as the tendons and flesh (actions/processes) eventually come together.

## TESTIMONY AFTER LEARNING ABOUT THE BREATH OF GOD

One of our young people who faithfully attended our monthly prayer and fasting sessions gave this testimony the month after she had learnt about the breath of God. Working in a bank, she had monthly targets that needed to be met. One morning a gentleman came into the bank and she began to assist him. The man, after careful consideration, decided that he would not take the loan.

She really needed that transaction and the voice of God told her to engage the breath of God in this difficult situation. She obeyed the voice and asked the Lord to breathe on this difficult situation. The man changed his mind and took the loan.

What a God!!!

## CHAPTER 9
# THE EAR OF GOD

*"...I cried to my God for help. From His temple He heard my voice; my cry came before Him, into His ears."*
*Psalm 18:6*

The ear is the organ of hearing and balance

### A. "DOES NOT THE EAR TEST WORDS..."
Job 12:11

**1. THE PSALMIST EXEMPLIFIES ONE WHO ENTREATS THE LORD TO LISTEN TO HIM, TO HIS PRAYERS:**

**Psalm 4:1**
Answer me when I call to you my righteous God. Give me relief from my distress. Have mercy on me and hear my prayer.

**Psalm 4:2-3**

How long will you people turn my glory into shame…know that the LORD has set apart His faithful servant for Himself; the LORD will hear when I call to Him. David rebukes those who turn away from His God to seek relief from the counterfeit gods. He assures them that the Lord will hear him.

**Psalm 5:1-3 (TLB)**

Give ear to my words O LORD, consider my sighing. Listen to my cry for help, my King and my God for to you I pray. In the morning O LORD you hear my voice; in the morning I lay my requests before you and wait in expectation. The Psalmist's appeal to be heard. This morning prayer is the psalmist's cry for help when his enemies spread malicious lies to destroy him.

**Psalm 18:6**

In my distress I called to the LORD, I cried to my God for help. From His temple he heard my voice, my cry came before Him into His ears.

**Psalm 28:1-2**

To you LORD I call; You are my Rock, do not turn a deaf ear to me…For if you remain silent…Hear my cry for mercy as I call to you for help.

**Psalm 39:12**

Hear my prayer LORD, listen to my cry for help, do not be deaf to my weeping.

**Psalm 55:1-2 (TLB)**

Listen to my prayer O God; don't hide yourself when I cry to you. Hear me LORD! Listen to me! (betrayal at the hands of friends)

**Psalm 55:17**

Evening, morning and noon I cry out in distress and He hears my voice.

**Psalm 59:7 (TLB)**

See what they spew from their mouths—they spew out swords from their lips and they say "Who can hear us?" But you O LORD, laugh at them.

**Psalm 69:13 (TLB)**

But I keep right on praying to you LORD. For now is the time you are bending down to hear.

**Psalm 71:2 (TLB)**

Bend down your ear and listen to my plea and save me

**Psalm 102:1-2 (TLB)**

Bend down your ear and give me speedy answers

## 2. GOD ALSO HEARD:

### THE ISRAELITES AFTER 400 YEARS OF SUFFERING

**Exodus 3:7-9**

⁷ The Lord said, "I have indeed seen the misery of my people in Egypt. I have heard them crying out because of their slave drivers, and I am concerned about their suffering. ⁸ So I have come down to rescue them from the hand of the Egyptians and to bring them up out of that land into a good and spacious land, a land flowing with milk and honey—the home of the Canaanites, Hittites, Amorites, Perizzites, Hivites and Jebusites. ⁹ And now the cry of the Israelites has reached me, and I have seen the way the Egyptians are oppressing them.

### THE CHILDREN OF ISRAEL, AT THE GIVING OF THE LAW

**Deuteronomy 5:28**

The LORD heard you when you spoke to me and the LORD said to me, "I have heard what this people said to you. Everything they said was good…"

**HIS SON**

**John 11:41-42**

So they took away the stone. Then Jesus looked up and said, "Father, I thank you that you have heard me. I knew that you always hear me, but I said this for the benefit of the people standing here, that they may believe that you sent me."

**CORNELIUS**

**Acts 10:1-4**

At Caesarea there was a man named Cornelius, a centurion in what was known as the Italian Regiment. ² He and all his family were devout and God-fearing; he gave generously to those in need and prayed to God regularly. ³ One day at about three in the afternoon he had a vision. He distinctly saw an angel of God, who came to him and said, "Cornelius!"

⁴ Cornelius stared at him in fear. "What is it, LORD?" he asked.

The angel answered, "Your prayers and gifts to the poor have come up as a memorial offering before God.

## B. WHAT DOES GOD HEAR?

### 1. THE CRY OF THE POOR
### /INJUSTICE AGAINST THE POOR

**Exodus 22:26-27**

If you take your neighbor's cloak as a pledge, return it by sunset, because that cloak is the only covering your neighbour has. What else can they sleep in? When they cry out to me, I will hear, for I am compassionate.

If all that a man had to offer as his pledge for a loan was his cloak, he was among the poorest of the poor. The law prohibited keeping a man's cloak overnight as a pledge (Deuteronomy 24:12-13) or taking a widow's cloak at all.

**Job 34:27-28 (TLB)**

For they (wicked men) turned aside from following Him, causing the cry of the poor to come to the attention of God. Yes, He hears the cries of those being oppressed.

**Psalm 9:12**

…He does not ignore the cries of the afflicted.

**Psalm 69:33 (TLB)**

The Lord hears the cries of His needy ones and does not look the other way.

**Psalm 102:17 (TLB)**

He will listen to the prayers of the destitute, for He is never too busy to heed their requests.

**Psalm 103:6**

He gives justice to all who are treated unfairly.

**Isaiah 11:3**

He will not judge by what He sees with His eyes or decide by what He hears with His ears; but with righteousness He will judge the needy.

### 2. THE RAVENS

**Job 38:41**

Who provides for the ravens when their young cry out to God as they try to struggle up from their nest in hunger.

### 3. THE DOWNHEARTED

**I Samuel 1:10-20**

In her deep anguish Hannah prayed to the Lord weeping bitterly as Eli observed her mouth. Hannah was praying in her heart and her lips were moving but her voice was not heard. Eli thought she was drunk. Not so my LORD, I am a woman who is deeply troubled…I was pouring out my soul to the LORD…I have been praying here out of my great anguish and grief…and the LORD remembered her petition. Eli did not hear Hannah but God heard.

## 4. THE PLEA FROM A FRIEND /THE RIGHTEOUS

**Genesis 19:29**

So when God destroyed the cities of the plain He remembered Abraham/He heeded Abraham's plea…

**Psalm 34:15**

"…His ears are attentive to the cry of the righteous…"

**Malachi 3:16**

"Then those who feared the Lord talked with each other and the LORD listened and heard."

**John 9:31**

"…God listens to the godly person who does His will."

## 5. YOUR DISBELIEF

**Genesis 18:12-15**

Then the Lord said…about this time next year…Sarah your wife will have a son. Now Sarah was listening…and she was past the age of childbearing. So Sarah laughed to herself as she thought "After I am worn out and my lord is old, will I now have this pleasure?" Then the LORD said to Abraham, "Why did Sarah laugh?"…Sarah was afraid, so she lied and said "I did not laugh." But He said, "Yes you did laugh.

## 6. LIES

**Psalm 5:6**

You destroy those who tell lies.

## 7. OPPRESSION

**Exodus 2:23**

The Israelites groaned in their slavery and cried out, and their cry for help because of their slavery went up to God. God heard their groaning and he remembered… 3:7 …I have heard them crying out because of their slave drivers and I am concerned about their suffering. So I have come down to rescue them...

**James 5:4 (TLB)**

For listen! Hear the cries of the field workers whom you have cheated of their pay; their cries have reached the ears of the LORD of hosts.

### 8. WHEN OTHERS TRY TO WRITE THE END OF YOUR STORY

**II Kings 19:14 (TLB)**

Hezekiah's prayer. V.16 He spread the troubling letter before the Lord...give ear O LORD and hear...listen to the words Sennacharib has sent to insult the living God. V.20 I have heard your prayer concerning Sennacharib...v.28 Sennacharib's insolence has reached my ears.

### 9. DEATH CRIES

**II Kings 20 (TLB)**

You are going to die...Hezekiah turned his face to the wall and prayed. V.5 I have heard your prayer and seen your tears.

**Psalm 56:8**

You have collected all my tears and preserved them in your bottle! You have recorded every one in your book.(TLB)//Record my lament; list my tears on your scroll—are they not in your record? (NIV)

## C. WHEN DOES GOD NOT HEAR?

### 1. WHEN SIN IS PRESENT

**Isaiah 59:1**

Surely...His ear (is not) too dull to hear...your sins have hidden His face from you so that He will not hear.//Listen now! The LORD isn't too weak to save you. And He isn't getting deaf! He can hear you when you call! But the trouble is that your sins have cut you off from

God. Because of sin He has turned His face away from you and will not listen anymore.

**John 9:31**

We know that God does not listen to sinners. He listens to the godly person who does His will.

### 2. WHEN WICKED WAYS ARE PRESENT

**II Chronicles 7:12-14**

If my people will humble themselves, pray, seek my face and turn from their wicked ways then I will hear from heaven and will forgive their sin and will heal their land…now my ears will be attentive to the prayers offered in this place…

### 3. WHEN THE WRONG KIND OF FASTING IS DONE

**Isaiah 58:3-4**

Yet on the day of your fasting, you do as you please, and exploit all your workers. Your fasting ends in quarreling and strife and in striking each other with wicked fists. You cannot fast as you do today and expect your voice to be heard on high.

When husbands are not considerate of their wives and treat them with respect.

### 4. WHEN HUSBANDS ARE NOT CONSIDERATE OF THEIR WIVES AND TREAT THEM WITH RESPECT

**I Peter 3:7**

Husbands, in the same way be considerate as you live with your wives, and treat them with respect as the weaker partner and as heirs with you of the gracious gift of life, so that nothing will hinder your prayers.

When leaders don't treat the people right. When they hate good and love evil.

## 5. WHEN LEADERS DON'T TREAT THE PEOPLE RIGHT. WHEN THEY HATE GOOD AND LOVE EVIL

**Micah 3:4**

Then they will cry out to the LORD but He will not answer them. At that time He will hide His face from them because of the evil they have done.

God does not listen to the prayers of those who flout the law.

## 6. GOD DOES NOT LISTEN TO THE PRAYERS OF THOSE WHO FLOUT THE LAW

**Romans 13:2**

So those who refuse to obey the laws of the land are refusing to obey God, and punishment will follow.

In the face of disobedience

## 7. IN THE FACE OF DISOBEDIENCE

**Deuteronomy 1:45**

You came back and wept before the LORD but He paid no attention to your weeping and turned a deaf ear to you.

## D. WHEN DOES GOD HEAR US?

### 1. AFTER THE PROPER KIND OF FASTING

**Isaiah 58:6-9**

"Is not this the kind of fasting I have chosen: to loose the chains of injustice, and untie the cords of the yoke, to set the oppressed free and break every yoke? Is it not to share your food with the hungry and to provide the poor wanderer with shelter…then you will call and the LORD will answer; you will cry for help and He will say "Here am I"".

**Isaiah 65:24**

Before they call I will answer while they are still speaking I will hear

### 2. WHEN WE PRAY ACCORDING TO HIS WILL

**I John 5:14**

This is the confidence we have in approaching God, that if we ask anything according to His will He hears us…

### 3. AFTER CONFESSING OUR SINS

**Psalm 66:17-19 (TLB)**

For I cried to Him for help, with praises ready on my tongue. He would not have listened if I had not confessed my sins. But He listened! He heard my prayer! He paid attention to it!

### 4. WHEN WE LIVE RIGHT

**I Peter 3:12**

For the eyes of the LORD are on the righteous and His ears are attentive to their prayer.

**Psalm 17:1-2, 6 (TLB)**

Hear O LORD, my righteous plea; listen to my cry. Give ear to my prayer, it does not rise from deceitful lips. May my vindication come from you…I call on you O God for you will answer me, give ear to me and hear my prayer.

## E. WHEN WE PRAY ASKING GOD TO HEAR SOMETHING, HOW DO WE PRAY?

When we are made aware of situations that we want God to hear, Solomon shows us the various ways to pray:

- Give attention to your servant's prayer and his plea for mercy
- Hear the cry and prayer that your servant is praying in your presence this day
- Hear the supplication
- Hear from heaven

Using Solomon's Prayer of Dedication in I Kings 8:22-53, as a model, we can get some guidelines. When we are asking God to hear about…

1. Insufficient evidence to support the legitimacy of a charge—hear and act by condemning the guilty and bringing down on his own head what he has done and declare the innocent not guilty and so establish his innocence. v.31-32
2. Defeat/trouble brought about by disobedience—hear and forgive and teach the right way to live. v.33
3. Disease or disaster striking the land (famine, plague, blight, insect invasion)—hear, forgive and act—deal with each man according to all he does since you know his heart… v. 37
4. Foreigners—hear and do whatever the foreigner asks so that people may know your name and fear you as do your own people.v.41
5. Our fight against our enemies—hear and uphold our cause. v. 44

## PERSONAL APPLICATION

But I keep right on praying to you, LORD. For now is the time… You are bending down to hear! You are ready with a plentiful supply of love and kindness. Psalm 69:1

CHAPTER 10

# THE FIST OF GOD
Your Possession of the Promised Land *(Victory)* is a Shout Away

*"With your help I can advance against a troop;*
*with my God I can scale a wall...*
*He trains my hands for battle..."*
*Psalm 18:29 & 34*

The fist is the hand with the fingers clenched into the palm as for hitting.

## A. DAGON

In Canaanite mythology he was the son or brother of El and the father of Baal. He was the principal god of the Philistines and was worshipped in the temples at Gaza (Judges 16:23) Ashdod (I Samuel 5) & Beth Sham (31:10-12) Dagon was one of the Philistine's most popular deities. He was a major member, or perhaps head of the pantheon of the Biblical Philistines and bore the titles LORD of the gods, lord of the land.

## 1. GAZA (JUDGES 16:20-23)

Then she called, "Samson, the Philistines are upon you!" He awoke from his sleep and thought I'll go out as before and shake myself free." But he did not know that the LORD had left him. Then the Philistines seized him, gouged out his eyes and took him down to Gaza. In shame and weakness, Samson was led to Gaza, the place where he had displayed great strength (16:1-3) Now the rules of the Philistines assembled to offer a great sacrifice to Dagon their god and to celebrate saying, "Our god has delivered Samson our enemy into our hands."

It was common to attribute a victory to the national deities.

Samson is a fallen hero…how are the mighty fallen II Samuel 1:19. However, Samson received the victory when he prayed to the LORD.

In October 21, 2011 while attending a conference in Guatemala the LORD revealed to me in a dream that the Spirit of Dagon=**5** and reminded me of this aspect of the anatomy that I was preparing. This number is seen in all of our accounts and confirms that the Spirit of Dagon was manifesting itself in each of these situations.

**Judges 16:28-29**

1 blow to get revenge for my 2 eyes…he…reached towards the 2 central pillars=5

**Judges 16:27**

The 5 Philistine leaders were present.

## 2. BETH SHAN (I SAMUEL 31:8-10)

"The next day, when the Philistines came to strip the dead, they found Saul and his three sons fallen on Mount Gilboa. They cut off his head and stripped off his armour, and they send messengers throughout the land of the Philistines to proclaim the news in the temple of their idols and among their people. They put his armour in the temple of the Ashtoreths and fastened his body to the wall of Beth Shan."

This was symbolic of ascribing victory to the Philistine gods. I

Chronicles 10:10-14 says "They put Saul's armor in the temple of their gods and hung up his head in the temple of Dagon…so the LORD put him to death…" caused by disobedience to the voice of God and the LORD turned His face away.

**I Samuel 15:26**

But Samuel said to Saul, I will not go back with you. You have rejected the word of the LORD, and the LORD has rejected you as king over Israel! 27 As Samuel turned to leave, Saul caught hold of the men of his robe and it tore. 28 Samuel said to him, The LORD has torn the kingdom of Israel from you today…35 Until the day Samuel died, he did not go to see Saul again, though Samuel mourned for him. And the LORD was grieved that he had made Saul king over Israel.

**I Samuel 28: 5-6**

When Saul saw the Philistine army he was afraid; terror filled his heart. 6 He inquired of the Lord, but the LORD did not answer him by dreams or Urim or prophets."

Upon hearing of the death of Saul & Jonathan, David did a lament recorded in II Samuel 1:19. "How the mighty have fallen!.." How the mighty have fallen! Tell it not in Gath, proclaim it not in the streets of Ashkelon…25 How the mighty have fallen in battle!"

As the major Philistine cities located the closest and farthest from Israel's borders, Gath and Ashkelon represent the entire Philistine nation. David does not want the enemies of God's covenant people to take pleasure in Israel's defeat and thus bring reproach on the name of the Lord:

**Numbers 14:13**

Moses desires to protect the Lord's reputation

**Joshua 7:9**

"The Canaanites and the other people of the country will hear about this and they will surround us…what then will you do for your own great name?" Joshua pleads, as Moses had that God's honor in the eyes of all the world was at stake in the fortunes of his people.

**Micah 1:10**

Tell it not in Gath

Remember the Spirit of Dagon=5—I Samuel 31:6 So Saul (1) and his 3 sons and his armor bearer (1)…died together (5) that same day.

Veneration of this deity, Dagon, was widespread in the ancient world, extending from Mesopotamia to the Armean and Canaanite area and attested in non-Biblical sources dating from the late third millennium BC until Maccabean times.

The precise nature of the worship of Dagon is obscure. Some have considered Dagon to be a fish god, but more recent evidence suggests either a storm or grain god.

### 3. ASHDOD (I SAMUEL 5)

The Ark in Ashdod and Ekron

After the Philistines had captured the ark of God, they took it from Ebenezer to Ashdod. ² Then they carried the ark into Dagon's temple and set it beside Dagon. ³ When the people of Ashdod rose early the next day, there was Dagon, fallen on his face on the ground before the ark of the Lord! They took Dagon and put him back in his place. ⁴ But the following morning when they rose, there was Dagon, fallen on his face on the ground before the ark of the Lord! His head and hands had been broken off and were lying on the threshold; only his body remained. ⁵ That is why to this day neither the priests of Dagon nor any others who enter Dagon's temple at Ashdod step on the threshold.

⁶ The Lord's hand was heavy upon the people of Ashdod and its vicinity; he brought devastation upon them and afflicted them with tumors. ⁷ When the men of Ashdod saw what was happening, they said, "The ark of the god of Israel must not stay here with us, because his hand is heavy upon us and upon Dagon our god." ⁸ So they called together all the rulers of the Philistines and asked them, "What shall we do with the ark of the god of Israel?"

They answered, "Have the ark of the god of Israel moved to Gath." So they moved the ark of the God of Israel.

⁹ But after they had moved it, the Lord's hand was against that city, throwing it into a great panic. He afflicted the people of the city, both young and old, with an outbreak of tumors. ¹⁰ So they sent the ark of God to Ekron.

As the ark of God was entering Ekron, the people of Ekron cried out, "They have brought the ark of the god of Israel around to us to kill us and our people." ¹¹ So they called together all the rulers of the Philistines and said, "Send the ark of the god of Israel away; let it go back to its own place, or it will kill us and our people." For death had filled the city with panic; God's hand was very heavy upon it. ¹² Those who did not die were afflicted with tumors, and the outcry of the city went up to heaven.

It was customary to dedicate the spoils taken from an enemy to their gods 1) as a gratitude offering for the help which they supposed them to have furnished 2) as proof that their gods were more powerful than those of the conquered. It was an insult to the God of Israel.

The ark was placed **next** to the image of Dagon by the Philistines in order to demonstrate Dagon's superiority over the God of Israel, but the symbolism was reversed when Dagon was toppled to a position of homage **before** the ark of the LORD.

**Isaiah 40:20**

"A person too poor to present such an offering selects wood that will not rot. They look for a skilled worker to set up an idol that WILL NOT TOPPLE."

**Isaiah 41:7**

"The other nails down the idol so it WILL NOT TOPPLE."

**Jeremiah 10:4**

"…they fasten it with hammer and nails so it will not totter."

**Zephaniah 1:9**

On that day I will punish all who avoid stepping on the threshold, who fill the temple of their gods with violence and deceit.

**I Samuel 5:3**

*"When the people of Ashdod rose early the next day, there was Dagon…they took Dagon and put him back in his place."* This suggests that the people of Ashdod/ worshippers of the god Dagon assumed that he had toppled over i.e. a fault of the craftsman and therefore not set up properly. There was no spiritual connection between Dagon falling and the presence of the LORD. They did not recognize the hand of God.

**I Samuel 5:4**

*"But the following morning when they rose, there was Dagon, fallen on his face on the ground before the ark of the Lord! His head and hands had been broken off and were lying on the threshold; only his body remained*

Just in case you missed the connection last night between my presence and your idol, between my glory and your idol, between Jehovah the King of Kings, LORD of lords and something that you have created with your hands. When you bring the presence of God into your situations, things do not remain the same.

You have to bow. At the name of Jesus every knee shall bow and every tongue confess that Jesus Christ is Lord to the glory of God the father.

**I Samuel 5:6**

"The LORD's hand was heavy upon the people of Ashdod and its vicinity; He brought devastation upon them and afflicted them with tumors."

Dagon's broken hand lay on the ground but the LORD shows the reality and strength of his own hand by bringing a plague on the people of Ashdod and the surrounding area. God would not be manipulated by His own people (4:3) nor would He permit the Philistines to think that their victory over the Israelites and the capture of the ark demonstrated the superiority of their god over the God of Israel.

So God allowed the ark of the LORD to be captured…go into enemy hands and also defeated the same enemy. His glory He will not share with another.

The revelation from God is that the Spirit of Dagon/Dagima = **5** as seen in the following examples:

**Judges 16:28-29**

1 blow to get revenge for my 2 eyes…he reached towards the 2 central pillars; 5

**I Samuel 31:6**

So Saul (1) and his 3 sons and his armor bearer (1)…died together (5) that same day.

**I Samuel 6:4**

There were 5 gold tumors and 5 gold rats according to the 5 Philistine rulers—Ashdod, Gaza, Ashkelon, Gath & Ekron

The number 5 represents bondage including debt, sickness, phobias, prisons, sin etc.

## WHAT IS THE WORD OF THE LORD TO US TODAY?

The LORD sees the walls that have been built up around us by our enemies. Walls are obstacles. They prevent access to our Promised Land.

- Walls of injustice,
- walls of indifference;
- walls of silent resistance;
- walls of financial insecurities/debt;
- walls of doubt;
- walls of past failures;
- walls of despair, hopelessness;
- walls of discouragement;
- walls of fear of the unknown;

- walls of abuse;
- walls of spiritual wickedness in high places
- walls of excessive worldliness

The Berlin Wall built in August 13, 1961 had 14,000 border guards, 300 towers and 600 dogs and the walls came down.

The Wall of Jericho—a stone retaining wall 12-15 feet high, on top of it another mud brick wall 6 feet thick and 25 feet tall at the crest of this embankment was another wall 45 feet above ground. Therefore the wall was over 70 feet tall…The walls came down.

The enemy is gloating and seems to have the upper hand. There are times that God allows these situations to exist in our lives. Psalm 78:59-66 "When God saw their deeds, his wrath was strong and He despised His people..He…allowed His Ark to be captured; He surrendered His glory into enemy hands…The the LORD rose…He routed His enemies and drove them back and sent them to eternal shame.

The Psalmist says "How long, O God, will you allow our enemies to dishonor your name? Will you let them get away with this forever? Why do you delay? Why hold back your power?

LORD, we know you can do it!! You have delivered before, and yes, You can do it again! God, we are tired! We have come before you time and time again and while you have given us the strength to hold on inspite of; when we have exhausted our store of endurance, you have given us the grace to carry on, but the situations remain unchanged. God, we are saying to you today, "Enough is enough!!!"

**Unleash your fist and give them a final blow!!** //finish them off!!(Psalm 74:11) We are asking God to unleash His fist for action without the shadow of a doubt. Gaza will be abandoned…at midday Ashdod will be emptied. Zephaniah 2:4

## B. TIMES WHEN GOD SAYS "ENOUGH IS ENOUGH!!!" AND HE RELEASES HIS FISTS AGAINST US:

**1. REJECTION–**When we forsake Him

**Jeremiah 15:6 (TLB)**

You have forsaken me and turned your backs upon me. Therefore I will clench my fists against you to destroy you. I am tired of always giving you another chance.//I am weary with repenting. God had had enough!!

**Isaiah 9:12 (TLB)**

The Lord's reply to your bragging is to bring your enemies against you—the Syrians on the east and the Philistines on the west. With bared fangs they will devour Israel. And even then the LORD's anger against you will not be satisfied—His fist will still be poised to smash you. For after all this punishment you will not repent and turn to Him...

**2. REVERENCE TO ANOTHER**

**Psalm 76:11-12 (TLB)**

Fulfill all your vows that you have made to Jehovah your God. Let everyone bring Him presents. He should be reverenced and feared for He cuts down princes and does awesome things to the kings of the earth.

**Ezekiel 7:3-5 (TLB)**

No hope remains, for I will loose my anger on you for your worshipping of idols...with one blow after another I will finish you.

**Ezekiel 16:26-7 (TLB)**

"...in addition to all your other wickedness—woe, woe upon you says the LORD God, you built a spacious brothel for your lovers and idol altars on every street...you added lustful Egypt to your prostitutions by your alliance with her. My anger is great. Therefore, I have **crushed**

**you with my fist**; I have reduced your boundaries and delivered you into the hands of those who hate you—the Philistines—and even they are ashamed of you//shocked by your lewd conduct.

**Zephaniah 1:4 (TLB)**

I will crush Judah and Jerusalem with my fist, and destroy every remnant of those who worship Baal; I will put an end to their idolatrous priests, so that even the memory of them will disappear."

## PERSONAL APPLICATION

**Unleash your fist and give them a final blow!!** (Psalm 74:11) We are asking God to unleash His fist for action without the shadow of a doubt.

**Against our enemies:**

The children of Israel & Pharaoh—The LORD's hand was upon the Egypt…plague after plague and then finally Pharaoh says to Moses"… leave us; please go away, all of you; go and serve Jehovah…take your flocks and herds and be gone." Exodus 12:31 BUT THEN 14:5 "what is this we have done, letting all these slaves get away?...so Pharaoh pursued the people of Israel. Enough was enough Exodus 15:3ff The LORD is a warrior…your right hand, O LORD, is glorious in power; it dashes the enemy to pieces…you reached out your hand and the earth swallowed them…"

**Psalm 138:7 (TLB)**

Though I am surrounded by troubles, you will bring me safely through them. You will clench your fist against my angry enemies! Your power will save me.

**Isaiah 31:3 (TLB)**

For these Egyptians are mere men, not God! Their horses are puny flesh, not mighty spirits! When the LORD clenches His fist against them, they will stumble and fall among those they are trying to help. All will fail together."

**Ezekiel 25:12-13 (TLB)**

"And the LORD God says: Because the people of Edom have sinned so greatly by avenging themselves upon the people of Judah, I will smash Edom with my fist and wipe out her people, her cattle and her flocks. The sword will destroy everything…"

**Ezekiel 35:3-4 (TLB)**

"The LORD God says: I am against you (the people of Mount Seir) and I will smash you with my fist and utterly destroy you because you hate my people Israel…"

**Zechariah 2:8-9 (TLB)**

"The LORD of Glory has sent me against the nations that oppressed you…I will smash them with my fist and their slaves will be their rulers…"

There are situations in our lives where God has already intervened and brought about a change. Like the first fall of Dagon. However, our family, friends, close associates see everything that is broken in our lives, they see a toppling over of what used to be and set about restoring/fixing it back to its original status.

Matthew Henry in his commentary highlights the following: "…the ark triumphs over Dagon. Thus the Kingdom of Satan will certainly fall before the Kingdom of Christ, error before truth, profaneness before godliness and corruption before grace in the hearts of the faithful. When the interests of religion seem to be ready to sink, even then we may be confident that the day of their triumph will come. When Christ, the true Ark of the covenant really enters the heart of fallen man, which is indeed Satan's temple, all idols will fall, every endeavour to set them up again will be vain, sin will be forsaken and unrighteous gain restored."

**Ezekiel 6:6 (TLB)**

"All your cities will be smashed and burned, and the idol altars abandoned. Your gods will be shattered; the bones of their worshippers will lie scattered among the altars. Then at last you will know I am the Lord."

**Isaiah 2:17-18 (TLB)**

"…the LORD alone will be exalted in that day, and the idols will totally disappear."

## TESTIMONY

This is the testimony of another individual who used the *fist* of God after having learnt about it in our Prayer & Fasting session. She employed the *fist* of God in a situation where unforgiveness had existed over a 4 year period, because she had had enough. Two days later she received a phone call from the individual seeking her forgiveness!!

It was a friendship shared for over thirteen years, one which was similar to that of Jonathan and David from scriptures. We shared family history, childhood experiences, living space and an intimacy that was truly based on friendship.

After all that we have been through - the good and indifferent times - our friendship ended after more than fourteen years. It was indeed a hard pill to swallow, since I never quite understood what happened. Days, weeks and years I realized how much I missed my friendship, but I had to move on and I did just that. However, there came a time when we both met to resolve the matter but it just never did work out.

Moving out from the place I called home broke my heart; having little or no communication, ***I prayed continuously that God would work this situation out for me.*** Then one day after learning about the "Fist of God" and what it can do when prayer is channeled in the right direction, I began to pray that the "Fist of God" be applied in my situation.

Four days after praying and calling on the "Fist of God" to intervene in the matter concerning my friendship, I received an early morning phone call from my friend apologizing for what took place over four years ago. At first it was a surprise, but then came the reality. Elated that this had happened I started to cry because I knew that God had intervened in this matter that had caused me such grief.

As I write this note the friendship never did resume from where we left it, but I am satisfied that the situation was resolved. To God be the glory great things He has done!!!

CHAPTER 11

# THE BACK OF GOD
The Afterglow of His Presence

*"Out of the brightness of
His presence clouds advanced..."*
*Psalm 18:12*

The back is the part of or side of anything less often seen or used. Something that supports, covers, or strengthens the rear of an object.

**Exodus 33:11-34:29**
Inside the tent the LORD spoke to Moses face to face, as a man speaks to his friend...Moses talked there with the LORD and said to him, "You have been telling me "Take these people to the Promised Land," but you haven't told me whom you will send with me. You say you are my friend, and that I have found favour before you; please, if this is really so, guide me clearly along the way you want me to travel so that I will understand you and walk acceptably before you. For don't forget that this nation is your people."

14 And the LORD replied, I myself will go with you and give you success." 15 For Moses had said, "If you aren't going with us, don't let us move a step from this place. 16 If you don't go with us, who will ever know that I and my people have found favour with you and that we are different from any other people upon the face of the earth?" 17 And the Lord replied to Moses, Yes I will do what you have asked for you have certainly found favour with me and you are my friend."

18 Then Moses asked to see God's glory. 19 The LORD replied, "I will make my goodness pass before you, and I will announce to you the meaning of my name Jehovah, the LORD. I show kindness and mercy to anyone I want to. 20 But you may not see the glory of my face, for many may not see me and live. 21 However, stand here on this rock beside me. 22 And when my glory goes by, I will put you in the cleft of the rock and cover you with my hand until I have passed. 23 Then I will remove my hand and you shall see my back, but not my face."

34:4 So Moses took two tablets of stone like the first ones and was up early and climbed Mount Sinai as the LORD had told him to, taking the two stone tablets in his hands. 5, 6 Then the LORD descended in the form of a pillar of cloud and stood there with him and passed in front of him and announced the meaning of His name. "I am Jehovah, the merciful and gracious God, He said, "slow to anger and rich in steadfast love and truth. 7 I, Jehovah, show this steadfast love to many thousands by forgiving their sins; or else I refuse to clear the guilty and require that a father's sins be punished in the sons and grandsons and even later generations."

8 Moses fell down before the LORD and worshipped. 28 Moses was up on the mountain with the LORD for forty days and forty nights and in all that time he neither ate nor drank. At that time God wrote out the Covenant—the Ten Commandments—on the stone tablets.

29 Moses didn't realize as he came back down the mountain with the tablets that his face glowed from being in the presence of God.

Because of this radiance upon his face, Aaron and the people of Israel were afraid to come near him.

We are looking at the back of God—the afterglow of His presence.

The reference to "behind God's back" is not usually a positive one. It suggests a forgotten place; it suggests a place where even God Himself is not present. But according to Scripture, it is the safest place where you can see Him, His glory, and live.

There are two truths about the back of God that I want to pull from Moses' encounter.

## A. GOD IS WILLING TO REVEAL HIMSELF TO US WHEN WE EMBARK ON THAT JOURNEY OF INTIMACY WITH HIM

We can begin our journey of intimacy with God because:

### 1. NOT ONLY DID HE PUT OUR SINS OUT OF SIGHT

**Isaiah 38:17**

You have put all my sins behind your back;

### 2. HE HAS ALSO PUT THEM OUT OF REACH

**Micah 7:19**

You will tread our sins underfoot and hurl all our iniquities into the depths of the sea;

**Psalm 103:12**

As far as the east is from the west so far has He removed our transgressions from us.

### 3. OUT OF EXISTENCE

**Isaiah 43:25**

I, even I, am He who blots out your transgressions, for my own sake and remembers your sins no more.

**Isaiah 44:22**

I have swept away your offenses like a cloud, your sins like the morning mist.

**Acts 3:19**

Repent then and turn to God so that your sins may be wiped out that times of refreshing may come from the LORD.

Moses' desire to see God's face came out of His intimate relationship with God. He and God were constantly in dialogue. Moses took the time to stay with God. The essence of Moses' encounter with his Friend speaks of closeness, friendship, intimacy.

Here are some other attributes of this unique friendship:

- It highlights Moses' dependency on God. As the leader of God's people, Moses knew that in order for him to succeed as the leader of God's people, he had to consult with God regularly, touch base with Him frequently and the children of Israel knew this. ***(33:8-10 Whenever Moses went to the Tabernacle, all the people…stood and would rise and stand in their tent doors…then all the people worshipped from their tent doors, bowing low to the pillar of cloud.)***
- It shows the importance, value that Moses placed on ensuring that there was always access to the presence of God ***(33:7 Moses ALWAYS erected the sacred tent of meeting with God as he called it, far outside the camp, and everyone who wanted to consult with Jehovah went out there.)***
- It shows that Moses was comfortable in God's presence, he conversed with God, the Creator of the universe as with a friend. ***(33:11 Inside the tent the LORD spoke to Moses face to face, as a man speaks to his friend.)***
- It reveals that Moses was in no hurry whenever he was in the presence of God. God anticipated Moses' company ***(33:9 As Moses entered, the pillar of cloud would come down and stand at the door while the Lord spoke with Moses.)***

## WHAT A GOD!

- It reveals that Moses knew the importance of practicing and being in the presence of God.
    1. Every step we take must be in the presence of God, there is security in God's presence *(33:15 if you aren't going with us, don't let us move a step from this place) (Psalm 18:30 He is a shield for everyone who hides behind Him.)*
    2. God's presence in our lives indicates His pleasure with us, His favour *(33:16 if you don't go with us, who will ever know that I and my people have found favour with you.)*
    3. God's presence in our lives distinguishes us from those who have no relationship with God *(33:16 "…we are different from any other people upon the face of the earth…")*
- Moses was not satisfied with the level of intimacy that he was experiencing with God…he wanted more. Wanting more got Oliver Twist in trouble. God wants us to desire Him; to want more of Him; to never be satisfied with the level of intimacy that we are experiencing. That is why our growth in the LORD is not a matter of comparing ourselves with our brothers and our sisters in Christ and thinking that compared to them, we are okay.

As we become more and more intimate, it is not about staying away from sin but more about staying in His presence, wanting more of the Lover of our souls. How do we increase our level of intimacy? By increasing the amount of time that we spend with him; the grabbing of opportunities that present themselves to us. Like a lover God prompts us when those opportunities come…a little quiet time and the Spirit says…time to pray…obey that still, small voice of God.

Dr. Woodrow Kroll in a devotional writes "in the March 1776 issue of The Gospel Magazine, Augustus Toplady maintained that if a man lived to the age of 80, he would have the opportunity to commit more than two and a half billion sins. Obviously it would be impossible for a person to pay for all those sins. Therefore, Toplady offered this solution in a hymn he wrote, He pled, "Rock of Ages, cleft for me, let me hide myself in Thee."

Moses found that this was his solution also. Sinful as he was, he had a great longing to see God more fully, to know Him more intimately. But the sinfulness of man and the glory of God could not coexist. To see God in all His glory would have meant instantaneous annihilation for Moses. So God provided a compromise. He placed Moses in a fissure of a rock and protected him as His glory passed by. Then God allowed him to see the "afterglow" of His presence.

Deep in all of our hearts lies the longing to see God more fully, to discover His presence to a greater degree. But there is also an innate fear because we know, and rightly so, that we cannot exist in the presence of His unapproachable glory. Only those hidden in God can safely see God revealed. *(Lesson on Living from Moses: The Practice of God's Presence pg.24-25)*

God is a Spirit but yet He often speaks of Himself in human terms. Why? God wants us to have a better understanding of Him as much as we with our finite minds are able to grasp. God desires for us to experience intimacy with Him.

## B. WHATEVER HE REVEALS OF HIMSELF (BACK) IS JUST ENOUGH OR AS GOOD FOR US

**Verse 18**

Now show me your glory. God, his Friend explains, "I will put you in the cleft of the rock and cover you with my hand until I have passed. Then I will remove my hand and you shall see my back, but not my face." As God is passing by He announces the meaning of His name. Name goes hand in hand with His presence. Likewise, Jesus is as near as the mention of His name//face. When we spend rich, quality time in the presence of God, wooing the King of kings, we leave His presence with a glow on our face. Whenever I experience that kind of time with him, afterwards someone will tell me that there is a glow about me…of course I give credit where credit is due.

**Psalm 34:5**

Those who look to Him are radiant; their faces are never covered with shame.

He who has asked to see God's glory now quite unawares reflects the divine glory. Today however, II Corinthians 3:12-18 we are not like Moses who would put a veil over his face to keep the Israelites from gazing at it while the radiance was fading away…we who with unveiled faces all reflect the LORD's glory are being transformed into his likeness with ever-increasing glory, which comes from the LORD who is the Spirit.

We who believe are made partakers of this glory by being gradually transformed into the likeness of Christ. Let us take the time to gaze upon His face so that we can be true reflectors of what we see.

**II Corinthians 4:6**

For God who said, "Let there be light in the darkness," has made us understand that it is the brightness of His glory that is seen in the face of Jesus Christ." The light that now shines in Paul's heart, qualifying him to be the proclaimer of Christ, is the knowledge of the glory of God as it was displayed in the face of Christ who has come, not just from an earthly tabernacle, but from the glorious presence of God in heaven itself.

In a sense Moses' prayer was finally answered on the Mount of Transfiguration where he shared a vision of the Lord's glory with Elijah and 3 disciples in Luke 9:30-32. Two men Moses and Elijah appeared in glorious splendor talking with Jesus.

## WHY MOSES & ELIJAH?
## WHY NOT NOAH? ABRAHAM?

Moses was the great Old Testament deliverer and lawgiver, and Elijah, the representative of the prophets. Moses' work had been finished by JOSHUA (means the Lord saves) Elijah's work by Elisha (another form of the name JOSHUA). Elijah is given someone to finish His work just as Moses was, and Elisha channels the covenant blessings to the faithful in Israel just as Joshua brought Israel into the Promised Land. They now spoke with Jesus (whose Hebrew name was JOSHUA) about the "exodus" he was about to accomplish, by which He would deliver His people from the bondage of sin and bring to fulfillment the work of both Moses and Elijah.

**Luke 9:29**

"Jesus' face began to shine, clothes…dazzling white and blazed with light…"

**Luke 9:30**

"They were splendid in appearance, glorious to see…"

## PERSONAL APPLICATION

**Jeremiah 15:1**

Then the LORD said to me, even if Moses and Samuel stood before me pleading for these people even then I wouldn't help them.

## WHY MOSES & SAMUEL?

They were famed for their intercession for sinful Israel.

**Exodus 32:11-14**

But Moses sought the favour of the Lord His God, "O LORD … why should your anger burn against your people, who you brought out of Egypt with great power and a mighty hand? Why should the Egyptians say, It was with evil intent that He brought them out, to kill them in the mountains and to wipe them off the face of the earth? Turn from your fierce anger; relent and do not bring disaster on your people. Remember your servants Abraham, Isaac and Israel, to who you swore by your own self. I will make your descendants as numerous as the stars in the sky and I will give your descendants all this land I promised them and it will be their inheritance forever. Then the LORD relented and did not bring on His people the disaster He had threatened."

**Exodus 32:30-34**

The next day Moses said to the people, you have committed a great sin. But now I will go up to the LORD; perhaps I can make atonement for your sin. So Moses went back to the LORD and said Oh what a great sin these people have committed! They have made themselves gods of gold. But now please forgive their sin but if not, then blot me out of the book you have written. Then LORD replied to Moses. Whoever has sinned against me I will blot out of my book. Now go lead the people to the place I spoke of…However, when the time comes for me to punish, I will punish them for their sin. And the LORD struck the people with a plague because of what they did with the calf Aaron had made.

**Numbers 14:13-23**

"Moses said to the LORD, then the Egyptians will hear about it! By your power you brought these people up from among them and they will tell the inhabitants of this land about it. They have already heard that you, O LORD, are with these people and that you O LORD have been seen face to face, that your cloud stays over them and that you go before them in a pillar of cloud by day and a pillar of fire by night. If you put these people to death all at one time, the nations who have heard this report about you will say The LORD was not able to bring these people into the land He promised them on oath; so He slaughtered them in the desert…The LORD replied, I have forgiven them as you asked. Nevertheless as surely as I live and as surely as the glory of the Lord fills the whole earth, not one of the men who saw my glory and the miraculous signs I performed in Egypt…will ever see the land I promised on oath to their forefathers."

**Deuteronomy 9:18- 21; 25-29**

Then once again I fell prostrate before the LORD for forty days and forty nights; I ate no bread and drank no water because of all the sin you had committed, doing what was evil in the Lord's sight and so provoking Him to anger. I feared the anger and wrath of the LORD for He was angry enough with you to destroy you. But again the LORD listened to me. And the LORD was angry enough with Aaron to destroy him but at that time I prayed for Aaron too.

**The back is also known for support:**

- Your back not broad for nuttin (nothing)…implying that you can take pressure.
- We carry our children on our backs

The LORD is calling us out to support and undergird the ministry of His church through intercessory prayer like we have never done before. The LORD is calling us to intercede on behalf of this part of His vineyard. Meaningful support comes out of intimacy. Because you know your friend you know how to approach, how to ask, what to ask, confidence to approach etc.

**Isaiah 62:1-6**

Because I love Zion, because my heart yearns for Jerusalem, I will not cease to pray for her or to cry out to God on her behalf until she shines forth in His righteousness and is glorious in His salvation. The nations shall see your righteousness. Kings shall be blinded by your glory; you will be called by a new name that the mouth of the LORD will bestow. You will be a crown of splendor in the LORD's hand, a royal diadem in the hand of your God…for the LORD delights in you and will claim you as His own. Your children will care for you, with joy like that of a young man who marries a virgin and God will rejoice over you as a bridegroom with his bride. O Jerusalem I have set intercessors/posted watchmen on your walls who shall cry to God all day and all night for the fulfillment of His promises.

**Isaiah 52:8**

Listen! Your watchmen lift up their voices; together they shout for joy. Watchmen look out for the arrival of the messengers (II Samuel 18:24-27).

Read Isaiah 60 & 61. When God's people are enabled to live righteous lives through God's power, they are no longer a reproach to His name (face) but become a light to the world.

CHAPTER 12

# THE ARM OF GOD
God is your Jehovah Nissi, Your Banner of Victory

*"...my God is my rock*
*in whom I take refuge..."*
***Psalm 18:2***

The appearance of the arm of God is seen in Daniel 10:6
"His arms...like the gleam of burnished bronze (NIV)//shone like polished brass (TLB)

## A. THE ARM OF GOD

### 1. SYMBOLIZES STRENGTH /GOD'S POWER

**Exodus 15:16**
"...by the power of your arm they will be as still as a stone until your people pass by, O LORD..." Dread will fall on them.

**Deuteronomy 4:34**

"Has any god ever tried to take for himself one nation out of another nation, by testings, by signs and wonders, by war, by a mighty hand and an outstretched arm…"

**Deuteronomy 7:19**

"You saw with your own eyes the great trials, the signs and wonders, the mighty hand and outstretched arm with which the LORD your God brought you out."

**Deuteronomy 9:29**

"But they are your people your inheritance that you brought out by your great power and your outstretched arm."

**Psalm 77:15**

"…with your mighty arm you redeemed your people…"

**Psalm 79:11**

"…with Your strong arm preserve those condemned to die."

**Psalm 89:10**

"You crushed Rahab like one of the slain with your strong arm you scattered your enemies."

**Psalm 89:13**

"Strong is your arm." (TLB)//Your arm is endued with power (NIV)

**Psalm 136:11-12**

"…and brought Israel out from among them…with a mighty hand and outstretched arm."

**Isaiah 30:30**

"The LORD will cause people to hear His majestic voice and will make them see His arm coming down with raging anger and consuming fire, with cloud burst, thunderstorm and hail."

**Isaiah 30:32**

"Every stroke the LORD lays on them with His punishing club will be to the music of timbrels and harps as He fights them in battle with the blows of His arm."

**Isaiah 40:10**

"See the Sovereign LORD comes with power and He rules with a mighty arm."

**Isaiah 51:9**

"Awake, awake! Arm of the LORD, clothe yourself with strength."

**Isaiah 62:8**

"The LORD has sworn by His right hand and by His mighty arm."

**Isaiah 63:5, 11b-12**

"…so my own arm achieved salvation for me and my own wrath sustained me…Where is He who…sent His glorious arm of power to be at Moses' right hand."

**Jeremiah 21:5**

"I myself will fight against you with an outstretched hand and a mighty arm in furious anger and in great wrath."

**Jeremiah 27:5**

"With my great power and outstretched arm I made the earth and its people and the animals that are on it."

**Jeremiah 32:17, 21**

"You have made the heavens and the earth by your great power and outstretched arm. Nothing is too hard for you….You brought your people Israel out of Egypt with signs and wonders by a mighty hand and an outstretched arm and with great terror." This describes God's powerful redemption of Israel at the exodus.

**Luke 1:51**

"He has performed mighty deeds with His arm; He has scattered those who are proud in their inmost thoughts."

### 2. SYMBOLIZES SALVATION/RESCUE/JUSTICE

**Psalm 98:1**

"Sing to the LORD a new song for He has done marvelous things; His right hand and His holy arm have worked salvation for him. The LORD has made His salvation known and revealed His righteousness to the nations." God's saving acts in behalf of His people are also His self-revelation to the nations; in this sense God is His own evangelist. God's saving acts reveal His righteousness.

**Isaiah 50:2**

"When I came, why was there no one?...was my arm too short to deliver you? Do I lack the strength to rescue you?"

**Isaiah 51:5**

"My righteousness draws near speedily, my salvation is on the way and my arm will bring justice to the nations."

**Isaiah 52:10**

"The LORD will lay bare His holy arm in the sight of all the nations and all the ends of the earth will see the salvation of our God." God is strong enough to bring His promised redemption and salvation.

**Isaiah 53:1**

"Who has believed our message and to whom has the arm of the LORD been revealed?"

**Isaiah 59:1,16**

"Surely the arm of the LORD is not too short to save…His own arm worked salvation for Him."

Rescued Moses while demonstrating His power

**Numbers 11:10-23**

Moses heard the people of every family wailing…he asked the LORD, "Why have you brought this trouble on your servant? What have I done to displease you that you put the burden of all these people on me? 12 Did I conceive all these people? Did I give them birth? Why do you tell me to carry them in my arms, as a nurse carries an infant to the land you promised…21 Here I am among six hundred thousand men on foot and you say, "I will give them meat to eat for a whole month!" 22 Would they have enough if flocks and herds were slaughtered for them? Would they have enough if all the fish in the sea were caught for them?" 23 The LORD answered Moses, "Is the LORD's arm too short? You will now see whether or not what I say will come true for you." 31 Now a wind went out from the LORD and drove quail in from the sea. It brought them down all around the camp to about three feet above the ground as far as a day's walk in any direction.

### 3. SUPERIOR TO THE ARM OF FLESH

**II Chronicles 32:1-23**

When Sennacherib, king of Assyria threatened Jerusalem Hezekiah assembled his officers and people before him and encouraged them with these words from verses 7-8: "Be strong and courageous, do not be afraid or discouraged because of the king of Assyrian and the vast army with him, for there is a greater power with us than with him. With him is only the arm of flesh but with us is the Lord our God to help us and to fight our battles."

**Job 40:9**

"Do you have an arm like God's?"

**Psalm 44:3**

"…nor did their arm bring them victory; it was your right hand, your arm…"

**Jeremiah 17:5**

"Cursed is the one who trusts in man who depends on flesh for his strength."

> *Stand up, stand up for Jesus;*
> *Stand in His strength alone*
> *The arm of flesh will fail you-*
> *Ye dare not trust your own*
> *Put on the gospel armour*
> *And watching unto prayer*
> *Where duty calls or danger*
> *Be never wanting there.*

Here are some insights into the Arm of God based on the song of Moses and Miriam:

**Exodus 15:16**

**"...terror and dread will fall upon them. By the power of your arm they will be as still as a stone until your people pass by, O LORD ...."**

**Exodus 15:9-12**

The enemy boasted, "I will pursue, I will overtake them, I will divide the spoils, I will gorge myself on them. I will draw my sword and my hand will destroy them. But you blew with your breath and the sea covered them. They sank like lead in the mighty waters. Who among the gods is like you, LORD? Who is like you majestic in holiness, awesome in glory, working wonders 12 You stretch out your right hand and the earth swallows your enemies."

Recall the hand of God on Israel's behalf near the Red Sea (light to Israel, darkness to Pharaoh; confusion in the camp; LORD fighting for them; horse and rider thrown; not ONE of them survived)

- Most of the references to the arm of God use the descriptive word "outstretched". This suggests outspread, extended, stretched out, spread out, widely spread, open, unfolded. It has the capacity to be stretched out; it can provide more than an adequate covering.

    In the movie "The Incredibles" there was a scene in which the Parr family was involved in a plane crash. The mother, Elastigirl, who was flying the plane, had the flexibility superpower to stretch any part of her body up to 100' (30 m) to a minimum thickness of 1mm and mold it into several shapes and sizes.

    The plane suddenly came under attack and just before a missile hit the aircraft Elastigirl enveloped the children into a human ball and the plane was blown to smithereens. As they were rapidly freefalling to the ground Elastigirl recovered sufficiently and saw the plight that they were in. Both of her children, on either side of her were screaming while falling headlong to earth.

Elastigirl then elongated each arm a little distance and pulled each child to her. She used her body as a parachute, sheltered them from the wreckage around them and they landed safely in the water.

- When we are assailed, overwhelmed by heavy onslaught of the enemy, long battle, enemy comes in like a flood; we employ the arm of God. (the fist of God is used also in a long battle, but the fist is for an immediate shattering of the situation; the arm of God shelters us during the storm)
- The plan of the enemy is to pursue, overtake, plunder, draw their hand, divide, gorge themselves, but the arm of God ensures complete victory—until your people pass by. The arm of flesh cannot hold on until the victory is assured. The arm of God ensures that the job is done; the arm of flesh cannot hold on to the end…good intentions
- The arm of God is our refuge and strong tower, our shelter in the time of storm.

> *The LORD's our Rock; in Him we hide…*
> *Secure whatever ill betide…*
> *A shade by day, defense by night…*
> *no fears alarm no foes affright…*
> *The raging storms may round us beat…*
> *we'll never leave our safe retreat…*
> *O Rock divine, O Refuge dear…*
> *Be thou our Helper ever near…*

- The arm of God protects us against the assault of the enemy…an assault over a period of time, no ordinary quick attack. That protection/covering is available to us, we have access. Kings were spoken of as the "shade" of those dependent on them for protection. Similarly the LORD is the protective "shade" of His people. The wings are the protective outreach of God's power.

**Ruth 2:12**

May you be richly rewarded by the LORD the God of Israel, under whose wings you have come to take refuge."

**Psalm 17:8**

Keep me as the apple of your eye; hide me in the shadow of your wings from the wicked who are out to destroy me, from my mortal enemies who surround me."

**Psalm 28:9 (TLB)**

Defend your people LORD …Lead them like a shepherd and carry them forever in your arms."

**Psalm 36:7 (TLB)**

All humanity takes refuge in the shadow of your wings.

**Psalm 57:1 (NIV)**

I will take refuge in the shadow of your wings until the disaster has passed.

**Psalm 57:1 (TLB)**

I will hide beneath the shadow of your wings until this storm is past.

**Psalm 63:6-7**

"On my bed I remember you; I think of you through the watches of the night. 7 Because you are my help, I sing in the shadow of your wings."

**Psalm 91:1-2**

"Whoever dwells in the shelter of the Most High will rest in the shadow of the Almighty. I will say of the Lord, "He is my refuge and my fortress, my God, in whom I trust." If you make the Most High your dwelling, even the LORD, who is my refuge then no harm will befall you, no disaster will come near your tent." The godly find safety under the protective wings of the LORD.

**Psalm 121:5**

The LORD watches over you—the LORD is your shade at your right hand.

**Isaiah 25:4**

"You have been a refuge for the poor, a refuge for the needy in their distress, a shelter from the storm and a shade from the heat."

**Isaiah 49:2**

"...in the shadow of His hand He hid me; He made me into a polished arrow and concealed me in His quiver."

**Isaiah 51:16**

"I have put my words in your mouth and covered you with the shadow of my hand..."

The arm of God keeps the enemies at bay by inflicting his terror upon them. There is something about this terror that keeps them still...as still as a stone. I am reminded of deer, when caught in the headlights of a car, they stand still with fright in the middle of the road, unable to move.

**Genesis 35:5 (TLB)**

"Then they (Jacob & his family) started on again and the terror of God was upon all the cities they journeyed through, so that they were not attacked."

**Deuteronomy 2:24**

"Beginning today I will make people throughout the whole earth tremble with fear because of you, and dread your arrival."(TLB) "...and be in anguish because of you..."(NIV)

**Deuteronomy 11:25**

"No one will be able to stand against you. The LORD your God, as He promised you, will put the terror and fear of you on the whole land, wherever you go."

**I Samuel 25:37**

"Then in the morning when Nabal was sober, his wife told him all these things and his heart failed him and he became like a stone."

## COMFORT

**Isaiah 40:11**

He tends His flock like a shepherd; He gathers the lambs in His arms and carries them close to His heart.

**Matthew 23:37**

"Jerusalem, Jerusalem, you who kill the prophets and stone those sent to you, how often I have longed to gather your children together, as a hen gathers her chicks under her wings, and you were not willing."

## PERSONAL APPLICATION

**Exodus 17:8-16**

*The Amalekites came and attacked the Israelites at Rephidim. Moses said to Joshua, "Choose some of our men and go out to fight the Amalekites. Tomorrow I will stand on top of the hill with the staff of God in my hands." 10 So Joshua fought the Amalekites as Moses had ordered, and Moses, Aaron and Hur went to the top of the hill. (NIV) 11 As long as Moses held up the rod in his hands Israel was winning, but whenever he rested his arms at his sides, the soldiers of Amalek were winning. Moses' arms finally became too tired to hold up the rod any longer. (TLB) 12 (NIV) ... they took a stone and put it under him and he sat on it. Aaron and Hur held his hands up—one on one side, one on the other—so that his hands remained steady till sunset. 13 So Joshua overcame the Amalekite army with the sword. 14 Then the LORD said to Moses, "Write this on a scroll as something to be remembered and make sure that Joshua hears it, because I will completely blot out the memory of Amalek from under heaven." 15 Moses built an altar and called it "Jehovah Nissi, Jehovah is my flag (TLB) The LORD is my Banner...for hands were lifted up to the throne of the LORD."*

Joshua fights, Moses prays; both minister to Israel. The rod was held up, as the banner, to encourage the soldiers, and also to God, by way of appeal to Him. Moses was tired. The strongest arm will fail with being long held out; it is God only whose hand is stretched out still. We do not find that Joshua's hands were heavy in fighting, but Moses' hands were heavy in praying; the more spiritual any service is, the more apt we are to fail and flag in it. God encourages Moses to write so that Israel will know that the hand of Moses did more for their safety than their own hands, his rod than their sword. ***(Matthew Henry's commentary, p.124)***

VICTORY Flags, banners mark victory. It is well understood that the conquering army in any battle has the right to remove the defeated country's flag and replace it with their own, depicting that the country with the conquering flag has won and are now in control.

In Psalm 60 we see a national prayer for God's help after suffering a severe blow by a foreign nation. Verses 4-5 shows their plea for help grounded in confidence because banners were used as rallying points for troops in preparation for battle and for leading them into action. "But you have given us a banner to rally to; all who love truth will rally to it; then you can deliver your beloved people. Use your strong right arm to rescue us."

Moses called God Jehovah Nissi because he understood the revelation that God Himself is our banner, our victory. He is the one who wins our battles. God said v.14b that "he will utterly blot out the remembrance of Amalek from under heaven. That means that this enemy would not rise again, he was defeated utterly…When you gather under Jehovah Nissi as your banner, trust Him that the outcome of your battle will be the same as it was for Moses and Joshua at Rephidim. God is saying there will always be war…but He is always the winner. The arm of God is our Jehovah Nissi, our banner.

Queen Elizabeth II of England has three royal residences (Buckingham Palace, Windsor Castle and the Palace of Holyrood), plus two private homes. This could be confusing for those who want to find her except for one important fact: the queen's banner always flies over whichever residence she is currently occupying. As Christians we should raise the LORD's banner over our lives. No matter how difficult our situation becomes, God will not abandon His residence in our midst. If the King is present, His banner should fly. Is it obvious to those around you that the King is in residence in your life? Make sure that His flag, colored with faith, hope and love, flies high over the castle of your life. ***(Lessons on Living from Moses: Living in the Valleys Woodrow Kroll)***

**Psalm 118:10-16 (TLB)**

*Though all the nations of the world attack me, I will march out behind His banner and destroy them. Yes, they surround and attach me; but with His flag flying above me I will cut them off. They swarm around me like bees; they blaze against me like a roaring flame. Yet beneath His flag, I shall destroy them…He is my Strength and Song in the heat of battle and now He has given me the victory…the strong arm of the LORD has done glorious things!*

The arm of God is our Jehovah Nissi, our Banner!

## CHAPTER 13

# THE TEETH OF GOD
### Trust EvEn in The Heat

*"...my God turns my darkness into light."*
***Psalm 18:28***

The tooth is defined as any of various bonelike structures set in the jaws of most vertebrates and used for biting, tearing or chewing

### A. REFERENCES TO MAN'S TEETH

#### 1. SKIN OF MY TEETH

**Job 19:20-21**
I am nothing but skin and bones; I have escaped only by the skin of my teeth (only my gums)...for the hand of God has struck me.
**The NIV text note** understands the phrase to imply that even Job's teeth are gone.

**A WEAPON OF THE WICKED**

**Job 4:8-11**

As I have observed, those who plow evil and sow trouble, reap it. At the breath of God, they are destroyed...the lions may roar and growl, yet the teeth of the great lions are broken.

**Job 29:17**

I broke the fangs of the wicked and snatched the victims from their teeth.

**Psalm 3:7**

Arise LORD, Deliver me my God! Strike all my enemies on the jaw; break the teeth of the wicked.

**Psalm 57:4**

I am in the midst of lions; I lie among ravenous beasts - men whose teeth are spears and arrows.

**Proverbs 30:14**

There are those whose teeth are swords and whose jaws are set with knives to devour the poor from the earth, the needy from among mankind.

**2. TEETH SET ON EDGE**

**Jeremiah 31:29**

In those days people will no longer say, "The parents have eaten sour grapes, and the children's teeth are set on edge." Instead, everyone will die for his own sin; whoever eats sour grapes—his own teeth will be set on edge."

**Ezekiel 18:2**

"What do you people mean by quoting this proverb about the land of Israel: "The fathers eat sour grapes; and the children's teeth are set on edge."

**NIV note--*This proverb*** indicates that the proverb arose first in Jerusalem. Jeremiah predicted the cessation of the proverb and Ezekiel said its end had come. The proverb, though it expresses self-pity, fatalism and despair, and though it mocks the justice of God, had its origin in Israelite belief in corporate solidarity. In Lamentations 5:7 the thought appears as a sincere confession. **Set on edge** The Hebrew for this phrase perhaps means "blunted" or "worn" but it may refer to the sensation in the mouth when eating something bitter or sour.

**Exodus 20:5**

"…punishing the children for the sin of the parents to the third and fourth generation of those who hate me…"

Those Israelites who blatantly violate God's covenant and thus show that they reject the LORD as their King will bring down judgment on themselves and their households…"households were usually extended to three or four generations." The proverb was apparently a popular one that originated in a misunderstanding of such passages above (Exodus 20:5) which teach that a man's sins can have a negative effect on his descendants. In the time of Jeremiah and Ezekiel, many people felt that God's hand of judgment against them was due not to their own sins, but to the sins of their ancestors.

Note however that the LORD said "As surely as I live…you will no longer quote this proverb in Israel, for every living soul belongs to me, the father as well as the son—both alike belong to me. The soul who sins is the one who will die." Ezek.18:3-31

### 3. GNASH

- To grind or strike (the teeth, for example) together.
- To bite (something) by grinding the teeth.

### SIGN OF SUFFERING DUE TO EXTREME REGRET

**Matthew 8:12**

But the subjects of the kingdom will be thrown outside into the darkness, where there will be weeping and gnashing of teeth." (occurs 6 times in Matthew's gospel)

**Matthew 13:42/50**

"They will throw them into the blazing furnace, where there will be weeping and gnashing of teeth."

**Matthew 22:13**

Then the king told the attendants, "Tie him hand and foot, and throw him outside into the darkness, where there will be weeping and gnashing of teeth."

**Matthew 24:51**

"He will cut him to pieces and assign him a place with the hypocrites, where there will be weeping and gnashing of teeth."

**Matthew 25:30**

"And throw that worthless servant outside, into the darkness, where there will be weeping and gnashing of teeth."

### SIGN OF MALICE

**Psalm 35:15-17**

But when I stumbled, *(not morally; He was brought low by circumstances)* they gathered in glee; assailants gathered against me without my knowledge. They slandered me without ceasing. 16 Like the ungodly they maliciously mocked, they gnashed their teeth *(in malice)* at me…rescue my life…from these lions.

**Psalm 37:12-13**

The wicked plot against the righteous and gnash their teeth at them 13 but the LORD laughs at the wicked for He knows their day is coming.

### SIGN OF GLOATING

**Lamentations 2:16**

All your enemies open their mouths wide against you; they scoff and gnash their teeth and say, "We have swallowed her up. This is the day we have waited for; we have lived to see it."

## SIGN OF VEXATION, ANGER

*(RESPONSE TO THINGS THEY HAVE NO CONTROL OVER AND WISHED IT WAS THE OPPOSITE SITUATION)*

### Psalm 112:10

The wicked will see (the good deeds and state of the righteous man) and be vexed, they will gnash their teeth and waste away.

### Acts 7:54

When the members of the Sanhedrin heard this, they were furious and gnashed their teeth at him. But Stephen full of the Holy Spirit looked up to heaven and saw the glory of God, and Jesus standing at the right hand of God.

They were furious at the message that Stephen gave. They had no control of the word of God as given to them neither could they change the record of events as outlined in Stephen's address.

## B. REFERENCES TO GOD'S TEETH

Job's description about how he felt about his situation:

### Job 16:9

God assails me and tears me in his anger and gnashes His teeth at me..."

**NIV note:** The figure here is graphic and disturbing; God, like a ferocious lion attacks and tears at Job's flesh. Job sees himself as God's target "God has turned me over to evil men and thrown me into the clutches of the wicked. All was well with me, but He shattered; He seized me by the neck and crushed me...He pierces my kidneys...he bursts upon me; He rushes at me like a warrior..." Job 16:11-14

### Psalm 7:1-2

"...save and deliver me from all who pursue me or they will tear me apart like a lion and rip me to pieces." Here the attack of the enemy was likened to that of ferocious animals especially the lion.

# C. JUDGMENTS

## 1. JUDGMENT AGAINST SPIRITUAL PROSTITUTION

**Hosea 5:2-6:1**

"The rebels are knee-deep in slaughter, I will discipline all of them…Their deeds do not permit them to return to God. A spirit of prostitution is in their heart; they do not acknowledge the LORD …When they go with their flocks and herds to seek the LORD they will not find Him; He has withdrawn Himself from them. They are unfaithful to the LORD …I will pour out my wrath on them…I will be like a great lion to Judah. I will tear them to pieces and go away; I will carry them off, with no one to rescue them. Then I will return to my lair until they have borne their guilt. And they will seek my face; in their misery they will earnestly seek me. 6:1 Come let us return to the Lord; He has torn us to pieces; but He will heal us; He has injured us but He will bind up our wounds."

**NIV note** 6:1 this was a shallow proposal of repentance in which Israel acknowledged that God, not Assyria was the true physician.

**Job 12:13-14**

"To God belong wisdom and power…what He tears down cannot be rebuilt; the man He imprisons cannot be released…"

## 2. JUDGMENT AGAINST GOD – DEFYING SIN AND COVENANT-BREAKING REBELLION

**Lamentations 3:3-23**

"…He has turned His hand against me…He has made my skin and my flesh grow old and has broken my bones. He has besieged me and surrounded me with bitterness and hardship…He has walled me in…He has weighed me down...even when I call out…for help He shuts out my prayer. He has barred my way…like a lion in hiding He dragged me from the path and mangled me…"

**Lamentations 3:16**

"**He has broken my teeth with gravel...**because of the LORD's great love we are not consumed, for His compassions never fail. They are new every morning; great is your faithfulness. For men are not cast off by the LORD forever. Though He brings grief, **He will show compassion.**"

**NIV note:** The author of Lamentations understands clearly that the Babylonians were merely the human agents of divine retribution and that God Himself has destroyed His city and temple. Nor was the LORD's action arbitrary; blatant, God-defying sin and covenant-breaking rebellion were the root causes of His people's woes. Although weeping is to be expected and cries for redress against the enemy are understandable, the proper response in the wake of judgment is sincere, heartfelt contrition. This book reminds us that justice and love come together in perfect balance in a holy God. In wisdom and grace, God does not allow sin to go unchecked. His standards are maintained... though He brings grief, He will show compassion. Trust His teeth; when you can't trace His hand trust His teeth.

**II Samuel 24:12-14**

"...this is what the LORD says: I am giving you three options. Choose one of them for me to carry out against you...Shall there come upon you three years of famine in your land? Or three months of fleeing from your enemies while they pursue you? Or three days of plague in your land? David said...I am in deep distress, Let us fall into the hands of the Lord, **for His mercy is great**; but do not let me fall into the hands of men."

**Job 42:12**

"The Lord blessed the latter part of Job's life more than the first..."

**NIV note:** The cosmic contest with the accuser is now over and Job is restored. No longer is there a reason for Job to experience suffering unless he was sinful and deserved it which is not the case. God does not allow us to suffer for no reason and even though the reason may be hidden in the mystery of His divine purpose we must trust in Him as the God who does only what is right.

### 3. JUDGMENT TO PURIFY GOD'S PEOPLE/SUFFERING FOR BEING A CHRISTIAN

**I Peter 4:12-16**

Dear friends, do not be surprised at the fiery ordeal that has come on you to test you…but rejoice inasmuch as you participate in the sufferings of Christ, so that you may be overjoyed when His glory is revealed. If you suffer, it should not be as a murderer or thief or any other kind of criminal, or even as a meddler. However, if you suffer as a Christian, do not be ashamed but praise God that you bear that name…So then those who suffer according to God's will should commit themselves to their faithful Creator and continue to do good.

## PERSONAL APPLICATION

**James 1:2-12**

Consider it pure joy, my brothers and sisters whenever you face trials of many kinds, because you know that the testing of your faith develops perseverance. Let perseverance finish its work so that you may be mature and complete, not lacking anything…Blessed is the one who perseveres under trial, because having stood the test, that person will receive the crown of life that the LORD has promised to those who love Him.

It is in the darkest moments that God pulls the gems out of us. Trust His teeth.

**Psalm 46:1-5**

God is our refuge and strength, an ever present help in trouble. Therefore we will not fear, though the earth give way and the mountains fall into the heart of the sea, though its waters roar and foam and the mountains quake with their surging…God is within her she will not fall. God will help her at break of day.

This is a triumphant confession of fearless trust in God, though the continents break up and sink beneath the resurging waters of the sea.

CHAPTER 14

# THE SIDE OF GOD
If You Believe You Will Receive

*"He is…the horn of my salvation…"*
**Psalm 18:2**

The side of God reflects proof of His laying down His life (death); proof of His life (resurrection from the dead) and proof of His love.

## A. PROOF OF HIS LAYING DOWN HIS LIFE *(HE DIED)*

"Crucifixion was never intended to kill anybody. People actually lived on the cross, crucified for up to six days. If you can, imagine a man hanging on a cross outside the gates of a city with the birds pecking at his eyes and roosting on his head, as he hangs there naked as a spectacle for the whole city. That was the point of crucifixion, it was part of the shame and humiliation that a man hang there so people could come by for a day or two and stand and mock and jeer and shout accusations and railing and blasphemy at him. The idea was to make him suffer as much as possible.

It was never intended to kill anybody. It was only intended to make a human being suffer as much as could be inflicted upon him before killing him by breaking his legs (crucifracture). Crucifracture is what they would do when they simply grew tired of watching this agony and suffering or when they had something better to do and wanted to end a crucifixion. They would take a spear and swing it like a ball bat and hit the victim in the shins to break his shin bones. They'd break the tibula and the fibula bone. Many times they would have to beat the legs for five or ten minutes until they finally could break the shin bones—it takes a lot of force to break your shin bone. With the shin bone broken, the victim could no longer push up to breathe." *(Excerpt from* **"Jesus' Suffering and Crucifixion From A Medical Point of View"** *Tripta Kapur. South Asian Connection)*

Why didn't they break Jesus' legs? Psalm 34:20 "He protects all his bones, not one of them will be broken." This is why the Roman centurion didn't break His legs. That was totally uncharacteristic of the crucifixion, because that's how crucifixion victims died. When they grew tired of you and got bored with the situation they'd break your legs and in about four to six minutes they would asphyxiate. That's how the two thieves died. But Jesus had already laid down His life.

**Exodus 12:46** Passover Restrictions

"Do not break any of the bones (Numbers 9:12) When Jesus our Passover Lamb was crucified, it was reported that none of His bones were broken in fulfillment of Scripture.

**John 19:30, 32-33**

When He had received the drink, Jesus said "It is finished." With that, He bowed His head and gave up His spirit…Because the Jewish leaders did not want the bodies left on the crosses during the Sabbath, they asked Pilate to have the legs broken and the bodies taken down. 32 The soldiers therefore came and broke the legs of the first man who had been crucified with Jesus, and then those of the other. But when they came to Jesus and found that he was already dead, they did not break His legs." It was extraordinary that Jesus was the only one of the three men whose legs were not broken and that He suffered an unusual spear thrust that did not break a bone.

**John 19:34-37**

Instead one of the soldiers pierced Jesus' side with a spear, bringing a sudden flow of blood and water. 35 The man who saw it has given testimony and his testimony is true. He knows that He tells the truth, and he testifies so that you also may believe. These things happened so that the Scriptures would be fulfilled. Not one of His bones will be broken and as another Scripture says "they will look on the One they have pierced."

The spear wound to the Lord's side was not the cause of his death either. Jesus' side was pierced to make doubly sure that Jesus was dead but perhaps simply as an act of brutality. The spear thrust was Biblical prophecy fulfilled.

"Blood & water—the result of the spear piercing the pericardium (the sac that surrounds the heart) and the heart itself.

The blow to Jesus' side was no doubt delivered from the right side through the right lung into the heart and on into the spine. If you take a unit of blood, drain it out of a human being's body, put it in a quart jar and set it on top of a desk, in about 30 minutes the red blood cells begin to settle out and the plasma rises to the top. The plasma separates from the red blood cells. When the soldier thrust the spear into the Lord's side, Jesus had already been dead 30-45 minutes. The spear wound did not take the life of the Lord Jesus; he was dead already when they thrust the spear into His side." (*Excerpt from* "***Jesus' Suffering and Crucifixion From A Medical Point of View***" *Tripta Kapur. South Asian Connection)*

So what took the Lord's life? No man did; no Roman centurion did, no cross took Jesus' life. He was able to do something that no human has done, He laid down His life. When it was finished and with a loud voice, He gave up the ghost.

**John 10:17-18**

The reason my Father loves me is that I lay down my life—only to take it up again. No one takes it from me, but I lay it down of my own accord. I have authority to lay it down and authority to take it up again. This command I received from my Father."

## B. PROOF OF HIS LIFE *(HE LIVES)*

John's Gospel is the only one of the four accounts that give such details relating to Jesus' pierced side, the showing of His side *(hands and feet were shown in Luke 24 not the side)* to Thomas as proof that He laid down His life and Thomas' response. The purpose of John's Gospel is found in

**John 20:31**

These are written that you may believe that Jesus is the Christ, the Son of God and that by believing you may have life in His name.

**John 20:20**

After He said this, He showed them His hands and side… "This is where the wounds were." Jesus was clearly identifying Himself.

Thomas doubted his resurrection.

**John 20:25-29**

"…unless I see the nail marks in His hands and put my finger where the nails were and put my hand into His side, I will not believe it." A week later…then Jesus said to Thomas "Put your finger here; see My hands. Reach out your hand and put it into My side. Stop doubting and believe. Thomas said to Him, My LORD and My God. Then Jesus told him, Because you have seen me you have believed, blessed are those who have not seen and yet have believed."

To acknowledge Jesus as Lord and God is the highest point of one's faith. Thomas had an "aha" moment. I learnt that Thomas was killed in India and that all of the churches started by him are still in existence at the time of writing.

**Revelation 1:7**

"Look, He is coming with the clouds and every eye will see Him, even those who pierced Him."

## UNBELIEF

**John 12:37-50**

37 Even after Jesus had performed so many signs in their presence, they still would not believe in him. 38 This was to fulfill the word of Isaiah the prophet: "LORD, who has believed our message and to whom has the arm of the Lord been revealed?" 39 For this reason they could not believe, because, as Isaiah says elsewhere: 40 "He has blinded their eyes and deadened their hearts, so they can neither see with their eyes, nor understand with their hearts, nor turn—and I would heal them." 41 Isaiah said this because he saw Jesus' glory and spoke about him. Yet at the same time many even among the leaders believed in him. But because of the Pharisees they would not acknowledge their faith for fear they would be put out of the synagogue; 43 for they loved human praise more than praise from God.

44 Then Jesus cried out, "Whoever a man believes in me, does not believe in me only, but in the One who sent me. 45 The one who looks at me is seeing the One who sent me. 46 I have come into the world as a light, so that no one who believes in me should stay in darkness. 47 "If anyone hears my words but does not keep them, I do not judge him. For I did not come to judge the world, but to save the world. 48 There is a Judge for the one who rejects me and does not accept my words; the very words I have spoken will condemn them at the last day. 49 For I did not speak on my own, but the Father who sent me commanded me to say all that I have spoken. 50 I know that his command leads to eternal life. So whatever I say is just what the Father has told me to say."

Unbelief can render you powerless to handle situations that you have the power to deal with.

**Mark 9:14-29**

If you can?!! said Jesus, "Everything is possible for him who believes." The question was not whether Jesus had the power to heal but whether the father had faith to believe.

"This kind can come out only by prayer" Lack of prayer indicated that the disciples had forgotten that their power over the demonic spirits was from Jesus.

**Unbelief can cause you to waver, hesitate and miss out on the promises of God.**

**Romans 4:20**

"Yet Abraham did not waver through unbelief regarding the promise of God, but was strengthened in his faith and gave glory to God."

Faith does not refuse to face reality but looks beyond all difficulties to God and His promised. Because Abraham had faith to believe that God would do what He promised…faith brings glory to God.

**Unbelief will cause you to be disobedient to God's guidance and direction so that you act on what you see and reason, and not on faith in God.**

**Hebrews 3:18-19**

"And to whom did God swear that they would never enter His rest, if not to those who disobeyed? So we see that they were not able to enter because of their unbelief."

The people who failed to enter Canaan were the ones who had heard God's promise concerning the land and that they refused to believe what God had promised—an action described as rebellion v.16; sin v.17; and disobedience v.18. Consequently, God, in His anger, closed the doors of Canaan in the face of that whole generation of Israelites.

## C. PROOF OF HIS LOVE

**Isaiah 53:5**

"But He was pierced for our transgressions. He was crushed for our iniquities..." the sins of the world weighed heavily upon Him.

## PERSONAL APPLICATION

**James 4:8**

And when you draw close to God, God will draw close to you.

Let us draw near to God with a sincere heart in full assurance of faith (belief) (NIV)

**Hebrews 10:21-22 (TLB)**

And since this great High Priest of ours rules over God's household, let us go right in, to God Himself, with true hearts fully trusting Him to receive us, because we have been sprinkled with Christ's blood to make us clean, and because our bodies have been washed with pure water.

Four conditions for drawing "near to God" in **NIV notes** are:

*"...a sincere heart..."*—undivided allegiance in the inner being; no divided loyalties; clean hands, pure heart;

*"...full assurance of faith..."*—faith that knows no hesitation in trusting in and following Christ;

*"...hearts sprinkled...from a guilty conscience..."*—total freedom from a sense of guilt, a freedom based on the once-for-all sacrifice of Christ;

*"...bodies washed with pure water..."*—not an external ceremony such as baptism but a figure for inner cleansing, of which the washing of the priests under the old covenant was a symbol (Exodus 30:19-21; Leviticus 8:6)

Jesus wants you to draw near to His side. He wants to identify Himself in some way to you. Do not hold back; do not doubt, do not be afraid to launch out into the deep—His depth of love for you. If you believe, you will receive.

**Luke 24:35**

"…and how Jesus was recognized by them when He broke the bread."

CHAPTER 15

# THE FINGER OF GOD
## God is in The Details

*"It is God who...makes my way perfect."*
***Psalm 18:32***

The finger of God is a concise and colourful figure of speech referring to God's miraculous power. (NIV Text Note on Exodus 8:19). The finger of God also suggests His personal attention to details. In the case of Pharaoh, he already had God's attention through the hand of God, but his continued stubbornness attracted the finger of God. The other references to creation, the giving of the Law, the driving out of demons and being an advocate for one accused all point to the fact that details are not missed by the King of the Universe. The song writer asked "How big is God?" His reply was that He's big enough to rule the mighty universe yet small enough to live within my heart.

God micro-manages our lives, but only if we allow Him to. Micromanagement is defined as:

Management with excessive control or attention on details (Merriam-Webster's Online Dict.)

Management or control with excessive attention to minor details *(Dictionary.com)*

Attention to small details in management; control of a person or a situation by paying extreme attention to small details. (Encarta)

They say it is not good to have a boss who micromanages you BUT I submit to you that God micromanages our lives and there is nothing negative about that.

We are going to look at the various examples in Scripture where God takes the time to attend to the details.

## A. THE FINGER OF GOD WORKS ON THE DETAILS ON STONE

**Exodus 31:18**

When the Lord finished speaking to Moses on Mount Sinai, He gave him two tablets of the covenant law, the tablets of stone inscribed by the finger of God. NIV//…on which the Ten Commandments were written with the finger of God. TLB

**Exodus 32:15-16**

They were inscribed on both sides front and back. The tablets were the work of God, the writing was the writing of God, engraved on the tablets.

**Deuteronomy 9:10**

The Lord gave me 2 stone tablets inscribed by the finger of God.

God, the Creator of the Universe, takes the time to write out 10 commandments on a stone tablet for mortal man. The ancient Near Eastern practice was that each party of the covenant gets a copy. Israel's copy was placed in the presence of God in the Ark. It was God's covenant (Exodus 19:5-6) and the stipulations of the covenant (Exodus 20:1-17) were His.

## B. THE FINGER OF GOD WORKS ON THE DETAILS IN THE SKY

### Psalm 8:3

When I consider your heavens, the work of your fingers, the moon and the stars which you have set in place, what is mankind that you are mindful of them; human beings that you care for them?

The vastness and majesty of the heavens as the handiwork of God evoke wonder for what their Maker has done for little man who is here today and gone tomorrow. God worked on the details of the seasons, natural disasters, climate, the solar system etc. He did not set up a select committee to coordinate the interior/exterior design of creation…He did it Himself.

## C. THE FINGER OF GOD WORKS ON THE DETAILS RE THE SPIRIT'S ROLE

### Luke 11:20

But if I drive out demons by the finger of God, then the kingdom of God has come upon you. The context suggests that the "unpardonable sin" was attributing to Satan Christ's authenticating miracles done in the power of the Holy Spirit. The Kingdom of God was present in the form of Jesus and that the powers of evil being overthrown by the finger of God.

He did not meet with the Human Resource Manager to ensure that all the employees get a copy of the Holy Spirit's job description. He clarified the matter Himself.

## D. THE FINGER OF GOD WORKS ON THE DETAILS IN THE FACE OF STUBBORNESS

### Exodus 8:19

**The magicians said to Pharaoh "This is the finger of God." But Pharaoh's heart was hard and he would not listen just as the LORD had said."**

It's all about God, it has nothing to do with us. All of life, situations, thoughts, is an initiative of God to move us towards Him, towards relationship with Him. When we make the choice to refuse Him, to spurn His advances, to stubbornly reject His holiness and His love we chart a course towards darkness and eventually death.

Some choices move us away from God's presence and plan. If we can identify the stages of the slide of stubbornness, therefore, it would help us to make a conscious decision to turn away from the folly of our ways.

God is light and in Him is no darkness at all. If God is not present there is darkness. Where there is no light there is darkness. To refuse God, who is light, means that we choose darkness.

Let's look at an individual who took a blatant stand contrary to the plans and wishes of God. He dismissed God's desires, plans and wishes for His people. He tried to engage in a tug of war of wills as he played God and tried to get God to do things according to his terms and conditions.

Pharaoh thought that he had something with which to bargain. He thought he possessed bargaining rights over the people of Israel, but they were God's people under God's rule. If Pharaoh had been able to read the book before he would realize that it was all about God, and had nothing to do with him. In taking a stand against the King of Kings and LORD of Lords he did not stand a chance. Pharaoh thought he was dealing with only the 2 middle management representatives in Moses and Aaron. He didn't realize that their Supervisor/Shepherd was into the details of these travelling officers / couriers / messengers.

Moses and Aaron brought a message to Pharaoh from Jehovah, the God of Israel. "Let my people go, for they must make a holy pilgrimage out into the wilderness, for a religious feast, to worship ME there." In Exodus 5:2 (TLB) we see Pharaoh's response to God's request. "Is that so?" retorted Pharaoh. "And who is Jehovah that I should listen to him, and let Israel go? I don't know Jehovah and I will not let Israel go." This was the purpose for the ensuing plot in Exodus 7-11. You don't know Jehovah, well at the end of this you will know who Jehovah is.

God's response is found in Exodus 6:1, "Now you will see what I shall do to Pharaoh," the LORD told Moses, "For he must be forced to let my people go; he will not only let them go, but will drive them out of his land. I am Jehovah, the Almighty God…I will use my mighty power and perform great miracles…and they shall know that I am Jehovah…The Egyptians will find out that I am indeed God when I show them my power and force them to let my people go."

Pharaoh represents those who refuse to get in line. Persons who choose not to get into line with God digress in the following ways:

## STEP #1
## THEY VIEW THE SPECTACULAR
## HAND OF GOD AS ORDINARY

**Exodus 7:20**

Aaron hit the surface…river turned to blood…

**Exodus 7:22**

The magicians of Egypt used their secret arts and turned water to blood. The action of the magicians reminds me of a game that we used to play in primary school…what can you do punchinella little fella (rept.); we can do it too punchinella little fella or There's a brown girl in the ring…show me your motion fallalalala…

**Exodus 7:22**

Pharaoh's heart remained hard and stubborn and he wouldn't listen. He returned to his palace unimpressed.

Because his magicians could do it too, Pharaoh was unimpressed with water in ALL rivers, canals, marshes, reservoirs, bowls and pots in homes turning to blood!! The fish died and the water became stink so that the Egyptians could not drink it and there was blood throughout the land, wherever there was water. Think about that!! But Pharaoh was unimpressed.

God does mighty things in our lives on a minute basis. But because we don't think it's spectacular enough we miss the little things, we miss His hand in our lives, we miss His working things out for our good. Or we credit His work to other things such as timing, following our minds, unaware that it's not who you know but who knows you.

**Exodus 8:5**

Aaron did and frogs covered the nation

**Exodus 8:7**

But the magicians did the same with their secret arts

**Exodus 8:9,15**

Plead with God to take the frogs away and I will let the people go…But when Pharaoh saw that the frogs were gone he hardened his heart.

We also miss out on the little things that God is doing among His people. We rationalize and explain in the natural why things happen. We are ungrateful for the small benefits in our lives. Time is a great deceiver. It can minimize the impact of a message. Whenever there is a great tragedy, people think of God, see His hand at work, talk about Him and pledge to be more mindful of Him. It has a great effect initially, but with the passage of time, that effect wears off and all promises are forgotten.

## STEP #2
### WE ENGAGE THE FINGER OF GOD

When the people remain unmoved, the finger of God will move.

**Exodus 8:17**

So Moses and Aaron did as God commanded and suddenly lice infested the entire nation.

**Exodus 8:18**

Then the magicians tried to do the same thing with their secret arts but **this time** they failed. Something was different this time around. They checked the expiry date on their potions; some of their wands had to go for servicing. They are now taking notice. We can't explain this one. This one is out of our realm.

**Exodus 8:19**

"This is the finger of God," they exclaimed to Pharaoh. Imagine those around Pharaoh who knew the situation recognized exactly what had happened and now tried to talk some sense into Pharaoh.

**Exodus 8:19**

But Pharaoh's heart was hard and stubborn and he wouldn't listen to them.

As a young Christian I had difficulty with the phrase "…the Lord hardened Pharaoh's heart…" It was the Hebrew thought that nothing happens without God's approval. The hardening of Pharaoh's heart was not a direct action of God but an indirect action of not persuading Pharaoh to do otherwise. God did not intervene, but rather, He withdrew His hand. There are consequences of our actions. God's actions with Pharaoh were more an allowance rather than a persuasion to keep Pharaoh's heart hardened. God does not override our will.

God permitted it rather than prevented it. God never becomes so persuasive as to cause Pharaoh to change his mind. God was moving Pharaoh to a point at which he recognized and acknowledged who God was but Pharaoh continually made the choice to disobey God.

Do you remember Pharaoh's question?

**Exodus 5:2**

And who is Jehovah, that I should listen to him…I don't know Jehovah…"

**Exodus 10:8**

"All right, go and serve Jehovah your God."

**Exodus 10:16**

"I confess my sin against Jehovah your God…"

**Exodus 12:32**

"Take your flocks and herds and be gone and give me a blessing as you go…" the greater blesses the lesser.

God gave Pharaoh opportunities to relent:
**Exodus 5:23 (TLB)**

Ever since I gave Pharaoh your message, he has only been more and more brutal to them.

Every time Pharaoh promised to let His people go, even though God in His sovereignty knew that Pharaoh was going to go back on his word, He allowed the plague to cease. He took Pharaoh at his word. Any goodly move towards God is honoured. Pharaoh's intent to respond under pressure was honoured by God. Pharaoh's baby steps were an inclination to seek God. In the worst of people God looks for the best in them. God is looking for graduation to His maturity. God is not willing that any should perish but that all should come to repentance.

There was an entourage of witnesses so that Pharaoh in the end could not doubt that God was love. God's actions were a move towards Pharaoh becoming repentant even though he knew that Pharaoh was not going to honour it. God is more concerned about redemption than condemnation. Every move of God is towards redemption.

When we engage the finger of God, the writing for us is on the wall, and we have been weighed in the scales and found wanting. Do you recall the story of King Belshazzar in Daniel 5? He threw a party and took the vessels from the temple that were holy to the LORD and used them to drink wine, etc. He used the sacred vessels for common purposes, profaned them and by doing so dishonoured God. It's all about God! He just saw some vessels and used them. Daniel 5:5 tells us that "suddenly the fingers of a human hand appeared and wrote on the plaster of the wall near the lamp stand."

When we engage the finger of God, things will not remain the same for us. It will not be business as usual. If there is a situation and you recognize that this had to be the finger of God, then listen to those around you. Stop the slide of stubbornness; God is working, He is moving up and down trying to get your attention. Wake up before it is too late!!

## WHAT A GOD!

The finger of God does not affect His people in a negative way…

**Exodus 8:24**

"…there were terrible swarms of flies in Pharaoh's palace and in every home."

**Exodus 8:22-23**

"I will make a distinction between your people and my people thus you will know that I am the LORD God of all the earth." There was no harm to God's people.

**Exodus 8:25**

Pharaoh hastily summoned Moses and Aaron. All right, go ahead but do it here.

I will obey, but conditionally, on my terms. Partial obedience is the half-brother of disobedience.

**Exodus 9:3**

"…the power of God will send a deadly plague to destroy…will only affect the cattle of Egypt. None of the herds and flocks of the Israelites will even be touched. Listen the Word of God tells us that when we live within the shadow of the Almighty, sheltered by the God who is above all gods…no plague shall come nigh thy dwelling; He will protect you from the fatal plague…the plague cannot even come near you!!

**Exodus 9:10**

So they took ashes…became boils

**Exodus 9:10**

"…magicians couldn't stand before Moses for the boils appeared on them too.

**Exodus 9:12**

Pharaoh refused to listen.

Things are happening but this time you have no rational explanation. However, you still remain in your stubbornness and you continue your slide into darkness.

## STEP #3
## WE DISMISS THE VOICE OF GOD
## AS EVIDENCED THROUGH ACTIONS & ADVICE
## OF THOSE WHO ONCE WALKED WITH US

### ACTIONS

**Exodus 9:19 (TLB)**

"…hailstorm…"

**Exodus 9:20 (TLB)**

"…some of the Egyptians terrified by this threat brought their cattle and slaves in from the fields but those who had no regard for the word of Jehovah left them out in the storm." Do you remember the message from God last week about towing the line in 2009? The first point was "Know that some may not be interested in what you are saying. Some may not be interested in your message. Some will respond to the message, others will not."

Illustration: Hurricane Gilbert, some heeded and others did not. Why? We got warnings all the time. Then, why was this one different? The finger of God!!

People who did not even belong to God or claim Him as their God were protected because of their obedience to His warnings.

**Exodus 9:27**

Pharaoh "I finally see my fault. Jehovah is right…"

**Exodus 9:34**

When Pharaoh saw this he and his officials sinned yet more by their stubborn refusal to do what they had promised.

They didn't know who they were playing with.

### ADVICE

**Exodus 10:4-5**

"…a thick layer of locusts."

**Exodus 10:7**

"…the court officials now came to Pharaoh and asked him, Are you going to destroy us completely? Don't you know that even yet all Egypt lies in ruins, let the men go…"

These officials were the ones who had originally been in FULL support of Pharaoh's previous decisions. They had also stubbornly refused to let them go. But now, they were advising Pharaoh differently. They used to be on the same wavelength as Pharaoh, they used to lime with Pharaoh, they were in his circle. Pharaoh used to listen to them… why not now? Pharaoh probably thinking, you used to side with me why are you now against me? It's not that they are against Pharaoh, they are against the path of destruction that he is on and so they have automatically moved out of the line they were in. They are seeing what is happening around Pharaoh. They have now ceased to engage God in battle and have withdrawn and can see clearly now that it really was not about them but all about God. But Pharaoh still could not see that.

The officials now became the voice of conscience, the voice of God. But they were familiar to Pharaoh What do they know? If they want to stop liming with you, that's their business. Those around you have surveyed the situation with different lenses to you and they see that what concerns you, what you had responsibility for now lies in ruins, not as flourishing as it was. They are trying to warn you!

**Exodus 10:16**

"I confess my sin against Jehovah your God and against you. Forgive my sin…I solemnly promise.

## STEP #4
## WE GIVE GOD AN OPPORTUNITY
## TO SHOW UP AND SHOW OFF

**Exodus 12:9**

"Pharaoh won't listen and this will give me the opportunity of doing mighty miracles to demonstrate my power."

**Exodus 12:29**

"…that night, at midnight…" ***Specific time***

"…Jehovah killed all the firstborn sons in the land of Egypt from Pharaoh's oldest son to the oldest son of the captive in the dungeon; also all the firstborn of the cattle…there was not a house where there was not one dead…" ***Specific plan***

"…there was bitter crying…Pharaoh summoned Moses and Aaron during the night…get out as quickly as possible…" ***Specific results***

Pharaoh's disobedience of Moses' request was direct disobedience of God's command and blatant challenge to God's authority. God gives His leaders His mandate and this must be carried out. Leaders are accountable to God not to man.

**Joshua 5**—the dread of God.

God used this to keep the Israelites in a pocket of safety for the 5 days they needed to heal after circumcising the males. Though the scale was tipped years ago, the implication years later God was able to use. The ability that He has to balance who He is and how He represents Himself.

**I John 4:4**

The One who is in you is greater than the one who is in the world. What confronts you is at the level of great and when you get to the point where your adversary seems to be at his best, God steps in and shows that He is greater.

## E. THE FINGER OF GOD WORKS ON THE DETAILS OF MY PERSONAL SECURITY

**Psalm 144:1**

Praise be to the LORD my Rock who trains my hands for war and my fingers for battle.

## F. THE FINGER OF GOD WORKS ON THE DETAILS OF RESTORING A MAN'S SPEECH

**Mark 7:32-35**

There some people brought to him a man who was deaf and could hardly talk, and they begged Jesus to place His hand on him. 33 After He took him aside, away from the crowd, Jesus put His fingers into the man's ears. Then He spit and touched the man's tongue. 34 He looked up to heaven and with a deep sight said to him "Ephphatha! (which means, Be opened!") 35 At this, the man's ears were opened, his tongue was loosened and he began to speak plainly.

## G. THE FINGER OF GOD WORKS ON THE DETAILS OF SOLOMON'S TEMPLE

David was a man of war through most of his life in contrast to Solomon, who is referred to in I Chronicles 22:9 as the man of "peace and rest" and who will build the temple. In I Kings 5:3 Solomon explains that David could not build the temple because he was too busy with wars. The nuance of the author of Chronicles is slightly different—not just that wars took so much of his time, but that David was in some sense defiled by them because of the bloodshed.

I Chronicles 28 recounts that he had it in his heart to build a house as a place of rest for the ark of the covenant of the LORD, for the footstool of God. But God said to him "You are not to build a house for my Name, because you are a warrior and have shed blood." David continues by saying that Solomon was chosen to build God's house and courts.

**I Chronicles 28:11-18**

*Then David gave his son Solomon the plans for the portico for the temple, its buildings, its storerooms, its upper parts, its inner rooms and the place of atonement. He gave him the plans of all that the Spirit had put in his mind for the courts of the temple of the Lord and all the surrounding rooms, for the treasuries of the temple of God and for the treasuries for the dedicated things. He gave him instructions for the divisions of the priests and Levites and for all the work of serving in the temple of the LORD. He designated the weight of gold for all the gold articles to be used in various kinds of service and the weight of silver for all the silver articles to be used in various kinds of service…He also gave him the plan for the chariot…the cherubim of gold that spread their wings and shelter the ark of the covenant of the LORD.*

David sums this up by saying in verse 19 "Every part of this blueprint was given to me in writing from the hand of the LORD … Don't be frightened by the size of the task, for the LORD my God is with you; He will not forsake you. He will see to it that everything is finished correctly." (details)

## H. THE FINGER OF GOD WORKS ON THE DETAILS IN THE SAND

In John 8:3-11 we see the account of a woman who was caught in adultery and brought to Jesus by the teachers of the law and the Pharisees. They made her stand before the group and said to Jesus, "Teacher, this woman was caught in the act of adultery. In the Law, Moses commanded us to stone such women. Now what do you say? They were using this question as a trap in order to have a basis for accusing Him.

Verse 6 tells us that Jesus bent down and wrote on the ground with His finger. 7 When they kept on questioning Him, He straightened up and said to them "If any one of you is without sin let him be the first to throw a stone at her." Again He stooped down and wrote on the ground.

We do not know what Jesus wrote on the ground with his finger. What we do know, however, is that whatever He took the time to write in the dust caused the woman's accusers to depart. The Son of God took the time to attend to the details of a woman who had committed a sinful act. How much more His children.

## I. THE FINGER OF GOD WORKS ON THE DETAILS OF OUR EVERY STEP

### PERSONAL APPLICATION

A popular expression used by many is that the devil is in the details. All of the meanings for the term boil down to the fact that it is often the small details of something which make it difficult or challenging. These details can prolong a task, or foil an otherwise straightforward dealing. However, as children of God, when we come into a better understanding of the finger of God we will recognize that it is God who is in the details as well as He is the One who takes care of every detail.

**Job 23:10 (TLB)**
But He knows every detail of what is happening to me.

**Job 31:4 (TLB)**
Does He not see my ways and count my every step?

**Job 34:21 (TLB)**
His eyes are on the ways of men; He sees their every step.

**Psalm 1:6** tells us that God watches over ALL the plans and path of godly men. God is a God of the details. He takes exquisite care of His children. Nothing is left to chance.

**Psalm 37:23**
The steps of the godly are directed by the Lord. He delights in every detail of their lives (NLT) God is a strategic planner. The book of Esther is a classic example of how God orchestrates every detail of our lives. Let us focus on Mordecai...

We have all heard that Queen Esther was a great, courageous woman, a woman of prayer and faith. The individual behind this strong woman, however, was her uncle Mordecai. Esther's life was an indication of Mordecai's own walk with God. Mordecai walked the talk and God took care of the details of his life and concerns.

**(3:2)**

Mordecai refused to compromise and did not bow

**(4:1)**

His first response was to God

**(2:19)**

The Lord granted Mordecai favour and he became a government official

**(2:22)**

The Lord then allows Mordecai to overhear a plot against the king He reports it to Esther who in turn reports it to the King giving the credit to Mordecai. After the investigation the individuals were executed. This was duly recorded in the records of the kingdom.

**Esther 6:1** marks the literary center of Esther…When things could not look worse, a series of seemingly trivial coincidences marks a critical turn that brings resolution to the story. All the events testify to the sovereignty of God over the events of the narrative.

Five years later the king cannot sleep and calls for the records of the kingdom to be read for him. The account of Mordecai's good deed in 2:22 is read and the king realizes that Mordecai was not honoured.

At just the time Haman appears before the king to request his permission to hang Mordecai, the king asks Haman what should be done to the man whom the king delights to honour.

Mordecai is honoured through the streets of the nation, on the king's horse, wearing the king's robe and heralded by his very enemy. After Haman's death, Haman's estate is eventually managed by Mordecai. Only a Master Strategic Planner could orchestrate these events.

I know that you, the reader, can identify with this aspect of God's anatomy. I am sure that you have your own testimony of how the LORD has worked out the details in so many of your situations. To highlight the miraculous working power of the finger of God, I have added testimonies from three individuals:

## TESTIMONY OF EDITH KHAN, JAMAICA

One evening my son and I were on our way to the country to visit relatives and when I left home I had my cell phone but there was no credit on it and I had a small amount of money in my purse. About 2 hours into the journey I heard a sound coming from the car and when I looked I saw smoke coming from the bonnet. I stopped the car and could not go any further.

When I stopped there was a mechanic who was right behind me. He immediately came out of his vehicle, came to me and said "Miss I am a mechanic and I saw the smoke coming out of your car." He went towards the engine to diagnose the problem. When he looked at it he said that it was the water hose that burst. He said that at this time of the evening the shop that he was thinking of to purchase the part would be closed but he would try. So I gave him the little money that I had in my purse to see if he could get the part.

Initially, when we had stopped a wrecker had passed and the man in the wrecker recognized the mechanic and called out to him and continued on his way. The mechanic then left with the money to get the part. While the mechanic was gone to get the part, a friend of mine who usually does not drive that way decided to drive this route this particular evening. She saw my car and recognized me by my head and so she drove up and stopped. She was on her way to the supermarket to purchase items for her restaurant. When the mechanic returned he realized that the problem was greater than he thought because the radiator had burst as well and would need to be changed.

By this time we realized that the car would have to be towed but I was telling the mechanic that I had no money. The wrecker returned just at this time and we were in discussion about payment the wrecker guy said "Miss, it's not all the time I charge; there is a place that sells radiators; it might be closed at this time but I will try." When he called the shop it was still open so he made enquiries about a radiator. They had the radiator in stock. So the car was lifted unto the wrecker and I was without a vehicle.

The mechanic followed the wrecker and my friend took us to the radiator shop. When we got there I had no funds to purchase the radiator but my friend was able to assist me with funds that she had. So we had the funds to purchase the radiator, pay the mechanic and within 1 ½ hours inspite of the problems encountered my car was repaired back on the road and ready for the journey.

The LORD is worthy of our praise!

## TESTIMONY OF GARTH MARSHALL, TRINIDAD & TOBAGO

*Garth was a new employee of a travel agency downtown and over time gained the respect and confidence of his employers. He was asked to take a pouch filled with passports for local businessmen to the US Embassy. This being the practice at the time was for the purpose of submitting their applications for obtaining a US visa. Garth got on his motorcycle and headed for the Embassy. Upon his arrival at the Embassy, he noticed that the pouch was missing! It had, at some point in his journey, slipped off the back of the motor cycle.*

*With heart in hand he made a number of trips around the Queens Park Savannah to see if he could locate this pouch. After much searching it proved to be futile as no pouch turned up. With a heavy heart he returned to the office and informed his boss of his calamity. His boss told him to go on home and that they would deal with the situation the following day.*

*When he arrived at home Garth relayed the misfortune to his mother. She prayed with him and told him not to worry about it but to go and rest. This he did.*

*The next morning he was up very early and his mother prayed with him once more and he made his way to the office. When he arrived it was so* early that the office was unopened. While waiting, he saw a man who made his way hesitantly toward the travel agency as if to verify some information. When he saw Garth he asked for confirmation of the name of the agency. When he was told the name of the agency he walked back to his vehicle, took out a pouch from his car and gave it to Garth. It was the missing pouch with all the passports intact!!

This gentleman then related how he happened to be in possession of the pouch. He told Garth that he was sitting at the back of a Ministry of Works truck that was loaded with office furniture. It was going around the Savannah some distance away from the motorbike. From his vantage point sitting on one of the desks he saw when the pouch happened to slide off the bike, fall to the ground and roll into a drain under the pavement!! He stopped and decided to retrieve the pouch from the drain. As he was an employee of the Ministry of Works he was not only dressed in clothes that would facilitate such a rescue but he also had the tools necessary to retrieve the pouch from the drain! He explained that whenever offices had to be moved it was his job to move the furniture.

The interesting thing was that his route to work took him past this travel agency on mornings so actually it was the only one he was familiar with. Because the name of the travel agency on the pouch was faded, he was not sure which agency it was hence his hesitancy at the outset. The reason he brought the pouch to this agency, he told Garth, was that he would leave the pouch with him so that he could make enquiries and get it to the right people.

The finger of God takes care of the details of our lives!!!

## TESTIMONY OF REV. DONNAMIE ALI, TRINIDAD & TOBAGO

### GOD SHOWED UP

My younger brother, Andrew, lost his short term memory in September 2012, following surgery to drain fluids from his head. He suffers from *epileptic seizures and had undergone two brain surgeries the previous year. I decided that I would go to Arizona to be with him and help sort out some of his paperwork which he was now unable to. Thankfully God led me to ask my husband David to accompany me on that journey from Trinidad to Arizona. What's more, even while we were preparing to leave, Andrew had to have further surgery about one month after the previous one that left him without his short term memory.*

Words cannot describe my emotional state of mind even while journeying to that far off place. I did not really know what we were going to do. All I knew is that we had to be there for him and do something. We went straight from the airport to the hospital even though the flights took us the greater part of one day. I wanted him to be assured that we were there for him. I still had not fully grasped the extent of his memory loss. He knew me and all those who he had interacted with prior to the latter part of 2010 but forgot everything else within ten minutes!

We journeyed to the hospital almost every one of those 12 days, talking to Andrew and trying to meet with doctors and the all-important social worker who would help us to find a safe home for him. You see he was now unable to care for himself as far as taking medications and even eating was concerned. He would take the meds, forget that he did and take them again. At times he just did not take them. He could not prepare his own meals or go anywhere to purchase them.

We found a place that would take him for the amount of his social disability check but he walked out on the second night and was found wandering by the police and taken to a local hospital. He knew himself but did not know where he was and could not of course get back to the home-he did not remember he was ever there.

An entire day was spent at that hospital with their social worker trying to find a place for him-one with locked doors, and one that his disability cheque could afford. We felt harassed and emotionally drained but at last a place was found where he could be taken and be safe. This was just about 36 hours before we were due to return to Trinidad.

I would not lie - I cried quite a number of times. I felt as if we were all faced with an impossible situation most of the time. I could not perceive where we were going to get the money for his seizure and other medications. The set I had purchased two nights earlier cost approx. TT $3,000 for one month's supply. Because his company had terminated his employment in January, he was left only with the disability money. We found no evidence that he had other savings. If he has, it would have been a recent addition as a result of the company's payment to him of a lump sum. Since this was recent he has no memory of it and it was not reflected in his bank statements which we found at the house. His loss of employment meant there was no insurance to cover his hospital stay and medications.

However in the midst of all of this my God was there gently reminding me of his care for both my brother and for us who were trying to help but unsure of how to proceed. He showed up first in:

**Axel**, *a 23 year old Nicaraguan who has been renting a room from my brother for close to three years. This young man who could converse in English quite well, made himself and his vehicle available to us so we could go where we needed to. What is even more remarkable is that his job was terminated the week before we arrived and so he could have spent those 12 days looking for a job. What is even more remarkable again is that he took a week off from his work when my brother first suffered the memory loss and was prematurely sent home from the hospital. He said he just could not leave him alone in that condition! Sometimes I wonder if that is why he lost his job! God used this young man to help us, for my brother lived in the suburbs and there was no public transportation.*

## THE COMPASSIONATE STRANGER

*While we were in the hospital that Andrew was taken to after he was found wandering by the Phoenix police, an Eastern European man was sent by the social worker to see if his home could accommodate Andrew. We could not make the payment though. He was obviously compassionate because he was willing to drop his price to help us out. However since none of us had a legal power of attorney, he said he definitely could not accept him in the home. He left but returned about an hour later with a cell phone in his hand, which he handed to my husband, telling him to take it and use it while were in the USA. It was an AT&T postpaid phone! We were shocked at this stranger's generosity and could only thank and wish God's blessings on Him. Now wasn't that God showing up, reminding us that he would take care?*

**Dana Leka**

*Sometime after this man left, another Eastern European, this time a woman, entered with her friend. This was Dana who operated two homes and was willing to take Andrew for the money that was available. Dana is Romanian but has lived in the USA for many years. She asked several questions including the one about who had the power of attorney. My heart sank and I was feverishly praying inside- 'Lord, please let this work out.' It was about 7 pm and we were in that hospital for the entire day! I was tired and Andrew was getting agitated.*

*Dana warmed to us when she learned that we were Christians and was pleased that we were in the pastoral ministry. God had sent at this 10$^{th}$ hour- a Christian woman who was willing to house Andrew on November 10$^{th}$, even though his first payment could not be made until November 17$^{th}$. She trusted us. What was even greater was when she told us the next day that she can make arrangements for him to get his medication free through some agency she was linked with! I could hardly speak for the tears welled up in my eyes and I whispered a silent 'thank you' to my Lord. He was taking care of the details.*

**Andrew's friends**

*Andrew belongs to a small group in his church in Arizona (SDA). These friends have been there for him when no family members were around. Since he has been in the home they took him out on two occasions that I am aware of. One of them, who works in the area, visits him as often as he could. He is working with us and my sister in New York to get Andrew's business matters in order so that he can be moved closer to his family members eventually. We keep in touch via email and telephone conversations. God is working through them.*

The end has not come as yet. There are times when I feel emotionally oppressed but these are getting few and far between. I feel the prayers of the saints of God and am able to carry on with my day to day activities without being consumed by depressing thoughts all the time. I speak to Andrew almost every day and during those times I concentrate on showing him how much he still has to be thankful for. He knows his family and friends and his long term memory is intact. I encourage him to write in his memory book and pray with him.

There are a number of difficulties to be worked out still but I have seen enough to know that God is truly in the midst. I have asked saints of God who care, to pray and though I do feel sad at times that my brother has to be housed in an establishment, I remain confident in God and not in my feelings.

*TO GOD BE THE GLORY.*
*Donnamie*
*06/12/12*

I trust the details of my life to the finger of God—the Strategic Planner

CHAPTER 16

# THE MOUTH OF GOD
Jehovah Makkaeh, The Lord Who Moulds Me With His Word

*"...consuming fire came from His mouth..."*
*Psalm 18:8*

The mouth is the opening through which many animals issue vocal sounds; it is the system of organs surrounding this opening, including the lips, tongue, teeth etc.
**Job 37:2**
"Listen! Listen to the roar of His voice, to the rumbling that comes from His mouth (thunder)…"

## A. REFERENCES TO THE MOUTH OF GOD INDICATE THAT…

### 1. HE LAUGHS

With derisive laughter the LORD meets the rebellious world powers with the sovereign declaration that it is He who has established the Davidic king in His own royal city of Zion.

**Psalm 2:4**

The One enthroned in heaven laughs; the LORD scoffs at them (those who conspire against the LORD.)

**Psalm 37:13**

"But the LORD laughs at the wicked for He knows their day is coming." Strikingly, the Psalmist nowhere speaks of God's active involvement in bringing the wicked down though he hints at it in verse 22…those the LORD bless will inherit the land but those He curses will be cut off. The certainty that the life of the wicked "will be cut off" is frequently asserted but God's positive action is here reserved for His care for and protection of the righteous.

**Psalm 59:8 (TLB)**

The LORD laughs at His enemies for they have no power against Him.

### 2. HE SPEAKS

**Psalm 89:19**

"Once you spoke in a vision, to your faithful people…"

**Psalm 107:25**

For He spoke and stirred up a tempest that lifted high the waves.

**Isaiah 1:19-20**

If you are willing and obedient, you will eat the best from the land; but if you resist and rebel, you will be devoured by the sword." For the mouth of the LORD has spoken. Same Hebrew word.

**Isaiah 45:19, 23 (TLB)**

I, the LORD speak the truth; I declare what is right…By myself I have sworn, my mouth has uttered in all integrity a word that will not be revoked.

**Hosea 12:4-5 (TLB)**

Yes, he wrestled with the Angel and prevailed. He wept and pleaded for a blessing from him. He met God there at Bethel face to face. God spoke to him—the LORD, the God of heaven's armies—Jehovah is His name.

**Micah 2:7(TLB)**

Is that the right reply for you to make, O House of Jacob? Do you think the Spirit of the LORD likes to talk to you so roughly? No! His threats are for your good, to get you on the path again.

**Luke 4:38-39, 41**

"...Now Simon's mother-in-law was suffering from a high fever, and they asked Jesus to help her. 39 So He bent over her and rebuked the fever, and it left her. She got up at once and began to wait on them...Moreover, demons came out of many people, shouting "You are the Son of God!" But He rebuked them and would not allow them to speak..."

**Luke 22:70-71**

⁷⁰ They all asked, "Are you then the Son of God?" He replied, "You say that I am." ⁷¹ Then they said, "Why do we need any more testimony? We have heard it from His own lips."

### 3. THERE ARE TIMES TO BE SILENT

**Isaiah 53:7**

He was oppressed and He was afflicted, yet He never said a word. He was brought as a lamb to the slaughter; and as a sheep before her shearers is dumb, so He stood silent before the ones condemning Him.

**Mark 14:60-61**

⁶⁰ Then the high priest stood up before them and asked Jesus, "Are you not going to answer? What is this testimony that these men are bringing against you?" ⁶¹ But Jesus remained silent and gave no answer.

**Mark 15:3-5**

³ The chief priests accused him of many things. ⁴ So again Pilate asked him, "Aren't you going to answer? See how many things they are accusing you of."

⁵ But Jesus still made no reply, and Pilate was amazed.

#### 4. THERE IS NO DECEIT IN HIS MOUTH
…His words can be trusted

**Isaiah 53:9**

He was assigned a grave with the wicked, and with the rich in his death, though He had done no violence, nor was any deceit in His mouth.

#### 5. HE SINGS

**Zephaniah 3:17**

Is that a joyous choir I hear? No, it is the LORD Himself exulting over you in happy song.

## B. REFERENCES TO THE MOUTH OF GOD INDICATE THAT THE SWORD OF THE SPIRIT IS THE WORD OF GOD

**Psalm 78:1**

My people, hear my teaching, listen to the words of my mouth. I will open my mouth with a parable, I will utter hidden things, things from of old—things we have heard and known, things our ancestors have told us.

**Ephesians 6:17**

Take the helmet of salvation and the sword of the Spirit which is the word of God.

#### 1. THE POWER OF HIS SPOKEN WORD

**What He speaks comes into existence:**

##### A NEW WORLD

**Genesis 1:3**

And God said, "Let there be light," and there was light.

**Genesis 1:6**

And God said, "Let there be a vault between the waters to separate water from water." And it was so. God called the vault "sky".

**Genesis 1:9**

And God said, "Let there be water under the sky be gathered to one place and let dry ground appear. " And it was so.

**Genesis 1:11**

Then God said, "Let the land produce vegetation, seed-bearing plants and trees on the land that bear fruit with seed in it…And it was so.

**Genesis 1:14**

And God said, "Let there be lights in the vault of the sky to separate the day from the night…and it was so.

**Genesis 1:20**

And God said, "Let the water teem with living creatures, and let birds fly above the earth across the expanse of the sky…so God created.

**Genesis 1:24**

And God said, "Let the land produce living creatures according to their kinds; livestock, creatures that move along the ground and wild animals…And it was so.

**Genesis 1:26**

Then God said, "Let us make mankind in our image, in our likeness, so that they may rule over the fish of the sea and the birds of the air…so God created.

**Psalm 33:6, 9**

By the word of the LORD were the heavens made, their starry host by the breath of His mouth…For He spoke, and it came to be; He commanded, and it stood firm.

### A NEW SITUATION

**Psalm 107:20**

"He sent out His word and healed them…"

**Luke 4:33-36 (TLB)**

Once as He was teaching in the synagogue, a man possessed by a demon began shouting at Jesus, 34 "Go away! We want nothing to do with you, Jesus from Nazareth. You have come to destroy us. I know who you are---the Holy Son of God." 35 Jesus cut him short. "Be silent!" He told the demon. "Come out!" The demon threw the man to the floor as the crowd watched and then left him without hurting him further. 36 Amazed, the people asked, "What is in this man's words that even demons obey him?"

### A NEW COMMAND

**Psalm 147:15**

He sends His commands to the earth; His word runs swiftly." His word is here personified as messengers commissioned to carry out a divine order.

### A NEW NAME

**Isaiah 62:2**

The nations will see your vindication, and all kings your glory; you will be called by a new name that the mouth of the LORD will bestow.

### A NEW BIRTH

**I Peter 1:23**

"For you have been born again, not of perishable seed, but of imperishable, through the living and enduring word of God." The new birth comes about through the direct action of the Holy Spirit but the Word of God also plays an important role. James 1:18 says "He chose to give us birth through the word of truth, that we might be a kind of firstfruits of all he created." The Word of God presents the Gospel to the sinner and calls on him to repent and believe in Christ and "this is the Word that was preached to you." (I Peter 1:25)

### WHAT HE SPEAKS GIVES WISDOM

**Psalm 119:130**

The unfolding of your words gives light; it gives understanding to the simple.

**Proverbs 2:6**

For the LORD grants wisdom! His every word is a treasure of knowledge and understanding. He grants good sense to the godly—His saints (TLB) // For the LORD gives wisdom and from His mouth come knowledge and understanding. (NIV)

### WHAT HE SPEAKS IS RIGHT AND TRUE

**Psalm 33:4**

For the word of the LORD is right and true; He is faithful in all He does.

**Psalm 119:160**

"All your words are true…"

### 2. THE PROPHETIC NATURE OF HIS SPOKEN WORD
### …IT WILL COME TO PASS

God's word is sure; whatever He speaks will come to pass.

**Isaiah 40:8 says**

"The grass withers, the flowers fade, but the Word of our God shall stand forever."

### SPOKEN BY GOD HIMSELF

**Psalm 89:34**

I will not…alter what my lips have uttered.

**Psalm 119:89**

Your word, O LORD, is eternal; it stands firm in the heavens."

**Isaiah 34:16 (TLB)**

Search the Book of the LORD and see all that He will do; not one detail will He miss; not one kite will be there without a mate, for the LORD has said it, and His Spirit will make it all come true.

**Isaiah 40:5 (TLB)**

"…The glory of the LORD will be seen by all mankind together." The LORD has spoken—it shall be.

**Isaiah 48:3-7 (TLB)**

Time and again I told you what was going to happen in the future. My words were scarcely spoken when suddenly I did just what I said. 4 I knew how hard and obstinate you are. Your necks are as unbending as iron; you are as hardheaded as brass. 5 That is why I told you ahead of time what I was going to do, so that you could never say, "My idol did it; my carved image commanded it to happen!" 6 You have heard my predictions and seen them fulfilled, but you refuse to agree it is so. Now I will tell you new things I haven't mentioned before, secrets you haven't heard. 7 Then you can't say, "We knew that all the time!"

**Isaiah 46:10-11 (TLB)**

Who can tell you what is going to happen. All I say will come to pass, for I do whatever I wish. 11 I will call that swift bird of prey from the east—that man Cyrus from far away. And he will come and do my bidding. I have said I would do it and I will.

**Isaiah 55:10-11 (TLB)**

As the rain and snow come down from heaven and stay upon the ground to water the earth, and cause the grain to grow and to produce seed for the farmer and bread for the hungry, 11 so also is my Word. I send it out and it always produces fruit. It shall accomplish all I want it to, and prosper everywhere I send it.

### SPOKEN BY HIS PROPHETS

**Isaiah 51:16**

"I have put my words in your mouth…"

**Hosea 6:5 (TLB)**

I sent my prophets to warn you of your doom; I have slain you with the words of my mouth, threatening you with death. Suddenly, without warning, my judgment will strike you as surely as day follows night.

## C. REFERENCES TO THE MOUTH OF GOD INDICATE THAT OUT OF HIS MOUTH COMES

### 1. FIRE FOR JUDICIAL WRATH

Fire manifested in the storm cloud's lightning bolts; fire often signified God's judicial wrath.

**Deuteronomy 4:24**

For the LORD your God is a consuming fire, a jealous God.

**Deuteronomy 9:3**

"But be assured today that the LORD your God is the one who goes across ahead of you like a devouring fire. He will destroy them; he will subdue them before you…"

**Psalm 18:8 (TLB)**

"…consuming fire came from His mouth, burning coals blazed out of it."

**Psalm 21:9 (TLB)**

At the time of your appearing you will make them like a fiery furnace. In His wrath the LORD will swallow them up and His fire will consume them."

**Psalm 83:14**

As fire consumes the forest or a flame sets the mountains ablaze, so pursue them with your tempest and terrify them with your storm.

**Psalm 97:3**

Fire goes before Him and consumes His foes on every side.

**Daniel 7:10**

A river of fire was flowing coming out from before Him (the Ancient of Days).

**Isaiah 30:27, 30**

"See the Name of the LORD comes from afar, with burning anger and dense clouds of smoke; His lips are full of wrath, and His tongue is a consuming fire…The LORD will cause people to hear His majestic voice…"

**Isaiah 66:16 (TLB)**

For the LORD will punish the world by fire…and the slain of the LORD shall be many!

## A SWORD FOR JUDGMENT

The sword symbolizes divine judgment. This is a powerful rod like a long Thracian sword which comes from the mouth of the Messiah.

(He made my mouth like a sharpened sword.)

**Job 9:33-34**

If only there were someone to mediate between us, someone to bring us together, someone to remove God's rod.

**Job 21:7-9**

Why do the wicked live on, growing old and increasing in power? They see their children established around them, their offspring before their eyes. Their homes are safe and free from fear; the rod of God is not upon them.

**Psalm 89:32**

"I will punish their sin with the rod…"

**Isaiah 10:5-7, 24-25**

"Assyria is the whip of my anger (the rod of my anger in whose hand is the club of my wrath-NIV); his military strength is my weapon upon this godless nation, doomed and damned; he will enslave them and plunder them and trample them like dirt beneath his feet. 7 But the king of Assyria will not know that it is I who sent him. He will merely think he is attacking my people as part of his plan to conquer to the world…24 Therefore the LORD God says, "O my people in Jerusalem, don't be afraid of the Assyrians when they oppress you just as the Egyptians did long ago. It will not last very long; in a little while my anger against you will end, and then it will rise against them to destroy them." Assyria was God's rod of judgment against Israel but the Messiah will rule the nations with an iron scepter (Psalm 2:9; Psalm 45:6; Revelation 19:15)

**Isaiah 11:4**

"He will strike the earth with the rod of His mouth; with the breath of His lips He will slay the wicked…"

**Isaiah 27:1**

"In that day, the LORD will punish with His sword, His fierce, great and powerful sword, Leviathan, the gliding serpent, Leviathan the coiling serpent; He will slay the monster of the sea." The Leviathan monster is a symbol drawn from Canaanite myths of wicked nations such as Egypt.

**Isaiah 30:32**

Every stroke the LORD lays on them with His punishing rod will be to the music of tambourines and harps as He fights them in battle with the blows of His arm.

**Isaiah 66:16 (TLB)**

For the LORD will punish the world by…His sword, and the slain of the LORD shall be many!

Revelation 1:16 (TLB)

"Out of His mouth came a sharp double-edged sword."

**Revelation 2:12**

These are the words of Him who has the sharp, double-edged sword.

**Revelation 2:16**

Repent therefore! Otherwise I will soon come to you and will fight against them with the sword of my mouth.

**Revelation 19:15 & 21**

Out of His mouth comes a sharp sword with which to strike down the nations…The rest of them were killed with the sword that came out of the mouth of the rider on the horse." The rider is Christ returning as Warrior-Messiah-King.

### 3. SPIT THAT BRINGS HEALING

#### THE HEALING OF A DEAF & MUTE MAN

**Mark 7:32-35**

There some people brought to him a man who was deaf and could hardly talk, and they begged him to place His hand on the man. 33 After He took him aside, away from the crowd, Jesus put His fingers into the man's ears. Then He spit and touched the man's tongue. 34 He looked up to heaven and with a deep sight said to him "Ephphatha! (which means, Be opened!") 35 At this, the man's ears were opened, his tongue was loosened and he began to speak plainly.

#### THE HEALING OF A BLIND MAN

**Mark 8:22-25**

They came to Bethsaida, and some people brought a blind man and begged Jesus to touch him. 23 He took the blind man by the hand and led him outside the village. When He had spit on the man's eyes and put His hands on him, Jesus asked, "Do you see anything?" 24 He look up and said, "I see people; they look like trees walking around." 25 Once more Jesus put His hands on the man's eyes. Then his eyes were opened, his sight was restored, and he saw everything clearly.

#### THE HEALING OF A MAN BORN BLIND

**John 9:1-11**

As he went along, he saw a man blind from birth. 2 His disciples asked him, "Rabbi, who sinned, this man or his parents, that he was born blind?"

3 "Neither this man nor his parents sinned," said Jesus, "but this happened so that the works of God might be displayed in his life. 4 As

long as it is day, we must do the works of him who sent me. Night is coming, when no one can work. ⁵ While I am in the world, I am the light of the world."

⁶ Having said this, he spit on the ground, made some mud with the saliva, and put it on the man's eyes. ⁷ "Go," he told him, "wash in the Pool of Siloam" (this word means Sent). So the man went and washed, and came home seeing.

⁸ His neighbors and those who had formerly seen him begging asked, "Isn't this the same man who used to sit and beg?" ⁹ Some claimed that he was.

Others said, "No, he only looks like him. But he himself insisted, "I am the man."

¹⁰ "How then were your eyes opened?" they demanded.

¹¹ He replied, "The man they call Jesus made some mud and put it on my eyes. He told me to go to Siloam and wash. So I went and washed, and then I could see."

## D. REJECTING THE WORD THAT COMES FROM THE MOUTH OF GOD CAUSES...

### BITTER LABOR

**Psalm 107:11-12**

"…for they had rebelled against the words of God and despised the counsel of the Most High. 12 So He subjected them to bitter labor…"

## E. OUR RESPONSE TO THE WORD THAT COMES FROM THE MOUTH OF GOD

### PRAISE GOD FOR HIS WORDS

**Psalm 138:4 (KJV)**

All the kings of the earth shall praise thee, O LORD, when they hear the words of your mouth.

## PILE IT UP/STORE IT

**Job 22:22**

Accept instruction from His mouth and lay up His words in your heart.

## PROTECT/TREASURE HIS WORD

**Job 23:12**

I have treasured the words of His mouth more than my daily bread.

**Psalm 119:72**

The law from your mouth is more precious to me than thousands of pieces of silver and gold.

## HOPE IN HIS WORD

**Psalm 119:81**

My soul faints with longing for your salvation, but I have put my hope in your word.

## OBEY THEM

**Psalm 119:88**

"…I will obey the statues of your mouth."

## LIVE BY IT

**Psalm 119:9**

How can a young man keep his way pure? By living according to your word.

**Matthew 4:4**

Jesus answered, "It is written: 'Man does not live on bread alone, but on every word that comes from the mouth of God.'"

## RECOUNT THEM

**Psalm 119:13**

With my lips I recount all the laws that come from your mouth.

### BELIEVE IN IT

**Psalm 119:66**

Teach me knowledge and good judgment for I believe in your commands.

### DO NOT FORGET THEM

**Psalm 119:93**

I will never forget your precepts for by them you have preserved my life.

### LOVE THEM

**Psalm 119:97**

Oh how I love your law! I meditate on it all day long.

### DO NOT DEPART FROM THEM

**Job 23:12**

I have not departed from the commands of His lips

**Psalm 119:102**

I have not departed from your laws for you yourself have taught me.

### PERSONAL APPLICATION

This is the only part of the anatomy of God that has two applications for the believer:

1. The **rod that comes from the mouth of God** brings judgment on the wicked. However, to the righteous, it brings comfort.
2. The **sword that comes from the mouth of God** symbolizes divine judgment. Our personal application, however, to the Sword of the Spirit which is the Word of God, is to take heed to clothe ourselves with this piece of armor.

## A. THE ROD THAT GIVES COMFORT

**Psalm 23:4**
"…your rod and staff comfort me."

The rod is an instrument of authority used by shepherds for counting, guiding, protecting and rescuing sheep.

1. It is the shepherd's crook under which the sheep passed when they were being counted.
   **Leviticus 27:32**
   The entire tithe of the herd and flock—every tenth animal that passes under the shepherd's rod—will be holy to the LORD.
2. With the rod the shepherd rules and guides the flock to green pastures;
3. The "crook" was used to seize the legs of the sheep or goats when they were disposed to run away, and thus to keep them within the flock and prevent them from wandering off.
4. It was used to drive away the enemies of the flock e.g. dogs that would scatter or worry the sheep.
5. It was also used to lay hold of their horns or legs to pull them out of thickets, bogs, pits, or waters;
6. It was also used to correct the sheep when they were disobedient.
7. The LORD comforts His people with His rod. Thy rod and thy staff, by which you govern and rule your flock, the ensigns of your sovereignty and of your gracious care – they comfort me. I will believe that thou reignest still. The rod of Jesse shall still be over me as the sovereign succour of my soul.

The sight of the rod and staff brings comfort and consolation to the sheep, confirming that the Shepherd, by his presence and his office imparts confidence, proving that he will not leave them alone, but will defend them.

## THE LORD WILL BRING COMFORT TO HIS PEOPLE

**Psalm 71:21**

You will increase my honor and comfort me once more.

**Psalm 86:17**

Give me a sign of your goodness, that my enemies may see it and be put to shame for you, LORD, have helped me and comforted me.

**Isaiah 40:1**

Comfort, comfort my people says your God.

## B. THE SWORD THAT

### 1. GIVES PROTECTION…

**Ephesians 6:17**

Take…the sword of the Spirit which is the Word of God.

The battle that we face daily is a spiritual one and must be fought in God's strength depending on the Word. Bible scholars often note that in the armor of God only the sword of the Spirit is an offensive weapon; all the rest were used for defense. We are reminded that the weapons of our warfare are not carnal but are mighty through God to the pulling down of strongholds. (II Corinthians 10:4)

The metaphor of a sword is also used where reference is made to the words that come from the mouth of the enemy. The most frequent weapon used against the Psalmists is the tongue. The Psalmists experienced that the tongue is as deadly as the sword.

**Psalm 55:21**

His talk is smooth as butter, yet war is in his heart; his words are more soothing than oil, yet they are drawn swords.

**Psalm 57:4**

I am in the midst of lions; I am forced to dwell among men whose teeth are spears and arrows, whose tongues are sharp swords.

**Psalm 64:2-4**

² Hide me from the conspiracy of the wicked, from the plots of evildoers.

³ They sharpen their tongues like swords and aim cruel words like deadly arrows.

⁴ They shoot from ambush at the innocent; they shoot suddenly, without fear.

**Proverbs 5:3-4**

For the lips of an adulteress drip honey, and her speech is smoother than oil; but in the end she is bitter as gall, sharp as a double-edged sword.

**Job 20:12**

"Though evil is sweet in his mouth and he hides it under his tongue,

**Psalm 5:9**

"Not a word from their mouth can be trusted; their heart is filled with malice. Their throat is an open grave; with their tongue they tell lies."

**Psalm 10:7**

"His mouth is full of lies and threats; trouble and evil are under his tongue."

The three most common weapons of the tongue were curses, lies and threats. The ancient Near Eastern peoples thought that by pronouncing curses on someone they could bring down the power of the gods on that person. They had a large conventional stock of such curses. Slander and false testimony were used for malicious purposes. (NIV Text Note)

As believers we need to use the sword of the Spirit, which is available to us for our use and also for our protection. Unlike the enemy who uses the sword to steal, kill and destroy we can use the sword of the Spirit, the word of God to:

## SPEAK WORDS OF LIFE TO OTHERS

**John 6:68**

Simon Peter answered him, "LORD, to whom shall we go? You have the words of eternal life."

**Ephesians 4:29**

Do not let any unwholesome talk come out of your mouths, but only what is helpful for building others up according to their needs, that it may benefit those who listen.

## KEEP OUR LIPS PURE

**Proverbs 4:24**

Keep your mouth free from perversity, keep corrupt talk far from your lips.

## 2. PENETRATES

**Hebrews 4:12-13**

[12] For the word of God is living and active. Sharper than any double-edged sword, it penetrates even to dividing soul and spirit, joints and marrow; it judges the thoughts and attitudes of the heart. [13] Nothing in all creation is hidden from God's sight. Everything is uncovered and laid bare before the eyes of him to whom we must give account.

This dynamic word of God, active in accomplishing God's purposes, appears in both the Old Testament and the New Testament. When we speak the Word of God we are using the sword of the Spirit and engaging the penetrative action of bringing God into situations.

The word of God/sword of the Spirit that we are to be using as a part of our armor:

## HEALS

**Psalm 107:20**

He sent out his word and healed them; he rescued them from the grave.

### IS POWERFUL

**Psalm 147:18**

He sends his word and melts them; he stirs up his breezes, and the waters flow.

### IS IMPERISHABLE, LIVING AND ENDURING

**Psalm 119:89**

Your word O LORD is eternal; it stands firm in the heavens.

**Psalm 119:160**

"…all your righteous laws are eternal."

**I Peter 1:23**

For you have been born again, not of perishable seed, but of imperishable, through the living and enduring word of God.

### GIVES US WISDOM, MORE INSIGHT AND UNDERSTANDING

**Psalm 119:98-100**

[98] Your commands are always with me and make me wiser than my enemies, for they are ever with me. [99] I have more insight than all my teachers, for I meditate on your statutes. [100] I have more understanding than the elders, for I obey your precepts.

**Psalm 119:104**

I gain understanding from your precepts; therefore I hate every wrong path.

The author of Hebrews describes the sword of the Spirit as a living power that judges as with an all-seeing eye, penetrating a person's innermost being, soul and spirit, joints and marrow, the totality and depth of one's being. The author further associates the activity of the sword of the Spirit/the word of God with the activity of God as one and the same.

Jehovah Makkeh is the LORD who moulds us with His word. The LORD corrects and trains us with His word and this is how Jehovah Makkeh works in our lives.

CHAPTER 17

# THE WAIST OF GOD
Jehovah Tsidkenu, The Lord My Righteousness

*"To the faithful you show yourself faithful...*
*He brought me out into aspacious place;..."*
*Psalm 18:25 & 19*

The waist is the constricted part of the trunk between the ribs and hips.

The LORD started my study of this aspect of God's anatomy with Ephesians 6:14 which says, "Stand firm then with the belt of truth buckled around your waist." This was the springboard to the waist of God which highlights His character of faithfulness.

### A. REFERENCES TO THE WAIST OF GOD

**Ezekiel 1:26-28**

"For high in the sky above them was what looked like a throne made of beautiful blue sapphire stones, and upon it sat someone who appeared to be a Man. 27,28 From His waist up, he seemed to be all glowing bronze, dazzling like fire; and from his waist down he seemed to be entirely flame, and there was a glowing halo like a rainbow all around him. And when I saw it, I fell face downward on the ground…" (TLB)

The symbolic clothing of the Messiah is found in Isaiah 11:5 "Righteousness will be His belt and faithfulness the sash around His waist." Character, not brute force, wins the battle just as in the case of the Messiah.

## 1. FAITHFULNESS—
## THE SASH AROUND HIS WAIST

### GOD'S FAITHFULNESS IS BEYOND MEASURE

**Exodus 34:6**

"The LORD, the LORD the compassionate and gracious God, slow to anger, abounding in love and faithfulness." This is the Lord's proclamation of who He is.

**Psalm 18:25**

To the faithful you show yourself faithful.

**Psalm 57:10**

"…your faithfulness is higher than the skies." (TLB)

**Psalm 61:7**

May he (the king) be enthroned in God's presence forever; appoint your love and faithfulness to protect him. " Faithfulness is here personified as God's messenger.

**Psalm 89:1, 8**

I will sing of the LORD's great love forever; with my mouth I will make your faithfulness known through all generations. Who is like you, LORD God Almighty? You are mighty, LORD, and your faithfulness surrounds you.

**Psalm 91:4**

"…His faithfulness will be your shield and rampart."

**Psalm 108:4**

For great is your love, higher than the heavens; your faithfulness reaches to the skies.

**Psalm 115:1**

Not to us, LORD, not to us but to your name be the glory, because of your love and faithfulness.

**Lamentations 3:22-23**

Because of the LORD's great love we are not consumed, for his compassions never fail. 23 They are new every morning; great is your faithfulness.

**Romans 3:3-4**

What if some were unfaithful? Will their unfaithfulness nullify God's faithfulness? Not at all! Let God be true and every human beinga liar.

## 2. RIGHTEOUSNESS— THE BELT AROUND HIS WAIST

**Isaiah 11:5**

Righteousness will be His belt…"

    a. As the loins represent the reproductive area in a body God expects His people to reproduce and share His character.

**Psalm 7:17**

I will give thanks to the LORD because of His righteousness.

**Psalm 71:19**

"Your righteousness God reaches to the heavens, O God…"

**Psalm 85:13**

Righteousness goes before him and prepares the way for His steps.

The Psalmist personifies righteousness as a herald or guide leading the way and marking the course for God's engagement in His people's behalf. Righteousness is God's perfect faithfulness to all His covenant commitments.

b. When a man prepared for vigorous action He tied up his loose, flowing garments with a belt. This readiness or preparation for ease of movement is found in:

**Exodus 12:11**

"This is how you are to eat it; with your cloak tucked into your belt…"

**I Kings 18:46**

The power of the LORD came upon Elijah and tucking his cloak into his belt he ran ahead of Ahab all the way to Jezreel.

**Isaiah 5:27**

Not one of them grows tired or stumbles, not one slumbers or sleeps; not a belt is loosened at the waist.

### 3. FAITHFULNESS & RIGHTEOUSNESS

In Psalm 89:14 we see that righteousness and justice are the foundation stones of God's throne; love and faithfulness are personified as angelic attendants that herald His royal movements.

Just as a belt is normally used in conjunction with the waist, so too the elements of righteousness and faithfulness are used together in the following references:

**1 Samuel 26:23**

The LORD rewards every man for his righteousness and faithfulness. The LORD delivered you into my hands today, but I would not lay a hand on the LORD's anointed.

**Psalm 4:1**

"Answer me when I call to you, my righteous God. Give me relief from my distress." Give me relief literally means make a spacious place for me.

Often the righteousness of God in the Psalms refers to the faithfulness with which He acts. This faithfulness is in full accordance with His commitments (both expressed and implied) to His people and with His status as the divine King to whom the powerless may look for protection, the oppressed for redress and the needy for help. This God's righteous deeds express His righteous character. (NIV text note)

**Psalm 36:5-6**

"…your faithfulness (reaches) to the skies. Your righteousness is like the highest mountains."

**Psalm 40:10**

I do not hide your righteousness in my heart; I speak of your faithfulness and your saving help. I do not conceal your love and your faithfulness from the great assembly.

**Psalm 85:10-13**

Love and faithfulness meet together; righteousness and peace kiss each other. 11 Faithfulness springs forth from the earth, and righteousness looks down from heaven. 12 The LORD will indeed give what is good, and our land will yield its harvest. 13 Righteousness goes before him and prepares the way for His steps.

**Psalm 119:75**

I know, LORD, that your laws are righteous, and that in faithfulness you have afflicted me.

**Psalm 119:90**

"Your faithfulness continues through all generations."

**Psalm 143:1**

"LORD, hear my prayer, listen to my cry for mercy; in your faithfulness and righteousness come to my relief." The Psalmist's prayer for deliverance from enemies and for divine leading. He appeals to God's righteousness and His faithfulness.

**Isaiah 16:5**

In love a throne will be established; in faithfulness a man will sit on it— one from the house of David— one who in judging seeks justice and speeds the cause of righteousness.

**Revelation 19:11**

I saw heaven standing open and there before me was a white horse, whose rider is called Faithful and True. With justice he judges and wages war.

## 4. JUSTICE & RIGHTEOUSNESS

**Ephesians 6:14**

"Stand firm then with the belt of truth buckled around your waist; with the breastplate of righteousness in place." As we prepare for battle, for the war that wages against our souls we must be ready at all times. We must be in a state of readiness and one of the elements that must be in place for vigorous action is righteousness. Here again, the warrior's character is his defense. God himself is symbolically described as putting on a breastplate of righteousness when he goes forth to bring about justice.

**Psalm 9:8**

He rules the world in righteousness; and judges the peoples with equity.

**Psalm 33:4-5**

"For the word of the LORD is right and true; He is faithful in all He does. The LORD loves righteousness and justice…"

**Psalm 89:14 (TLB)**

Your throne is founded on two strong pillars the one is justice and the other righteousness.

**Psalm 96:13 (TLB)**

They will sing before the LORD, for he comes, he comes to judge the earth. He will judge the world in righteousness and the peoples in his truth.

**Psalm 98:9**

Let them sing before the LORD, for he comes to judge the earth. He will judge the world in righteousness and the peoples with equity.

**Isaiah 5:16**

But the LORD Almighty will be exalted by His justice and the holy God will be proved holy by His righteous acts.

**Isaiah 9:7**

"…He will reign on David's throne and over his kingdom establishing and upholding it with justice and righteousness from that time on and forever…"

**Isaiah 11:4**

But with righteousness He will judge the needy.

**Isaiah 59:7-17**

"Their feet rush into sin; they are swift to shed innocent blood. Their thoughts are evil thoughts; ruin and destruction mark their ways. 8 The way of peace they do not know; there is no justice in their paths…9 so justice is far from us and righteousness does not reach us…we look for justice, but find none…we acknowledge our iniquities: rebellion and treachery against the LORD, turning our backs on our God…so justice is driven back, and righteousness stands at a distance…the LORD looked and was displeased that there was no justice. He saw that there was no one He was appalled that there was no one to intervene…His own righteousness sustained Him. He put on righteousness as His breastplate…"

**Jeremiah 9:24**

But let the one who boasts boast about this that they have the understanding to know me, that I am the LORD who exercises kindness, justice and righteousness on earth for in these I delight, declares the LORD.

**Jeremiah 23:5-6**

The days are coming, declares the LORD when I will raise up to David a righteous Branch, a King who will reign wisely and do what is just and right in the land…this is the name by which he will be called: The LORD Our Righteous Saviour.

**Amos 5:7**

O evil men you make justice a bitter pill for the poor and oppressed. "Righteousness" and "fair play" are meaningless fictions to you!

## PERSONAL APPLICATION

With reference to the provision of armor for our waist, our **personal application** comes from the encouragement in Ephesians 6:14: "Stand firm then with the belt of truth buckled around your waist…"

This is the first piece of the armor given to us for the battle that is waging around us. This first piece deals with truth which is foundational to the other pieces of the armor.

The girdle that Paul was speaking of here was similar to those worn by Roman soldiers. Not simply a strip of cloth around his waist or even a narrow belt, but rather, it was generally a leather apron that helped to protect the lower part of his body. The girdle doubled in use also as a sheath for the soldier's sword.

What does the girdle of truth illustrate in the life of the believer?

In the Bible, the girdle had the function of pulling things together. In the culture of that day, men and women, including soldiers, wore flowing robes. When they wanted to move rapidly, they would gather up their robes and tuck the ends into their girdles so that their legs would be unencumbered as highlighted earlier. Likewise, the Christian must prepare his mind and heart for battle, eliminating any thoughts, habits or speech that would hinder his walk with the LORD. If we don't have on this girdle we will resort to lying, dishonesty, compromise and all manner of falsehood. Truth frees us from encumbrances and things that are designed to trip us up. God is truth; His Word is truth, and truth pulls everything together.

God wants to use us and we have to ensure that we are wearing the belt of truth.

**Psalm 15:1-5**

[1] Lord, who may dwell in your sacred tent? Who may live on your holy mountain? [2] The one whose walk is blameless and who does what is righteous, who speaks the truth from his heart [3] and whose tongue utters no slander, who does no wrong to a neighbor and casts no slur on others, [4] who despises a vile person but honors those who fear the Lord, who keeps an oath even when it hurts… whoever does these things will never be shaken.

**Proverbs 10:11**

The mouth of the righteous is a fountain of life, a source of life-giving wisdom. There is living truth in what a good man says. (TLB)

**Proverbs 22:11**

He who values truth is the king's friend (TLB)

The girdle of truth is represented by a life and mind that is pulled together by the truth of God's Word and one that is ready to serve for the glory of God. A life also that is ready to live righteously, spreading the gospel of peace, using faith to extinguish the enemy's flaming arrows, and praying in the Spirit. It speaks of integrity: truth in the inner being. Surely, God desires truth in our inner parts. It is therefore not enough just to carry the sword of the Spirit—the word of God — in the sheath of the girdle. The truth of God's word must be drawn; it must be used, it must penetrate our lives so that our actions, motives and speech are governed by integrity and truth.

If we are not wearing our belt of truth then we do not have our sword of the Spirit, which is the word of God. Truth and the word of God go hand in hand. Remember Psalm 33:4 says "For the word of the LORD is right and true…" If we want the blessing of the Word of God we need to be in possession of the truth and speak it always.

If there is no belt of truth around our waist, then there is no sword of the Spirit, the word of God, because His word is truth.

CHAPTER 18

# THE HAIR OF GOD
Jehovah M'kaddesh, The Lord My Sanctifier

*"...to the pure you show yourself pure..."*
*Psalm 18:26*

**APPEARANCE OF THE HAIR OF GOD**

**Daniel 7:9**

As I looked, thrones were set in place, and the Ancient of Days took his seat. His clothing was as white as snow; the hair of his head was white like wool. His throne was flaming with fire, and its wheels were all ablaze.

**Revelation 1:14**

The hair on His head was white like wool, as white as snow.

What is the parallel characteristic of wool and snow that would make them comparable to the preferred state of our spiritual life? The author of Revelation writes that "...his head and his hairs were white like wool, as white as snow". This suggests something that is exceedingly or perfectly white. The first suggestion to the mind of the apostle John being that of wool, and then the thought occurring of its extreme whiteness resembling snow — the purest white of which the mind conceives. The comparison with wool and snow to denote anything especially white is not uncommon. The whiteness of wool is used for comparison with snow also:

**Psalm 147:16**

"He spreads the snow like wool and scatters the frost like ashes."

## A. WHAT ARE PURE THINGS AS HIGHLIGHTED IN SCRIPTURE?

### THE FEAR OF THE LORD

**Psalm 19:9**

The fear of the LORD is pure enduring forever.

### THE LORD'S EYES

**Habakkuk 1:13**

Your eyes are too pure to look on evil; you cannot tolerate wrong doing.

### JESUS OUR HIGH PRIEST

**Hebrews 7:26**

Such a high priest meets our need—one who is holy, blameless, pure, set apart from sinners, exalted above the heavens.

### GOD'S WISDOM

**James 3:17**

But the wisdom that comes from heaven is first of all pure; then peace loving, considerate, submissive, full of mercy and good fruit, impartial and sincere.

As children of God we are called to purity in the 7 areas outlined below. As we look at each area let us prayerfully examine ourselves and allow our Supervisor, the Holy Spirit, to turn on his search light to ensure that we are not found wanting in any of these areas:

## 1. PURITY OF LIFE

The term "white as snow" is used in reference to cleansing and the purity of our lives as seen in the lines of the hymn "Lord Jesus I long to be perfectly whole…now wash me and I shall be whiter than snow."

**Isaiah 52:11**

"Depart, depart, go out from there! Touch no unclean thing! Come out from it and be pure…"

We must make a clean break from sin but we cannot do it on our own. It must be done with the help of our LORD and Saviour Jesus Christ.

**Psalm 51:7**

Cleanse me with hyssop and I will be clean; wash me and I will be whiter than snow.

This imagery pictured the renovation of the psalmist's inner being in response to his sinful condition. Like a filthy garment, he needs washing but if God washing him, he will be so pure that there is no figurative word that can describe him.

**Isaiah 1:18**

"Come now let us settle the matter," says the LORD. "Though your sins are like scarlet, they shall be as white as snow; though they are red as crimson, they shall be like wool."

This is a very powerful figurative description of the result of forgiveness. This offer of forgiveness is conditioned on the reformation of life.

**Acts 15:9**

"He did not discriminate between us and them, for he purified their hearts by faith."

The Spirit not only gives witness of divine acceptance, but also cleanses the inner life of believers.

**I John 1:7,9**

But if we walk in the light as He is in the light, we have fellowship with one another, and the blood of Jesus, His Son, purifies us from all sin. If we confess our sins, He is faithful and just and will forgive us our sins and purify us from all unrighteousness.

When we think of wool we think of sheep (holy nation, royal priesthood, a people belonging to God) and lambs (Jesus is our sacrificial lamb; the lamb of God slain before the foundation of the world)

**Revelation 5:6-13**

Then I saw a Lamb, looking as if it had been slain, standing at the center of the throne encircled by the four living creatures and the elders….fell down before the Lamb…Worthy is the Lamb who was slain to receive power and wealth and wisdom and strength…to him who sits on the throne and to the Lamb be praise and honor and glory and power, forever and ever!

## 2. PURITY OF HEART

The term 'heart' refers to the center of one's being, including the mind, will and emotions. Those who are pure in heart love and serve God with undivided loyalties as David asked God for:

**Psalm 86:11**

Teach me your way O LORD…give me an undivided heart that I may fear your name.

**Psalm 24:3-4**

"Who may ascend the mountain of the LORD? Who may stand in His holy place? 4 The one who has clean hands and a pure heart, who does not trust in an idol or swear by a false god."

God requires of His people guiltless actions and right attitudes and motives.

**Psalm 51:10-12**

"Create in me a pure heart, O God and renew a steadfast spirit within me. Do not cast me from your presence or take your Holy Spirit from me. 12 Restore to me the joy of your salvation and grant me a willing spirit, to sustain me."

In this Psalm we find a prayer for purity, for a pure heart.

**Psalm 73:13**

"…I kept my heart pure…"

**II Corinthians 7:1**

"Since we have these promises, dear friends, let us purify ourselves from everything that contaminates body and spirit, perfecting holiness out of reverence for God."

This is the goal of every Christian, who, in this life, is growing in God's grace to the attainment of perfect love.

**James 4:8**

Come near to God and He will come near to you. Wash your hands, you sinners and purify your hearts, you double-minded.

**To Those Who Are Pure In Heart:**

### GOD WILL BE GOOD TO THEM

**Psalm 73:1**

Surely God is good to Israel, to those who are pure in heart.

### WILL HAVE THE KING FOR A FRIEND

**Proverbs 22:11**

One who loves a pure heart and who speaks with grace will have the king for a friend.

### WILL SEE GOD

**Matthew 5:8**

Blessed are the pure in heart for they will see God.

### WILL BE FILLED WITH LOVE

**I Timothy 1:5 (TLB)**

What I am eager for is that all the Christians there will be filled with love that comes from pure hearts and that their minds will be clean and their faith strong.

## THEIR LIVES WILL HELP THE SPREAD OF THE GOSPEL

**Titus 2:3-5**

Teach the older women to be reverent in the way they live…then they can urge the younger women…to be self-controlled and pure…so that no one will malign the word of God.

### 3. PURITY OF ACTION

**Proverbs 20:11 (TLB)**

The character of even a child can be known by the way he acts - whether what he does is pure and upright?

**II Corinthians 6:4,6-7**

Rather as servants of God we commend ourselves in every way:… in purity, understanding, patience and kindness; in the Holy Spirit and in sincere love; in truthful speech and in the power of God;…"

**I Timothy 4:12**

Don't let anyone look down on you because you are young, but set an example for the believers in speech, in conduct, in love, in faith, and in purity.

**I Timothy 5:1-2**

Treat …younger women as sisters, with absolute purity.

**I Timothy 5:22 (TLB)**

Never be in a hurry about choosing a pastor; you may overlook his sins and it will look as if you approve of them. Be sure that you yourself stay away from all sin.

(Or as the NIV says) Keep yourself pure.

NIV text note: Paul is speaking of the ordination of an elder which should not be performed until the candidate has had time to prove himself. Do not ordain a person unworthy of the office of elder. Purity requires the refusal to become involved in the ordination of an unworthy man.

**Titus 2:13-14**

"…our Saviour Jesus Christ…died under God's judgment against our sins so that He could rescue us from constant falling into sin and make us His very own people, with cleansed hearts and real enthusiasm for doing kind things for others.

**James 1:27 (TLB)**

The Christian who is pure and without fault from God the Father's point of view, is the one who takes care of orphans and widows, and who remains true to the LORD not soiled and dirtied by his contacts with the world.

**I Peter 1:22**

Now that you have purified yourselves by obeying the truth so that you have sincere love for each other, love one another deeply from the heart.

### 4. PURITY OF THOUGHT

**Proverbs 15:26**

The LORD detests the thoughts of the wicked, but gracious words are pure in His sight.

**Philippians 4:8**

Finally brothers and sisters, whatever is true, whatever is noble, whatever is right, whatever is pure, whatever is lovely, whatever is admirable—if anything is excellent or praiseworthy—think about s uch things.

When we studied the mind of God, we saw that Paul understood the influence of one's thought on one's life. What a person allows to occupy his mind will sooner or later determine his speech and his action.

**Matthew 12:34**

"Out of the overflow of the heart the mouth speaks. The good man brings good things out of the good stored up in him, and the evil man brings evil things out of the evil stored up in him…for by your words you will be acquitted and by your words you will be condemned."

**Titus 1:15**

"To the pure all things are pure, but to those who are corrupted and do not believe, nothing is pure. In fact, both their minds and consciences are corrupted."

The Living Bible says "a person who is pure of heart sees goodness and purity in everything; but a person whose own heart is evil and untrusting finds evil in everything, for his dirty mind and rebellious heart color all he sees and hears."

To Christians who have been purified by the atoning death of Christ "everything God created is good, and nothing is to be rejected if it is received with thanksgiving."

### 5. PURITY OF ADORNMENT

References to the garments worn by angels and the redeemed show that they are dressed in white.

**Psalm 132:9**

We will clothe the priests in white, the symbol of all purity.

**Matthew 28:2-3**

"…an angel of the LORD came down from heaven…and his clothes were white as snow.

**Mark 16:5**

"As they entered the tomb, they saw a young man dressed in a white robe…"

**Revelation 3:4**

Yet you have a few people in Sardis who have not soiled their clothes. They will walk with me, dressed white, for they are worthy.

**Revelation 4:4**

Surrounding the throne were twenty-four other thrones, and seated on them were twenty-four elders. They were dressed in white and had crowns of gold on their heads.

**Revelation 6:11**

"Then each of them was given a white robe and they were told to wait a little longer…" This white robe was a symbol of blessedness and purity.

**Revelation 7:9**

After this I looked and there before me was a great multitude that no one could count, from every nation, tribe, people and language, standing before the throne and in front of the Lamb. They were wearing white robes and were holding palm branches in their hands.

**Revelation 7:13**

Then one of the elders asked me, "These in white robes—who are they, and where did they come from? I answered, "Sir, you know." And he said, "These are they who have come out of the great tribulation; they have washed their robes and made them white in the blood of the Lamb…."

**Revelation 19:14**

The armies of heaven were following him, riding on white horses and dressed in fine linen, white and clean. (Rev.19:8 Fine linen, bright and clean, was given her to wear. "Fine linen stands for the righteous acts of the saints.)

### 6. PURITY OF MARITAL RELATIONSHIPS

**Hebrews 13:4**

Marriage should be honored by all, and the marriage bed kept pure, for God will judge the adulterer and all the sexually immoral.

**Malachi 2:15**

Has not the LORD made them one? In flesh and spirit they are His. And why one? Because He was seeking godly offspring. So guard yourself in your spirit and do not break faith with the wife of your youth.

**I Peter 3:1-2**

Wives, in the same way, submit yourselves to your own husband, so that if any of them do not believe the word, they may be won over without words by the behavior of their wives, when they see the purity and reverence of your lives.

### 7. PURITY OF ENDING

**Titus 2:13-14**

While we wait for the blessed hope - the appearing of the glory of our great God and Savior, Jesus Christ, who gave himself for us to redeem us from all wickedness and to purify for himself a people that are his very own, eager to do what is good.

The colors of the horsemen in Revelation correspond to the character of the rider and white symbolizes conquest. When there is a battle and you want to call a truce, you show your intention to surrender to the other party by waving a white flag.

**Revelation 6:2**

I looked, and there before me was a white horse! Its rider held a bow, and he was given a crown, and he rode out as a conqueror bent on conquest.

## C. CHALLENGES TO PURITY AND SOLUTIONS TO THOSE CHALLENGES

### CHALLENGE #1

**Job asked in 14:4**

"How can God demand purity in one born impure?"

**Answer:**

Christ provided purification for sins:

**Hebrews 1:3**

The Son is the radiance of God's glory and the exact representation of His being, sustaining all things by His powerful word. After He had provided purification for sins, He sat down at the right hand of the Majesty in heaven.

**Titus 2:13-14**

"…our Saviour Jesus Christ…died under God's judgment against our sins so that He could rescue us from constant falling into sin and make us His very own people, with cleansed hearts…"

**I John 3:2-3**

"When He comes we will be like Him, as a result of seeing Him as He really is. And everyone who really believes this will try to stay pure because Christ is pure."

The standard of holiness for the believer is Christlikeness. Holy living is not only the responsibility, but also a possibility for every follower of Christ. Christ died, was resurrected, sent the Holy Spirit and intercedes for the believer all to that end. Holy living enables the possibility of not sinning, the most gracious liberty that humanity can experience in this life.

**I Peter 1:15-16**

"Be holy, because I am holy" is the emancipation proclamation of a gracious God  *("Spreading Holiness in the World", Darius Salter, NIV Text)*

Jehovah M'Kaddesh is our sanctifier and desires that we should be like Him.

### CHALLENGE #2

**Psalm 119:9**

How can a young person stay on the path of purity?

With all the encumbrance of this world how can young people keep free from all moral taint?

**Answer:**

By living according to the Word of God

**Psalm 119:9b**

Spend time in the Word of God.

By enjoying the company of those who have pure hearts

**II Timothy 2:22**

Run from anything that gives you the evil thoughts that young men often have, but stay close to anything that make you want to do right. Have faith and love, and enjoy the companionship of those who love the LORD and have pure hearts.

## PERSONAL APPLICATION

**Proverbs 16:31**

White hair is a crown of glory and is seen most among the godly (TLB). The NIV says "… it is attained by a righteous life."

**Proverbs 20:29**

The glory of young men is their strength, gray hair (experience) the splendor of the old.

White hair is something that is shunned by many individuals and it is an embarrassment to some. It is fought aggressively and effectively fought against with hair dyes, by being mercilessly uprooted and other means. But in the Scripture white or hoary hair speaks of wisdom and commands respect and reverence.

Whenever we see white hair let it help us to recall the purity that God desires in our life, our heart, in our actions, in our thoughts, in our adornment, in our marital relationships and in finishing well.

CHAPTER 19

# THE HEAD OF GOD
Elohim, the Sovereign, Mighty Creator

*"God is alive...Praise Him...
From His temple He heard my voice..."*
*Psalm 18:6b*

**Revelation 1:14**
His head and hair were white like wool, as white as snow.
**Revelation 19:12**
His eyes are like blazing fire and on his head are many crowns.

## A. SIGNIFICANCE OF AUTHORITY

The Oxford Dictionary defines authority as:

The power or right to give orders, make decisions, and enforce obedience: he had absolute **authority over** his subordinates rebellion against those **in authority**

The right to act in a specified way, delegated from one person or organization to another: military forces have the legal authority to arrest drug traffickers

A person or organization having political or administrative power and control: health authorities issued a worldwide alert.

The power to influence others, especially because of one's commanding manner or one's recognized knowledge about something.

## B. SYMBOLS OF AUTHORITY

### 1. CROWN

**Revelation 4:10**

The twenty-four Elders fall down before Him who sits on the throne and worship him, the Eternal Living One, and cast their crowns before the throne.

**Revelation 14:14**

"…seated on the cloud was one "like a son of man" with a crown of gold on his head…" This crown was a victory wreath of gold.

### 2. THRONE

In the Most Holy place of the temple, where God takes the reins of world into His hands; the LORD is often represented as sitting on a throne between the cherubim on the ark of the covenant in the temple.

**Psalm 9:4,7**

For you have upheld my right and my cause; sitting enthroned as the righteous judge…the LORD reigns forever; He has established His throne for judgment.

**Psalm 11:4**

The LORD is in His holy temple, the LORD is on His heavenly throne.

**Psalm 47:8**

God is seated on His holy throne.

**Psalm 89:14**

Your throne is founded on two strong pillars—the one is Justice and the other Righteousness. Mercy and Truth walk before you as your attendants.

**Psalm 113:4-5**

The LORD is exalted over all the nations, His glory above the heavens "who is like the Lord our God the One who sits enthroned on high."

**Revelation 4:2-5**

"I was, in spirit, there in heaven and saw…a throne and someone sitting on it! Great burst of light flashed forth from Him as from a glittering diamond or from a shining ruby, and a rainbow glowing like an emerald encircled His throne. Lightning and thunder issued from the throne…directly in front of His throne were seven lighted lamps representing the seven-fold Spirit of God.

**Revelation 7:15**

Therefore, they are before the throne of God and serve Him day and night in His temple and He who sits on the throne will shelter them with His presence.

**Revelation 19:4**

The twenty-four elders and the four living creatures fell down and worshipped God, who was seated on the throne.

**Revelation 21:5-6**

He who was seated on the throne said, "I am making everything new!" He said to me: "It is done. I am the Alpha and the Omega…"

### 3. APPAREL

**Psalm 93:1**

The LORD reigns He is robed in majesty; the LORD is robed in majesty.

### 4. DIVINE KNOWLEDGE/TEACHING

**Matthew 7:28**

"When Jesus had finished saying these things, the crowds were amazed at his teaching because he taught as one who had authority, and not as their teachers of the law."

The teachers of the law quoted other rabbis to support their own teaching but Jesus spoke with authority. The Jewish scholars of the day were professionally trained in the development, teaching and application of Old Testament law. Their authority was strictly human and traditional.

**Mark 1:22**

The people were amazed at His teaching, because He taught them as one who had authority not as the teachers of the law.

**Luke 4:32**

They were amazed at His teaching because His message had authority.

### 5. ABILITY TO LAY DOWN HIS LIFE

**John 10:17-18**

The reason my Father loves me is that I lay down my life only to take it up again. No one takes it from me, but I lay it down of my own accord. I have authority to lay it down and authority to take it up again. This command I received from my Father.

### 6. ABILITY TO FORGIVE SIN

**Matthew 9:6/Mark 2:10/Luke 5:24**

But so that you may know that the Son of Man has authority on earth to forgive sins…" Then he said to the paralytic, "Get up, take your mat and go home."

## C. SPECIFICS ON AUTHORITY

### 1. YOU MUST SUBMIT TO AUTHORITY

**Romans 13:1,5**

Everyone must submit himself to the governing authorities for there is no authority except that which God has established. Therefore, it is necessary to submit to the authorities, not only because of possible punishment but also because of conscience.

**Hebrews 13:17**

Obey your leaders and submit to their authority.

### 2. GOD HAS ESTABLISHED ALL AUTHORITY

**Romans 13:1 (TLB)**

Everyone must submit himself to the governing authorities for there is no authority except that which God has established. The authorities that exist have been established by God.

### 3. WHEN ONE REBELS AGAINST ESTABLISHED AUTHORITY ONE IS REBELLING AGAINST GOD.

**Romans 13:1-4**

Everyone must submit himself to the governing authorities for there is no authority except that which God has established. The authorities that exist have been established by God. Consequently, he who rebels against the authority is rebelling against what God has institution and those who do so will bring judgment on themselves. For rulers hold no terror for those who do right, but for those who do wrong...He is God's servant, an agent of wrath to bring punishment on the wrongdoer.

When you challenge the authority of leaders that God has put in place, God intervenes because you challenge His authority.

**I Samuel 15:23**

Rebellion is like the sin of divination and arrogance like the evil of idolatry.

Miriam & Aaron oppose Moses and led a rebellion against him. The attack was on the prophetic gift of Moses and his special relationship with the Lord.

**Numbers 12:1-15 (v.2)**

"Has the Lord spoken only through Moses...hasn't He also spoken through us?"

**God's response (v.9)**
"The anger of the LORD burned against them and He left them."
**God's action (v.10,15)**
When the cloud lifted from above the Tent, there stood Miriam—leprous like snow...so Miriam was confined outside the camp for seven days and the people did not move on till she was brought back.
**Numbers 16**
Korah, Dathan and Abiram  Korah, a first cousin, and his allies attack the leadership of Moses and Aaron. Korah was descended from Levi through Kohath.  As a Kohathite he had high duties in the service of the LORD at the tabernacle but he desired more.  His passion was to assume the role of priest and he used deception to advance his claim. Their charge was that Moses had "gone too far" (v.3) in taking the role of spiritual leadership of the people "the whole community is holy". To this abusive charge Moses retorts, "You Levites have gone too far!" (v.7)
**God's response  (v.23) Then the LORD said to Moses 24**
"Say to the assembly, 'Move away from the tents of Korah, Dathan and Abiram.'"
**God's action (v.31-33, 49)**
"...the ground under them split apart and the earth opened its mouth and swallowed them with their households and all Korah's men and all their possessions. They went down alive into the grave with everything they owned; the earth closed over them, and they perished and were gone from the community...but 14,700 people died from the plague in addition to those who had died because of Korah.

## 4. YOU HAVE AN OBLIGATION TO PAY TAXES

**Romans 13:6**
This is also why you pay taxes, for the authorities are God's servants, who give their full time to governing.  Give to everyone what you owe him: if you owe taxes, pay taxes; if revenue, then revenue; if respect, then respect; if honor, then honor.

### 5. A HAT IS A SYMBOL OF AUTHORITY

**I Corinthians 11:7-10**

God's glory is man made in His image, and man's glory is the woman. 8 The first man didn't come from woman but the first woman came out of man. 9 And Adam, the first man, was not made for Eve's benefit but Eve was made for Adam. 10 So a woman should wear a covering on her head as a sign that she is under man's authority, a fact for all the angels to notice and rejoice in…a woman should wear a covering when prophesying or praying publicly in the church.

### 6. BE OBEDIENT TO ESTABLISHED AUTHORITY

**Ephesians 6:5-6**

Slaves, obey your earthly masters with respect and fear, and with sincerity of heart, just as you would obey Christ. Obey them not only to win their favor when their eye is on you, but like slaves of Christ, doing the will of God from your hearts.

**Titus 3:1**

"Remind the people to be subject to rulers and authorities, to be obedient, to be ready to do whatever is good…"

### 7. THERE IS ESTABLISHED AUTHORITY IN THE HEAVENLY REALMS.

**Ephesians 6:12**

For our struggle is not against flesh and blood, but against the rulers, against the authorities…in the heavenly realms.

### 8. CHRIST IS SUPREME OVER ALL AUTHORITY

**Matthew 28:18**

"Then Jesus said to them, "All authority in heaven and on earth has been given to me. Therefore go and make disciples…"

**Colossians 1:15-16**

Christ…is the firstborn over all creation. For in him all things were created: things in heaven and on earth, visible and invisible, whether thrones or powers of rulers or authorities; all things have been created through him and for Him. He is the head of the body, the church; he is the beginning and the firstborn from among the dead so that in everything He might have the supremacy.

**I Peter 3:21-22**

Jesus Christ…has gone into heaven and is at God's right hand with angels, authorities and powers in submission to Him.

## 9. GOD TOOK AWAY SATAN'S AUTHORITY TO ACCUSE US OF SIN

**Colossians 2:15**

And having disarmed the powers and authorities, he made a public spectacle of them, triumphing over them by the cross.

## PERSONAL APPLICATION

**Matthew 8:7-10,13**

Jesus said to him, "I will go and heal him." 8 The centurion replied, "LORD, I do not deserve to have you come under my roof. But just say the word, and my servant will be healed. 9 For I myself am a man under authority, with soldiers under me. I tell this one, "Go," and he goes: and that one, "Come," and he comes. I say to my servant, "Do this," and he does it." When Jesus heard this, He was astonished and said to those following him. "I have not found anyone in Israel with such great faith…Go! It will be done just as you believed it would." And his servant was healed at that very hour.

The centurion's knowledge and clear understanding of earthly authority and what it means to submit to that authority gave him the revelation that sickness and even death was under the divine authority of God and so Jesus did not even have to be physically present to have these things submit to Him…He could just speak the word. This translated into great faith!

CHAPTER 20

# THE FOREHEAD OF GOD

*"You save the humble but bring
low those whose eyes are haughty."*
*Psalm 18:27*

The **forehead** of humans is the flat space of skin above the eyes, between the eyebrows and where your hair starts to grow. It exists to make room for the brain inside the skull.

A doctor or nurse will often touch someone's forehead to check whether or not they have a fever. This is because of the many blood vessels in the head and face.

### A. THE FOREHEAD IS A POINT WHERE

#### 1. AN IMPORTANT VICTORY WAS WON

**I Samuel 17:48-9**
David..reaching into his bag and taking out a stone, he slung it and struck the Philistine on the forehead. The stone sank into his forehead and he fell face down on the ground.

## 2. IMPORTANT THINGS TO BE REMEMBERED ARE PLACED

**Exodus 13:9**

This observance will be for you like a sign on your hand and a reminder on your forehead that the law of the LORD is to be on your lips

**Exodus 13:16**

And it will be like a sign on your hand and a symbol on your forehead that the LORD brought us out of Egypt with His mighty hand.

**Exodus 28:36**

Make a plate of pure gold and engrave on it "Consecrated to Jehovah"…attach it to the front of Aaron's turban. In this way Aaron will be wearing it upon his forehead and thus bear the guilt connected with any errors regarding the offerings of the people of Israel. It will be on Aaron's forehead continually so that they will be acceptable to the LORD.

**Deuteronomy 6:8**

These commandments…tie them as symbols on your hand and bind them on your foreheads.

**Deuteronomy 11:18**

Fix these words of mine in your hearts and minds; tie them as symbols on your hands and bind them on your foreheads.

## 3. IMPERATIVE MARKS ARE PLACED

**Revelation 7:3**

Do not harm the land or the sea or the trees until we put a seal on the foreheads of the servants of our God.

**Revelation 9:4**

They were told not to harm the grass of the earth or any plan or tree but only those people who did not have the seal of God on their foreheads.

**Revelation 13:16**

It also forced all people, great and small, rich and poor, free and slave to receive a mark on their right hands or on their foreheads.

**Revelation 14:1**

Then I looked, and there before me was the Lamb, standing on Mount Zion and with him 144,000 who had His name and His Father's name written on their foreheads.

**Revelation 14:9**

"If anyone worships the beast and his image and receives his mark on the forehead or on the hand he too will drink of the wine of God's fury…"

**Revelation 20:4**

And I saw the souls of those who had been beheaded because of their testimony for Jesus and because of the Word of God. They had not worshiped the beast or his image and had not received his mark on their foreheads…they came to life and reigned with Christ a thousand years."

**Revelation 19:12**

A name was written on His forehead and only He knew its meaning.

## B. WHATEVER WAS WRITTEN ON THE LORD'S FOREHEAD WAS CONCEALED. SOME CONCEALED, UNKNOWN THINGS ARE

### 1. SECRETS OF THE LORD

**Deuteronomy 29:29**

There are secrets the LORD your God has not revealed to us, but these words which he has revealed are for us and our children to obey forever.

## 2. SECRETS AMONG FRIENDS

**Proverbs 11:13**

A gossip betrays a confidence but a trustworthy person keeps a secret.

## 3. THE LORD'S RETURN

**Matthew 24:36**

No one knows about that day or hour, not even the angels in heaven, not the Son, but only the Father.

## 4. GOD'S JUDGMENTS

**Romans 11:33-34**

Oh, the depth of the riches of the wisdom and knowledge of God! How unsearchable his judgments and his paths beyond tracing out! Who has known the mind of the Lord? Or who has been his counselor?

## 5. THE ELAPSING TIME OR THE CHARACTER OF COMING EVENTS

**Acts 1:7**

He said to them "It is not for you to know the times or dates the Father has set by His own authority…"

## 6. GOD'S THOUGHTS

**Isaiah 55:8-9**

For my thoughts are not your thoughts, neither are your ways my ways, declares the LORD. As the heavens are higher than the earth so are my ways higher than your ways and my thoughts than your thoughts.

## 7. THE NAMES OF ANGELS

**Judges 13:18**

"Don't even ask my name" the Angel replied, "for it is a secret."

According to Wikipedia, a **bindi** from Sanskrit *bindu*, meaning "a drop, small particle, dot" is a forehead decoration worn in **South Asia**. Traditionally it is a bright dot of red color applied in the center of the forehead close to the eyebrows, but it can also consist of a sign or piece of jewelry worn at this location. The religious significance of this is that traditionally, the area between the eyebrows (where the bindi is placed) is said to be the sixth **chakra**, *ajna*, the seat of "concealed wisdom". According to followers of Hinduism, this chakra is the exit point for **kundalini** energy. The bindi is said to retain energy and strengthen concentration. It is also said to protect against demons or bad luck. The bindi also represents the **third eye**. *(http://soul-service.tumblr.com/post)*

## PERSONAL APPLICATION

### Matthew 23:12

**For those who exalt themselves will be humbled and those who humble themselves will be exalted.**

### Matthew 23:5

"Everything the Pharisees do is done for men to see (God conceals). They make their phylacteries wide..."

The phylacteries were boxes that contained 4 Scripture passages, worn on the forehead and arm. The four passages were:

### Exodus 13:1-10

The Lord said to Moses, ² "Consecrate to me every firstborn male. The first offspring of every womb among the Israelites belongs to me, whether human or animal."

³ Then Moses said to the people, "Commemorate this day, the day you came out of Egypt, out of the land of slavery, because the Lord brought you out of it with a mighty hand. Eat nothing containing yeast. ⁴ Today, in the month of Aviv, you are leaving. ⁵ When the Lord brings you into the land of the Canaanites, Hittites, Amorites, Hivites and Jebusites—the land he swore to your ancestors to give you, a land flowing with milk and honey—you are to observe this cer-

emony in this month: ⁶ For seven days eat bread made without yeast and on the seventh day hold a festival to the Lord. ⁷ Eat unleavened bread during those seven days; nothing with yeast in it is to be seen among you, nor shall any yeast be seen anywhere within your borders. ⁸ On that day tell your son, 'I do this because of what the Lord did for me when I came out of Egypt.' ⁹ This observance will be for you like a sign on your hand and a reminder on your forehead that this law of the Lord is to be on your lips. For the Lord brought you out of Egypt with his mighty hand.¹⁰ You must keep this ordinance at the appointed time year after year.

**Exodus 13:11-16**

¹¹ "After the Lord brings you into the land of the Canaanites and gives it to you, as he promised on oath to you and your ancestors, ¹² you are to give over to the Lord the first offspring of every womb. All the firstborn males of your livestock belong to the Lord. ¹³ Redeem with a lamb every firstborn donkey, but if you do not redeem it, break its neck. Redeem every firstborn among your sons.

¹⁴ "In days to come, when your son asks you, 'What does this mean?' say to him, 'With a mighty hand the Lord brought us out of Egypt, out of the land of slavery. ¹⁵ When Pharaoh stubbornly refused to let us go, the Lord killed the firstborn of both people and animals in Egypt. This is why I sacrifice to the Lord the first male offspring of every womb and redeem each of my firstborn sons.' ¹⁶ And it will be like a sign on your hand and a symbol on your forehead that the Lord brought us out of Egypt with his mighty hand."

**Deuteronomy 6:4-9**

Hear, O Israel: The LORD our God, the Lord is one. 5 Love the Lord your God with all your heart and with all your soul and with all your strength. 6 These commandments that I give you today are to be on your hearts. 7 Impress them on your children. Talk about them when you sit at home and when you walk along the road, when you lie down and when you get up. 8 Tie them as symbols on your hands and bind them on your foreheads. 9 Write them on the doorframes of your houses and on your gates.

**Deuteronomy 11:13-21**

[13] So if you faithfully obey the commands I am giving you today— to love the Lord your God and to serve him with all your heart and with all your soul— [14] then I will send rain on your land in its season, both autumn and spring rains, so that you may gather in your grain, new wine and olive oil. [15] I will provide grass in the fields for your cattle, and you will eat and be satisfied.

[16] Be careful, or you will be enticed to turn away and worship other gods and bow down to them. [17] Then the Lord's anger will burn against you, and he will shut up the heavens so that it will not rain and the ground will yield no produce, and you will soon perish from the good land the Lord is giving you. [18] Fix these words of mine in your hearts and minds; tie them as symbols on your hands and bind them on your foreheads. [19] Teach them to your children, talking about them when you sit at home and when you walk along the road, when you lie down and when you get up. [20] Write them on the doorframes of your houses and on your gates, [21] so that your days and the days of your children may be many in the land the Lord swore to give your ancestors, as many as the days that the heavens are above the earth.

So by the showy way they did things, the Pharisees made a point to let everyone know that they were righteous and they were following the law. They were puffed up with the knowledge that they had.

**I Corinthians 8:1** tells us that knowledge puffs up; it fills one with false pride.

**Mark 4:11**

The secret of the kingdom of God has been given to you. But to those on the outside everything is said in parables so that they may be ever seeing but never perceiving, and ever hearing but never understanding.

When a believer, the wisest and most knowledgeable Christian who shares God's secrets, realizes that his knowledge is limited and God is the only one who knows all, he will not become prideful.

**I Corinthians 8:2** tells us that the man who thinks he knows something does not yet know as he ought to know. But the man who loves God is known by God.

Wisdom comes from the Spirit of God, and those who are His, will share His secrets.

**I Corinthians 2:6-10** says we do, however, speak a message of wisdom among the mature, but not the wisdom of this age or of the rulers of this age, who are coming to nothing. 7 No we speak of God's secret wisdom, a wisdom that has been hidden and that God destined for our glory beforetime began. 8 None of the rulers of this age understood it…but God has revealed it to us by His Spirit.

Don't get puffed up like the Pharisees because of our relationship with the King. If we get puffed up and prideful the LORD will humble us. Jeremiah reminds us in 9:24 that the only thing we should showcase on our foreheads for all to see is this: but let the one who boasts boast about this: that they have the understanding to know me that I am the LORD who exercises kindness, justice and righteousness on the earth for in these I delight.

CHAPTER 21

# THE THIGH OF GOD
El Elyon, God Most High

*"...the God above all gods..."*
*Psalm 18:13*

The thigh is the part of the lower limb in humans between the hip and the knee.
**Revelation 19:16**
On His robe and on His thigh He has this name written "King of Kings and LORD of Lords."

In our study, when we looked at the head of God, we have already established that He rules and reigns in majesty. He is in control, in charge, and He is sovereign. The thigh of God addresses the fact that **'in comparison to"** our God is above ALL! El Elyon is above all gods, above all kings, above all lords, above all authorities, above all principalities, above all powers, and above all rulers. There is none as great as He is; there is just none like Him!

**Genesis 14:19**

Blessed be Abram by God Most High, Creator of heaven and earth (Elohim). And praise be to **God Most High** (El Elyon) who delivered your enemies into your hand.

**Deuteronomy 10:17**

For the LORD your ***God is God of gods and the LORD of lords***, the great God mighty and awesome.

**II Chronicles 2:5**

The temple I am going to build will be great because ***our God is greater*** than all other gods.

**Psalm 21:7**

For the king trusts in the LORD through the unfailing love of **the Most High,** he will not be shaken.

**Psalm 47:2**

For ***the LORD Most High*** is awesome***, the great King over all the earth***.

**Psalm 57:2**

I cry out to **God Most High**, to God who vindicates me.

**Psalm 77:13-18**

Your ways, God, are holy. ***What god is so great as our God?*** 14 You are the God who performs miracles; you display your power among the peoples. 15 With your mighty arm you redeemed your people… the waters saw you God…and writhed; the very depths were convulsed 18 your thunder was heard in the whirlwind, your lightning lit up the world."

**Psalm 78:35**

They remembered that God was their Rock, ***that God Most High*** was their Redeemer.

**Psalm 83:18**

Let them know that you, whose name is the LORD that ***you alone are the Most High over all the earth.***

### Psalm 89:6

For who in the skies above can compare with the LORD? Who is like the LORD among the heavenly beings? In the council of the holy ones God is greatly feared; He is more awesome than all who surround Him. Who is like you LORD God Almighty? You LORD are mighty, and your faithfulness surrounds you.

### Psalm 91:1 (TLB)

We live within the shadow of the Almighty, sheltered by the ***God who is above all gods.***

### Psalm 95:3

For the LORD is the great God ***the great King above all gods.***

### Psalm 99:1-5 (TLB)

Jehovah is King! Let the nations tremble! He is enthroned between the Guardian Angels. Let the whole earth shake. Jehovah sits in majesty in Zion, supreme above all rulers of the earth. Let them reverence your great and holy name…Exalt the LORD our holy God! Bow low before His feet.

### Psalm 135:5-7

I know that the LORD is great ***that our LORD is greater than all gods.*** The LORD does whatever pleases Him in the heavens and on the earth, in the seas and all their depths. He makes clouds rise from the ends of the earth; He sends lightning with the rain and brings out the wind from His storehouses.

### Psalm 136:2-3

Give thanks to the ***God of gods…the LORD of lords*** His love endures forever.

### Isaiah 46:9

***I am God, and there is no other; I am God, and there is none like me.*** I make known the end from the beginning, from ancient times, what is still to come. I say: My purpose will stand, and I will do all that I please.

**I Timothy 6:15-16**

"…God, the blessed and only Ruler, ***the King of kings and LORD of lords,*** who alone is immortal and who lives in unapproachable light…"

**Revelation 1:5**

"…and from Jesus Christ, who is the faithful witness, the firstborn from the dead, and the ***ruler of the kings of the earth***."

**Revelation 17:14**

They will wage war against the Lamb, but the Lamb will triumph over them because ***He is the LORD of lords and King of kings***—and with Him will be His called, chosen and faithful followers.

## A. CONQUEST OF gods CONFRONTED BY THE POWER OF EL ELYON

### 1. OVER THE GODS OF EGYPT

Jehovah was going to reveal Himself to the Egyptians by the plagues and judge the land of Egypt and her gods. In Exodus 12:12 El Elyon declared that He executed judgment on ALL the gods of Egypt. They were shown to be powerless in the display of El Elyon's power and many animals sacred to Egyptians in their worship of their gods would be killed.

Six (6) of the ten plagues are highlighted below:

### A. THE PLAGUE OF BLOOD

**Exodus 7:20-21**

"…Aaron raised his staff and struck the water of the Nile and all the water was changed into blood. The fish in the Nile died, and the river smelled so bad that the Egyptians could not drink its water. Blood was everywhere in Egypt." Egypt's dependence on the life-sustaining waters of the Nile led to its deification as the god Hapi.

## B. THE PLAGUE OF FROGS

**Exodus 8:3-4; 13-14**

"The Nile will teem with frogs. They will come up into your palace and your bedroom and onto your bed, into the houses of your officials and on our people and into your ovens and kneading troughs. The frogs will go up on you and your people and all your officials…the frogs died in the houses, in the courtyards and in the fields. They were piled into heaps and the land reeked of them."

The frog was deified in the goddess Heqt, the wife of the creator of the world and the goddess of birth who assisted women in childbirth. Heqt was always shown with the head and body of a frog. Frogs were so sacred in Egypt that even the involuntary slaughter of one was often punished with death. Imagine the people of the land as they went out to gather the decaying bodies of the frogs, and put them into heaps. (Against All the gods of Egypt, Padfield)

## C. THE PLAGUE OF GNATS

**Exodus 8:17**

Aaron stretched out his hand with the staff and struck the dust of the ground, gnats came upon people and animals. All the dust throughout the land of Egypt became gnats.

This plague would have been especially dreadful to the priests of Egypt, for they were required to shave their hair off every day, and wear a single tunic, that no lice would be permitted on their bodies. The daily rituals of the priests were not possible because of physical impurity. (Padfield)

## D. THE PLAGUE ON LIVESTOCK

**Exodus 9:3,6**

"…the hand of the LORD will bring a terrible plague on your livestock in the field--on your horses and donkeys and camels and on your cattle and sheep and goats…the next day the LORD did it. All the livestock of the Egyptians died."

The Egyptians worshiped many animals, and many animal-headed deities including the bull-gods Apis and Mnevis, the cow-god Hathor and the ram-god Khnum.

(Egypt) Why has Apis, your bull god, fled in terror? Because the LORD knocked him down before your enemies. Jeremiah 46:15 (TLB)

### E. THE PLAGUE OF DARKNESS

**Exodus 10:21-23**

Then the LORD said to Moses, "Stretch out your hand toward the sky so that darkness will spread over Egypt--darkness that can be felt." So Moses stretched out his hand toward the sky and total darkness covered all Egypt for three days. No one could see anyone else or leave his place for three days. Yet all the Israelites had light in the places where they lived.

This plague of darkness was an insult to Egypt's religion and entire culture. The sun god Amon-Ra was considered one of the greatest blessings in all of the land of Egypt.

Amon and Ra were originally two separate deities. (Padfield)

The Word of the LORD through Jeremiah the prophet declares, "I will punish Amon, god of Thebes and all the other gods of Egypt (Jeremiah 46:25 TLB)

### F. THE PLAGUE ON THE FIRSTBORN

The tenth plague destroyed only the Egyptians' firstborn males, whether human or animal. In Exodus 11:4-6 God told Moses that, "About midnight I will pass through Egypt. And all the oldest sons shall die in every family in Egypt, from the oldest child of Pharaoh, heir to his throne, to the oldest child of his lowliest slave; and even the firstborn of the animals. The wail of death will resound throughout the entire land of Egypt; never before has there been such anguish, and it will never be again." The Israelites and the entire male population of the nation were to be exempt from this plague. This plague was too selective to merely be a childhood epidemic.

The firstborn was not only an heir of a double portion of his father's inheritance, but represented special qualities of life and the major portion of a family estate would be inherited by the firstborn son when the father died (Deuteronomy 21:17). The death of the firstborn son would cripple a family legally and emotionally. This plague showed the total inability of the gods of Egypt to protect their subjects. In the face of unparalleled tragedy, "all of the gods of Egypt" were silent. (Against All the gods of Egypt, David Padfield, Padfield.com The Church of Christ in Zion, Illinois)

**Numbers 33:3-4**

They (the Children of Israel) left the city of Rameses, Egypt on the first day of April, the day after the night of the Passover. They left proudly, hurried along by the Egyptians who were burying all their eldest sons, killed by the LORD the night before. The LORD had certainly defeated all the gods of Egypt that night!

At the end of the display of God's miraculous power, the idols of Egypt trembled before Him. Isaiah 19:1

## 2. OVER LUCIFER, MORNING STAR, SON OF THE DAWN

**Isaiah 14:12-14**

"How you have fallen from heaven, morning star, son of the dawn! You have been cast down to the earth, you who once laid low the nations! 13 You said in your heart, I WILL ascend to heaven; I WILL raise my throne above the stars of God; I WILL sit enthroned on the mount of assemble, on the utmost heights of the sacred mountain. I WILL ascend above the tops of the clouds; I WILL make myself like the Most High (El Elyon). But you are brought down to the realm of the dead to the depths of the pit." He made 5 "I WILL" statements in five different ways. Remember in our study on the fist of God that the number 5=Spirit of Dagon

### 3. OVER BAAL, THE GOD OF FIRE

The account in I Kings 18:16-39 tells us about the showdown between Elijah, God's prophet and the prophets of Baal.

**Verses 24-39** reads as follows

"then you call on the name of your god, and I will call on the name of the LORD. The god who answers by fire—he is God. Then all the people said, "What you say is good." Then they called on the name of Baal from morning till noon. "Baal, answer us! They shouted. But there was no response; no one answered…At the time of sacrifice, the prophet Elijah stepped forward and prayed: "LORD, God of Abraham, Isaac and Israel, let it be known today that you are God in Israel and that I am your servant and have done all these things at your command…Then the fire of the LORD fell and burned up the sacrifice, the wood, the stones and the soil, and also licked up the water in the trench. When all the people saw this, they fell prostrate and cried "The LORD—He is God! The LORD—He is God!"

**Psalm 29:7**

The voice of God strikes with flashes of lightning.

**Psalm 104:3**

God makes "…flames of fire His servants…"

### 4. OVER THE GODS OF BABYLON

**Isaiah 46:1-2 (TLB)**

The idols of Babylon, Bel and Nebo are being hauled away on ox carts! But look! The beasts are stumbling! The cart is turning over! The gods are falling out onto the ground! Is that the best that they can do? If they cannot even save themselves from such a fall, how can they save their worshippers from Cyrus?

## Isaiah 46:1

Bel (Marduk) bows down, Nebo stoops low...they stoop and bow down together; unable to rescue the burden, they themselves go off into captivity (NIV).

## Jeremiah 50:2

Babylon will be captured; Bel will be put to shame, Marduk filled with terror. Her images will be put to shame and her idols filled with terror.

## Jeremiah 51:44, 52

I will punish Bel in Babylon and make him spew out what he has swallowed. The nations will no longer stream to him. And the wall of Babylon will fall...Yes, says the LORD, But the time is coming for the destruction of the idols of Babylon.

### 5. OVER THE GODS OF MOAB

– the land of the people of Chemosh.

The chief deity of Moab was Chemosh, a hideous god with the sacrifice of children as a burnt offering being a part of their worship of him.

We see this practice in the following account:

When the king of Moab saw that the battle had been lost, he led 700 of his swordsmen in a last desperate attempt to break through to the king of Edom but he failed. Then he took his oldest son, who was to have been the next king, and to the horror of the Israeli army, killed him and sacrificed him as a burnt offering upon the wall. II Kings 3:26-27 (TLB)

He (Solomon) even built a temple on the Mount of Olives for Chemosh the depraved god of Moab and another for Molech the unutterably vile god of the Ammonites. I Kings 11:7 (TLB)

## Isaiah 16:12

The people of Moab will pray in anguish to their idols at the tops of the hills, but it will do no good; they will cry to their gods in their idol temples, but none will come to save them.

**Jeremiah 48:7, 12-13**

For you (Moab) trusted in your wealth and skill; therefore you shall perish. Your god Chemosh, with his priests and princes, shall be taken away to distant lands…The time is coming soon, the LORD has said, when He will send troublemakers to spill her out from jar to jar and then shatter the jars! Then at last Moab shall be ashamed of her idol Chemosh, as Israel was of her calf-idol at Bethel.

### 6. OVER THE GODS OF THE AMMONITES

Milcom and Molech are alternate names for the same pagan deity and child sacrifice was included in the worship of this god. Solomon worshipped Ashtoreth the goddess of the Sidonians and Milcom the horrible god of the Ammonites. I Kings 11:5 (TLB)

**Jeremiah 49:3**

Weep daughter of Rabbah…for your god Milcom shall be exiled along with his princes and priests.

### 7. OVER THE GODS OF THE SIDONIANS

Ashtoreth (consort/wife of Baal) and Asheral (consort/wife of El--chief god of the Caananite pantheon). Ashtoreth was associated with the evening star and was the goddess of war and fertility. She was worshipped as Ishtar in Babylonia and as Athtart in Aram. To the Greeks she was Astarte or Aphrodite and to the Romans, Venus. Worship of the Ashtoreths involved extremely lascivious practices (NIV Text Note on Judges 2:13)

**Isaiah 23:4, 8-9**

"Be ashamed O Sidon, stronghold of the sea. For you are childless now! Who has brought this disaster on Tyre…the Commander of the armies of heaven has done it to destroy your pride and show His contempt for all the greatness of mankind."

### 8. OVER THE GODS OF ARAM, DAMASCUS
– capital of Syria.

The chief gods of Aram were Hadad (Baal), Mot, Anath and Rimmon which means Hadad the thunderer and war, was also known as Baal in Canaan & Phoenicia. This Aramean deity was the god of storm.

**II Kings 5:18**

But may the LORD forgive your servant (Naaman) for this one thing: When my master enters the temple of Rimmon to bow down and he is leaning on my arm and I have to bow there also--when I bow down in the temple of Rimmon, may the LORD forgive your servant for this.

**Isaiah 17:1-2,8**

Look, Damascus is gone! It is no longer a city--it has become a heap of ruins…the power of Damascus will end and the remnant of Syria shall be destroyed . They will no longer ask their idols for help in that day, neither will they worship what their hands have made! They will no longer have respect for the images of Ashtaroth and the sun idols.

**Zechariah 12:11**

On that day the weeping in Jerusalem will be great like the weeping of Hadad Rimmon in the plain of Megiddo.

### 9. OVER THE GOD OF THE STARS

**Amos 5:25-27**

" You sacrificed to me for forty years while you were in the desert, Israel--but always your real interest has been in our heathen gods--in Sakkuth your king, and in Kaiwan, your god of the stars, and in all the images of them you made. So I will send them into captivity with you far to the east of Damascus," says the LORD, the LORD Almighty.

**Psalm 97:7**

Let those who worship idols be disgraced--all who brag about their worthless gods--for every god must bow to Him!

**Psalm 135:15**

The heathen worship idols of gold and silver, made by men-idols with speechless mouths and sightless eyes and ears that cannot hear; they cannot even breath. Those who make them become like them! And so do all who trust in them.

## B. CONFESSIONS OF INDIVIDUALS WHO CAME IN CONTACT WITH THE POWER OF EL ELYON

### 1. JETHRO, PRIEST OF MIDIAN

**Exodus 18:9-11**

Jethro was delighted to hear about all the good things the LORD had done for Israel in rescuing them from the hand of the Egyptians… "*Now I know that the LORD is greater than all other gods,* for He did this to those who had treated Israel arrogantly."

### 2. NAAMAN, COMMANDER OF THE ARMY OF SYRIA

**II Kings 5:15**

Then Naaman and all his attendants went back to the man of God. He stood before him and said, "*Now I know that there is no God in all the world except in Israel.*

### 3. KING NEBUCHADNEZZAR, KING OF BABYLON

**Daniel 2:47**

The king said to Daniel, "*Surely your God is the God of gods and the* LORD *of kings* and a revealer of mysteries, for you were able to reveal this mystery.

**Daniel 3:26**

Nebuchadnezzar then approached the opening of the blazing furnace and shouted, "Shadrach, Meshach and Abednego, *servants of the Most High God*, come out! Come here!"

**Daniel 4:34**

At the end of that time, I, Nebuchadnezzar, raised my eyes toward heaven, and my sanity was restored. *Then I praised the Most High*; I honored and glorified Him who lives forever.

### 4. KING DARIUS THE MEDE

**Daniel 6:25-26**

Then King Darius wrote to all the peoples, nations and men of every language throughout the land: "May you prosper greatly! I issue a decree that in every part of my kingdom people must fear and reverence the God of Daniel. For **He is the living God and he endures forever;** His kingdom will not be destroyed, His dominion will never end."

### 5. THE SAILORS ON JONAH'S SHIP

Jonah received a word from the LORD for the people of Ninevah but instead of delivering the message he boarded a ship heading for Tarshish. On the journey there was a violent storm and all the sailors were afraid and each cried out to his own god. These sailors who would have come from different places worshipped several pagan gods. When Jonah was identified by lot as the cause of this trouble, he introduced himself as one who worshipped the LORD, the God of heaven who made the sea and the land.

The sailors would have understood Jonah's words as being descriptive of the highest divinity. Their recent experiences confirmed this truth, since, in the religions of the ancient Near East generally, the supreme god was master of the seas. (NIV Text Note)

Jonah advised them to throw him into the sea so that the storm would end. They reluctantly did so and the raging sea grew calm.

**Jonah 1:16**

The men stood there in awe before Jehovah and sacrificed to Him and vowed to serve Him.

## C. OUR RESPONSE TO THE KING OF KINGS AND LORD OF LORDS —THE GOD MOST HIGH, EL ELYON

### 1. HE IS TO BE FEARED

**I Chronicles 16:25-26/Psalm 96:4**

For great is the LORD and most worthy of praise; He is to be **feared above all gods**.

### 2. HE IS TO BE PRAISED

**Psalm 7:17**

I will sing the praises of the name of the LORD Most High

**Psalm 95:2-3**

Let us come before Him with thanksgiving and extol Him with music and song. For the LORD is the great God and great **King above all gods**.

### 3. HE IS TO BE EXALTED

**Psalm 97:9**

For you LORD, are the Most High over all the earth; you are **exalted far above all gods.**

### 4. HE IS TO BE WORSHIPED

**Psalm 96:4-5**

For the LORD is great beyond description, and greatly to be praised. **Worship only Him among the gods**! For the gods of other nations are merely idols, but our God made the heavens!

### PERSONAL APPLICATION

What is our personal application for the thigh of God?

**Isaiah 40:28-31**

Those who hope in the LORD will renew their strength

## Hosea 7:9

"...worshipping foreign gods has sapped their strength, but they don't know it. Ephraim...doesn't even realize how weak and old he is. His pride in other gods has openly condemned him; yet he doesn't return to his God nor even try to find him."

There is a sense of utter futility in the serving of other gods. They are powerless against El Elyon the God Most High; they cannot stand against Him. Our worship of other gods is not only fruitless but our strength is sapped; our energies drained. The enemy of our soul wants to steal, kill and destroy. There is nothing that we gain in serving other gods.

When you exalt El Elyon, you exalt Him over all of your situations and give Him the opportunity to take care of these situations. In this way He is glorified and the Everlasting God never tires of our circumstances.

## Isaiah 40:28-31

Do you not know? Have you not heard? The LORD is the everlasting God, the Creator of the ends of the earth. He will not grow tired or weary...He gives strength to the weary and increases the power of the weak....but **those who hope in the LORD will renew their strength**. They will soar on wings like eagles; they will run and not grow weary, they will walk and not be faint.

His strength is perfect when our strength is gone. He'll carry us when we can't carry on. Raised in His power the weak become strong; His strength is perfect.

## Habukkuk 3:19

The Sovereign LORD is my strength.

- Exalt El Elyon, and like Moses, He will give you the strength to deliver His people from under oppressive leaders and ordinances;
- Exalt El Elyon, and like Elijah, He will give you the extraordinary strength to demonstrate the impotence of other gods and to do supernatural acts;

- Exalt El Elyon, and like the 3 Hebrew boys, He will give you the strength to not bow down to other gods, not to compromise your faith;
- Exalt El Elyon, and like the 3 Hebrew boys, He will give you strength to go through your fiery trials;
- Exalt El Elyon, and like Daniel, He will give you the strength to face your lions' den experiences;
- Exalt El Elyon, and He will draw all men to Himself!

## THE SONG OF MOSES & MIRIAM IS A FITTING DESCRIPTION OF EL ELYON, THE GOD MOST HIGH

### Exodus 15:3-18 King James Version (KJV)

³ The Lord is a man of war: the Lord is his name.

⁴ Pharaoh's chariots and his host hath he cast into the sea: his chosen captains also are drowned in the Red sea.

⁵ The depths have covered them: they sank into the bottom as a stone.

⁶ Thy right hand, O Lord, is become glorious in power: thy right hand, O Lord, hath dashed in pieces the enemy.

⁷ And in the greatness of thine excellency thou hast overthrown them that rose up against thee: thou sentest forth thy wrath, which consumed them as stubble.

⁸ And with the blast of thy nostrils the waters were gathered together, the floods stood upright as an heap, and the depths were congealed in the heart of the sea.

⁹ The enemy said, I will pursue, I will overtake, I will divide the spoil; my lust shall be satisfied upon them; I will draw my sword, my hand shall destroy them.

¹⁰ Thou didst blow with thy wind, the sea covered them: they sank as lead in the mighty waters.

## WHAT A GOD!

¹¹ Who is like unto thee, O Lord, among the gods? who is like thee, glorious in holiness, fearful in praises, doing wonders?

¹² Thou stretchedst out thy right hand, the earth swallowed them.

¹³ Thou in thy mercy hast led forth the people which thou hast redeemed: thou hast guided them in thy strength unto thy holy habitation.

¹⁴ The people shall hear, and be afraid: sorrow shall take hold on the inhabitants of Palestina.

¹⁵ Then the dukes of Edom shall be amazed; the mighty men of Moab, trembling shall take hold upon them; all the inhabitants of Canaan shall melt away.

¹⁶ Fear and dread shall fall upon them; by the greatness of thine arm they shall be as still as a stone; till thy people pass over, O Lord, till the people pass over, which thou hast purchased.

¹⁷ Thou shalt bring them in, and plant them in the mountain of thine inheritance, in the place, O Lord, which thou hast made for thee to dwell in, in the Sanctuary, O Lord, which thy hands have established.

¹⁸ The Lord shall reign forever and ever.

# SUMMARY OF THE ANATOMY

What have you learned about God through the study of the various parts of His "anatomy"? When faced with situations we need to know the appropriate part to call upon.

## 1. THE HAND OF GOD REFLECTS
- His Power to save and to create
- His Protection from our enemies
- His Provision of possessions, promises, presence
- His Personal Care
- His Pouring Out of Judgment
- His Pierced Hands

**PERSONAL APPLICATION**

We are engraved in the palm of His hand (Isaiah 49:16)

**2. THE VOICE OF GOD**
- Is likened to/associated with thunder/power
- Can be heard/listened to
- Must be obeyed

What happens when you hear His voice and obey?
What happens when you hear His voice and don't obey?
The LORD selects those who hear His voice.
How can you hear God's voice?
How do you know it is the voice of God?

**PERSONAL APPLICATION**

God voices to us what we need to hear in that still small voice (I Kings 19:12b-13)


**3. THE EYE OF GOD**
- Sees
  – In the dark
  – And you cannot hide from Him
  – Records and stores
- Watches over the land
- Watches over the wicked
- Takes careful note of what you do and the condition of your life

Why does the LORD watch us so closely?
What is the danger of not seeing the LORD?

**PERSONAL APPLICATION**

We are the apple of God's eye
(Zechariah 2:8; Deuteronomy 32:10)

## 4. THE HEART OF GOD
- Gentle/Humble
- Compassionate
- Tender care/Protective of His own
- Can be reflected/He mentors His leaders

Who is a true worshipper?

What do we need to be a true worshipper?

## PERSONAL APPLICATION

We must be people after God's own heart who will do everything He wants us to. (Acts 13:22)

## 5. THE FACE OF GOD
- Responses to the face of God
  - Fear of Death
  - Friend with Friend
  - Fantastic
  - For I am a man of unclean lips..and my eyes have seen the King, the LORD Almighty—Isaiah
- Examining the face of God using the letters
  - **F**avour (when His face shines down on us blessing, deliverance and victory comes)
  - **A**ccess
  - **C**oncealment
  - **E**mbodiment/Essence
- We are encouraged to:
  - Seek His Face
  - Show His Face Again/Reflect His face
  - See His Face

## PERSONAL APPLICATION

Aaronic Blessing (Numbers 6:25)

## 6. THE FEET OF GOD
- Appearance—feet like bronze glowing
- References to the feet of God
  - Victory over His enemies
  - Ruler of everything
- Responses to the feet of Jesus
  - Sit at…to learn
  - Anoint…to show reverence, gratitude and love
  - Fall down…to worship
  - Pierced…for our salvation
  - Examine…to identify
  - Wash…to serve

**PERSONAL APPLICATION**

I have set you an example that you should do as I have done for you. (John 13:15)

## 7. THE MIND OF GOD

References to the mind of God:
- We do not know the mind of God
- He does not change His mind

God, nevertheless, will change His preannounced response to man, depending on what the latter does e.g. turning away from God; being extremely and genuinely sorry for sins and repenting, etc.

**PERSONAL APPLICATION**

Let this mind be in you which was also in Christ Jesus. (Philippians 2:5)

"The mind of sinful man is death, but the mind controlled by the Spirit is life and peace." (Romans 8:6)

Commit to memory the following verse:

"Whatever is true, whatever is noble, whatever is right, whatever is pure, whatever is lovely, whatever is admirable—if anything is excellent or praiseworthy—think about such things. (Philippians 4:8)

## 8. THE BREATH OF GOD
- Associated with life, giving understanding, wind, the Holy Spirit, destruction by fire, ice, water
- God wants to breathe:
  - On our political situations
  - Against unjust situations
  - On our difficult situations

### PERSONAL APPLICATION

The Breath of Restoration–The breath of God is always with us. "As for me, this is my covenant with them (those who repent of their sins), says the LORD, "My Spirit who is on you…will not depart from your mouth, or the mouths of your children, or from the mouths of their descendants from this time on and forever," says the LORD." (Isaiah 59:21)

## 9. THE EAR OF GOD
- What Does God Hear?
  - The Cry of the Poor//injustice against the poor
  - The Ravens
  - The Downhearted
  - The plea from a friend
  - Your disbelief
  - Lies
  - Oppression
  - When others try to write the end of your story
  - Death cries
- When Does God Not Hear?
  - When sin is present
  - When wicked ways are present
  - When the wrong kind of fasting is done
  - When husbands are not considerate of their wives

- When Does God Hear Us?
  - After the proper kind of fasting
  - When we pray according to His will
- How do we ask God to hear/deal with situations that He hears? I Kings 8:22-53
  - Insufficient evidence…hear and act
  - Trouble brought about by disobedience…hear, forgive and teach the right way…
  - Disease/disaster striking the land…hear, forgive and act
  - Foreigners…hear and do
  - Fight against our enemies…hear and uphold our cause

**PERSONAL APPLICATION**

"But I keep right on praying to you , Lord. For now is the time---you are bending down to hear! You are ready with a plentiful supply of love and kindness." (Psalm 69:1)


**10. THE FIST OF GOD**

*(Your Possession Of The Promised Land (Victory) Is A Shout Away)*
- Dagon
  - Gaza (Judges—Sampson)
  - Beth Shan (I Sam.31:8-10—Saul)
  - Ashdod (I Samuel 5—the Ark of God)

- God releases His fist against us when we
  - Reject Him—forsake Him; turn our backs on Him
  - Reverence others—turn to idols

**PERSONAL APPLICATION**

Unleash your fist from within your cloak and deliver one final blow (Psalm 74:11). Lord, break down the walls in my life, my church, my country.

## 11. THE BACK OF GOD *(Intimacy)*
- God is willing to reveal Himself to us when we embark on that journey of intimacy with Him
- Whatever He reveals of Himself (back) is just enough for us.

**PERSONAL APPLICATION**

The back is known for support. Moses was acknowledged by God as an intercessor for His people Israel. The call is for us to offer strong support for the ministry by interceding on its behalf.

## 12. THE ARM OF GOD
- Symbolizes strength
- Symbolizes salvation/rescue/justice
- Is superior to the arm of flesh

**PERSONAL APPLICATION**

The outstretched arm of God is our banner of victory—Jehovah Nissi. (Exodus 17:15)

## 13. THE TEETH OF GOD
*(**T**rust **Ev**En in **T**he **H**eat)*

A. References to Man's Teeth
- Skin of my teeth
- Teeth set on edge
- Gnash
  - Sign of suffering due to extreme regret
  - Sign of malice
  - Sign of gloating
  - Sign of vexation, anger

B. References to God's Teeth
- Judgment Against Spiritual Prostitution
- Judgment Against God-defying sin and covenant-

breaking rebellion
- Judgment to Purify God's People

**PERSONAL APPLICATION**

Consider it pure joy, my brothers, whenever you face trials of many kinds, because you know that the testing of your faith develops perseverance. Perseverance must finish its work so that you may be mature and complete. (James 1:2)

## 14. THE SIDE OF GOD

*(If You Believe You Will Receive)*

It reflects:
- Proof of His Laying Down His Life (death)
- Proof of His Life (resurrection from the dead)
- Proof of His Love

**PERSONAL APPLICATION**

Draw near to God, to His precious bleeding side, and He will draw near to you. (James 4:8)

## 15. THE FINGER OF GOD

*(Works on the Details)*
- On STONE
- In the SKY
- Re the SPIRIT'S Role
- In the face of STUBBORNESS
- Of my Personal SECURITY
- Of Restoring a man's SPEECH
- Of SOLOMON'S Temple
- In the SAND

**PERSONAL APPLICATION**

The Finger of God works on the details of our every STEP! The steps of the godly are directed by the LORD He delights in every detail of their lives. (Psalm 37:23)

## 16. THE MOUTH OF GOD

A. References to the Mouth of God indicate that:
- He Laughs
- He Speaks
- There are Times to be Silent
- There is no Deceit in His Mouth

B. The Sword of the Spirit is the Word of God
- The Power of His Spoken Word
  - What He Speaks Comes into Existence
  - What He Speaks Brings Wisdom
  - What He Speaks is Right and True
- The Prophetic Nature of His Spoken Word

C. That Out of His Mouth Comes
- Fire for judicial wrath
- A Sword for Judgment
- Spit That Brings Healing

**PERSONAL APPLICATION**

"…thy rod…comforts me." (Psalm 23:4) & "take…the sword of the Spirit which is the Word of God…" (Ephesians 6:17)


## 17. THE WAIST OF GOD
- References to the Waist of God:
- Faithfulness—the Sash Around His Waist
- Righteousness—the Belt Around His Waist
- Faithfulness and Righteousness
- Justice and Righteousness

**PERSONAL APPLICATION**

"Stand firm then with the belt of truth buckled around your waist." (Ephesians 6:14)

### 18. THE HAIR OF GOD
- What are pure things as highlighted in scripture
- Seven areas we are called to Purity:
  - Purity of Life
  - Purity of Heart
  - Purity of Action
  - Purity of Thought
  - Purity of Adornment
  - Purity of our Marital Relationships
  - Purity of our Ending
- Challenges to Purity and Solutions to those challenges

**PERSONAL APPLICATION**

"White hair is a crown of glory…the splendor of the old" (Proverbs 16:31; 20:29)

### 19. THE HEAD OF GOD
- Significance of Authority
- Symbols of Authority
- Specifics on Authority

**PERSONAL APPLICATION**

"Moreover, we have all had human fathers (fathers of flesh) who disciplined us and we respected them for it. How much more should we submit to the Father of our spirits and live!" (Hebrews 12:9)

### 20. THE FOREHEAD OF GOD
A. The forehead is a point where:
- An important victory was won
- Important things to be remembered are placed
- Imperative marks are placed

**PERSONAL APPLICATION**

For whoever exalts himself will be humbled and whoever humbles himself will be exalted. (Matthew 23:12)

## 21. THE THIGH OF GOD
   A. Conquest of gods Confronted by the Power of El Elyon
   B. Confessions of Individuals Who Came In Contact With the Power of El Elyon
   C. Our Response to the King of kings and LORD of lords —the God Most High

**PERSONAL APPLICATION**

"The LORD God is my strength, and He will make my feet like hinds' feet, and He will make me to walk upon mine high places." (Habakkuk 3:19)

# ANATOMY WORSHIP COMPANION

**The purpose of this worship companion to the study of The Anatomy of the Almighty is** to provide lists of recommended songs that can be used along with each aspect of the anatomy. These lists, though not exhaustive, when used in conjunction with the matching part of the anatomy, they go a long way to bring understanding and breathe new life into the songs that are sung regularly.

**The suggested format for studying the components of the anatomy of God is:**

a. Go through a period of prayer and fasting, before presenting any aspect of the anatomy;

b. On the day of the presentation, do the lesson on the particular part of the anatomy first;

c. This is to be followed by worship time as you are led by the Spirit of God. Worshippers can worship more intelligently when worship is done after having learnt about the specific part of the anatomy that they are now singing about.

There are times when the lesson can be interspersed with worship or specials that are specifically tied in with the particular part of the anatomy being taught.

Inasmuch as in you lies, the sessions should always begin and end with music for the prelude as well as the postlude. Suggestions will be given for both prelude and postlude music. This list too, is not exhaustive.

The suggested programme ideas should be used under the direction of the Holy Spirit, because, coming out of your personal time of meditation with Jehovah Rohi, He will give you guidance and other ideas.

## CHAPTER 1
## THE HAND OF GOD

Prelude: "Worship in the House" Keith Staten
SONGS:
- He Hideth My Soul
- Shout to the LORD
- He's Got the Whole World In His Hands
- The Right Hand of God
- Thank you for the Cross LORD
- Who Is Like Unto Thee?
- How Great is our God
- There is None Like You
- He Was Wounded For Our Transgression, He was Bruised
- Our God
- I Believe You're My Healer
- Potter's Hand
- I Will Run To You
- I Give Myself Away
- I Surrender—Bishops of the Faith #11
- He has His Hand on You – Marvin Sapp

- Take My Life and Let It Be
- Majesty, Your Grace Has Found Me

Response time the call to salvation "I Surrender All" Terry MacAlmon

**POSTLUDE**

"Worship in the House" Keith Staten
- #6 Shout to the LORD
- #9 You Are Awesome
- #11 LORD I Thirst

# CHAPTER 2
# THE VOICE OF GOD

Prelude: Holy, Holy, Holy "The Sound of Heaven" Terry MacAlmon

SONGS:
- We Need to Hear From You
- Open my Eyes LORD …Ears Lord and Help me To Listen
- I'll Say Yes, LORD, Yes
- I Am Thine O LORD
- How Great is our God
- Holy Spirit Rain Down
- #11 I Come to the Garden Alone-Thirsty by Marvin Sapp
- He is Here Hallelujah—Martha Manuzzi

(For the Exercises)
- Only you are holy
- Holy, Holy, Holy are you, LORD
- You are holy, holy, LORD, there is none like you
- I will lift my voice
- Hosanna in the highest, let our King be lifted up, hosanna

**SPIRITUAL EXERCISE**

Anoint ears of those present. Our physical ears are being anointed, but we need to listen with our spiritual ears.

Pray for Samuel's anointing for sensitivity and obedience to the voice of God.

## EXERCISE #1—
### To Listen to the Voice of God for yourself

We are going to enter a time of worship. As soon as worship is over you can keep standing, or sit, or kneel, no talking, close your eyes, no noise, no distractions. Nothing will be said after worship (just the music "Holy, Holy, Holy"—Terry MacAlmon)

1. After deliberately moving into the presence of God through worship, be willing, ready and eager to hear from Him;
2. Acknowledge His presence, praise Him, thank Him for His presence. Be still and know that He is God;
3. Then listen…
4. God might give you a song, a Scripture verse. Whatever He tells you, write it down.
5. Thank the LORD for speaking to you.
6. Leader—give some time, about 5-10 minutes, and then give opportunity for persons to share (if they are willing), what God has spoken to them. Then thank God for speaking.

## EXERCISE #2—
### To Listen to the Voice of God for someone else

1. Move into pairs with someone you are not familiar with;
2. After deliberately moving into the presence of God through worship, be willing, ready and eager to hear from Him;
3. Acknowledge His presence, praise Him, thank Him for His presence. Be still and know that He is God.
*(Music—You are Holy—Brooklyn Tabernacle "This is Your House Disc 2 #3; Bowed on my Knees—Brooklyn Tabernacle "Live Again" #7)*
4. Pray and ask God to give you a word for your partner.
5. Listen
6. Share with each other what you have heard no matter how silly or irrelevant it may seem.
7. Thank God for speaking.

Your ears have been anointed, sensitized to hear the voice of God. As you go, whatever He says to you, do it! Practice that, and make this song your lifestyle: *(Play "I Come to the Garden Alone" #11 Thirsty Marvin Sapp)*

## CHAPTER 3
## THE EYE OF GOD

Prelude: Here I Am To Worship

SONGS:
- Open the Eyes of my Heart, LORD
- Open my Eyes, LORD, I Want to See Jesus
- Light of the World…Here I am to Worship
- I Focus My Eyes on you
- Watch your eyes, watch your eyes what they see
- His Eye is on the Sparrow
- I See the LORD
- Potter's Hand
- "Journey" #4 Junior Tucker
- Change (Gates Praise) #7 & #12
- Israel & New Breed "Live From Another Level Disc 2 #1-4
- I Will Run to You—Alvin Slaughter
- Show Me Your Glory

Prayer time—Israel Disc 2 #10
- Those involved in activities that you know God is not pleased with and He is seeing…pornography, sexual activities
- Believer—you need clarity, direction, guidance for your unknown future.

Pray for healing of eyes

## POSTLUDE

Sound of Heaven, Terry MacAlmon #2; Change (GatesPraise) #12

# CHAPTER 4
## THE HEART OF GOD

This would be a great session for the music department of the local church which would include worship leaders, band members, chairpersons, and individuals who do specials, etc.

Anoint hands

**A. Clean hands—outstretch both hands up in the air, palms facing up**

Elohim, here are my hands that you created, wash them, cleanse them with your blood, break the chains that bind my hands to do evil. I dedicate them to you in the name of the Father, Son and Holy Spirit, they are yours. I consecrate them for your use now. Your word says that you are holding me by my right hand and telling me "Don't be afraid I am here to help you. Help me to keep my hands clean, help them not to be idle. Keep them from wrong doing and help me lift them to praise you.

**B. Pure heart—right hand outstretched in front of you, palm turned up, left hand on your heart and repeat after me**

El Elyon, examine my heart, create in me a new, clean heart filled with clean thoughts and right desires. God I give my heart to you. Give me an undivided heart that I may serve you without competing loyalties. Help me to seek you with all of my heart; help me to hide your Word in my heart so that I will not sin against you. Fix my thoughts on what is true and good and right. Help me to think about things that are pure and lovely and dwell on the fine, good things in others.

**C. Allegiance only to Elohim – right hand outstretched, left hand on your forehead.**

I pledge allegiance to you El Shaddai. Examine my mind. I give you permission to continuously transform my mind.

Take my heart and form it; take my mind transform it; take my will conform it to yours O LORD.

**D. Clean lips—both hands on lips and repeat after me**
LORD, take the coal, cleanse my lips. Forgive me for lying lips, a deceptive tongue and a mouth filled with slander and filthy language. May my spoken words and unspoken thoughts be pleasing to you El Shaddai (Psalm 19:14). Set a guard over my mouth, O LORD, keep watch over the door of my lips (Psalm 141:3) May my lips overflow with praise to you every day (Psalm 119:171). I want to be known as a wo/man after God's own heart.

## WORSHIPPERS FACE ALTAR TO AN AUDIENCE OF ONE

As Isaiah experienced that vision of God in His holiness, he became aware of His own sinful state and cried "Woe is me for I have unclean lips. So too as we look into God's holiness today, our cry to Him is…"Create in me a clean heart, O God!"

1. Outer Court Worship –Create in us clean hearts, O God, so that we can worship you.
   - (PURE HEART #7 "Lord make me pure in heart
   - Donnie McClurkin "Create in me a clean heart #7)
   - Create in me a clean heart, O God
2. Inner Court Worship—Lord, we long to be near to the throne of your glory; my soul thirsts for you, my flesh yearns for you. In a dry and weary land where there is no water.
   - (PURE HEART #8—Into Your Courts)
   - As the Deer
   - Draw me close to you
3. Holy of Holies—take us into the holy of holies, take us in by the blood of the Lamb; take the coal, cleanse our lips, here we are. We draw the curtain and we behold the Lamb of God who takes away the sin of the world.

(To Worship you I Live; Take me into the Holy of Holies)
Heart of worship

## CHAPTER 5
## THE FACE OF GOD—PENIEL

This session is ideal for the Hospitality Department, ushers, greeters, parking attendants, etc. as they are the first faces of the local church.

Prelude: The Sound of Heaven  Terry MacAlmon

SONGS:
- Isn't He?
- O Lord You're Beautiful
- You're Beautiful To Me
- You Are Beautiful Beyond Description
- I Worship You In The Beauty Of Holiness
- When I Look Into Your Holiness
- In Your Presence…Seeking Your Face
- The Worship Express With Terry Macalmon #10 My God & King
- Face To Face With Christ My Saviour
- On Christ The Solid Rock
- To See The Face Of God Is My Heart's Desire
- Turn Your Eyes Upon Jesus
- Let The Beauty Of Jesus Be Seen In Me
- Yes I Will Run To You
- You Are Awesome In This Place (Verse)
- To See Your Face Terry Macalmon "You're My Glory #4
- Change #7
- I See The Lord—Ron Kenoly
- Show Me Your Face Wm Mcdowell "As We Worship" #11
- Power Of Your Love

- Potter's Hand
- Your Presence Is Heaven To Me "Israel & New Breed"
- Jesus Name Above All Names

Memorise the Aaronic Blessing

"As We Worship" William MacDowell #11, #12: This is for those who just want more of Him, His grace, His power, His anointing for ministry, His presence, His love, His goodness. You just plain and simple want more of Him, and you are saying, "I want to know you."

The rendezvous area is confirmed. Let us meet at the altars

Prayer time: "Sound of Heaven" Terry MacAlmon #8 O The Glory

Postlude: " Sound of Heaven" Terry MacAlmon #3 To See Your Face; #4 You're My Glory"

# CHAPTER 6
# THE FEET OF GOD
SONGS:
- Trying to Walk in the Steps of the Saviour
- Sitting at the Feet of Jesus
- We Cry Holy, Holy, Holy
- We worship & adore you
- Consuming Fire sweet perfume, your awesome presence fills this room
- Bow down and worship Him
- Come let us worship and bow down
- For the Bride #10 & #8 Terry MacAlmon
- Revelation Son
- You Are Awesome
- Light of the World
- Alabaster Box—Dance
- The More I Seek You—Kari Jobe
- Highest Place (We Place You…)

- Hope of Nations #7
- Take My Life and Let It Be
- At Your Feet — Carlene Davis

The ritual of foot washing usually follows the study of this specific part of the anatomy. The purpose of the footwashing is to be the response of the hearer to go and do as Jesus did. The response also is a commitment to serve others to be His hands and His feet. As He set the example of service, go thou and do likewise.

During the exercise play Change (GatesPraise) #9

It is recommended that those who are washing the feet take their shoes off.

Do we have any worshippers who just want to fall down and worship Him? Come with your alabaster box and break it at His feet. Come broken (As We Worship Disc 2 #5)

**POSTLUDE**

"For the Bride" Terry MacAlmon #7-10

# CHAPTER 7
# THE MIND OF GOD

SONGS:
- Holiness, Holiness is what I long for
- Take My Life and Let it Be
- I Want to Be Like Jesus
- Glory To His Name

# CHAPTER 8
# THE BREATH OF GOD

SONGS:
- Breathe on Me Breath of God
- Fill Me Now
- Holy Spirit Rain Down

- Let Your Living Water
- Let the River Flow
- Let the Rain of your Presence fall on me
- How We Need the River—Sound of Heaven, Terry McAlmon #10
- Rain On Us Holy Spirit—Brooklyn Tabernacle:Live… We Come Rejoicing #6
- God is Moving by His Spirit—Brooklyn Tabernacle: BTC #11
- Holy Spirit Come and Fill this Place
- This is the Air I breathe
- Come Breathe on me breath of God  Terry MacAlmon
- You're All I Need  Hezekiah Walker
- Breathe Unto Me  Live From Another Level Disc 2 Israel #8
- Worthy is the/Lamb who was slain/Holy, Holy is He
- Eagles' Wings

1. Prelude–"Rain On Us Holy Spirit" B/Tab  Live… We Come Rejoicing  #6
2. Prayer
3. The Breath of God
4. Breathe on our Political situation
   a. Sharing
   b. Days of Elijah
   c. Prayer
5. Breathe on unjust situations/injustice
   a. Sharing
   b. Holy Spirit Rain Down
   c. Prayer
6. Breathe on our difficult situations
   a. Sharing
   b. Let Your Living Water

c. Let the River Flow
   d. Prayer
7. Breathe on us Holy Spirit
   a. Breathe on Me Breath of God
   b. Fill Me Now

## CHAPTER 9
## THE EAR OF GOD
SONGS:
- Hear My Cry O God
- Hear These Praises
- I Will Lift My Voice
- I Love You LORD —Let It Be A Sweet, Sweet Sound In Your Ear
- I Will Run To You—Alvin Slaughter
- I Am A Friend Of God

## CHAPTER 10
## THE FIST OF GOD
Your Possession of the Victory is a Shout Away
SONGS: (re: walls coming down)
- Blessed Be The Name Of The LORD
- For The LORD Is My Tower
- We Have The Victory
- Above All Else #283
- Change (GatesPraise) #1 "Break Down The Walls
- God Is Good
- See What The LORD Has Done For Us
- Around The Walls Of Jericho
- Shout For God Has Given Us The City
- In The Name Of Jesus

1. Prelude: Change #1 Break Down the Walls
2. Concert Prayer (ACTS)
3. The Fist of God
4. Praise
   a. Blessed be the Name of the LORD
   b. For the LORD is my Tower
   c. We have the victory
5. Identify the walls in our lives, church, society. Write them down. (Play Change GatesPraise #1) Walls are an obstacle. They prevent access to your Promised Land. The battle is not yours…it is the LORD's
6. Instructions
   a. Take off your shoes for this is holy ground  Joshua 5:15
   b. With leader in front, walk around the walls six times in silence, pause at the end of each lap. *"Let there be complete silence except for the trumpets…not a single word from any of you until I tell you to shout, then shout!!"* Joshua 6:10
   c. Begin the walk around the "walls" six times continuously (Play Change #1)
   d. When you hear one long, loud blast: all the people, give a mighty shout and the walls will fall down. *"So when the people heard the trumpet blast, they shouted as loud as they could. And suddenly the walls…crumbled and fell before them…"* Joshua 6:20  Shout for God has given you the city.
   e. Walk into your Promised Land Joshua 6:20 "…and the people…poured into the city from every side…"
7. Prayer
8. Walk

9. Celebration
    a. God is good
    b. See what the LORD hath done for us.
10. Prayer

# CHAPTER 11
# THE BACK OF GOD

The Afterglow of His Presence

This would be a great session for the Prayer groups of the local church which would include intercessors, prayer cell leaders, those responsible for organizing any prayer time in the church.
SONGS:
- Rock of Ages
- Glory in the House—Keith Staten
- In Your Presence
- More, More About Jesus
- I Want to Know You--As We Worship—Wm McDowell #11

1. Prelude  The Sound of Heaven  Terry MacAlmon
2. Prayer of Thanksgiving
3. Thanksgiving for an aspect of God as revealed throughout the year
4. Interlude  For the Bride Terry MacAlmon #7-10
5. Intercessory prayer for the church (details, by name, paper to write what God reveals to you through prayer) (Play You're My Glory)
    a. Departments e.g. Youth, Missions, Education
    b. Leaders, pastor, ministers, church board, board meetings, support of church, annual meeting, church projects e.g. roof, church facility, benches, equipment
    c. Married couples/marriages; young people in relationships, singles, babies who have been dedicated in our church

d. Ministries (hospitality, worship team & musicians, technical team, readers, chairpersons, altar workers, ushers/greeters (visitors), quiz, evangelistic outreach to the community, our witness in the community, follow-up re new converts)
e. Members (overseas, studying, walk with Christ, commitment to the things of God, intimacy with God, bereavement, financial situation, discipleship necessary, those not well, protection of members, exams

# CHAPTER 12
# THE ARM OF GOD

God is your Jehovah Nissi, Your Banner of Victory
PROPS: Red cloths to represent God is our Jehovah Nissi, our banner
SONGS:
- Jehovah Nissi reigns in victory
- Stand up, Stand up for Jesus "…the arm of flesh will fail you; you dare not trust your own…"
- What A Friend We Have in Jesus "…in His arms He'll take and shield thee…"
- Sheltered In The Arms Of God
- Leaning On The Everlasting Arms
- For The Bride #2 Terry Macalmon
- Wrap Me In Your Arms---Wm Mcdowell
- Cover Me--Bishops Of The Faith #7 #14
- Still (Hide Me Now Under Your Wing..)
- Sound Of Heaven #8 Terry Macalmon
- Falling In Love With Jesus…In His Arms…
- O God Our Help In Ages Past
- Love Is A Flag Flown High From The Castle Of My Heart

## CHAPTER 13
## THE TEETH OF GOD
**T**rust **E**v**E**n in **T**he **H**eat
SONGS:
- Great Is Your Mercy
- The Steadfast Love Of The Lord Never Ceases
- Great Is They Faithfulness
- For Every Mountain


## CHAPTER 14
## THE SIDE OF GOD
If You Believe You Will Receive

A showing of the crucifixion would be appropriate during the study of this part of the anatomy. This study is followed by communion.
SONGS:
- I Am Thine O LORD
- Power Of Your Love
- Draw Me Close To You
- Beautiful Lord, Wonderful Saviour
- Bishops Of The Faith CD #6 "I Believe"
- God Will Make A Way
- Give Thanks
- Thank You For The Cross LORD
- Light Of The World
- LORD I Lift Your Name On High
- King Of All Days
- I Will Never Let Go Of Your Love (The Bride #15, Terry Macalmon)

## CHAPTER 15
## THE FINGER OF GOD
God is in the Details
SONGS:
- He is Able
- God Will Make A Way
- Each Step I Take the Saviour Goes Before Me

Share testimonies of incidents where God took care of the details.


## CHAPTER 16
## THE MOUTH OF GOD
SONGS:
- Thy Word Is A Lamp Unto My Feet
- You Are The God That Healeth Me
- Take My Life And Let It Be
- The B-I-B-L-E
- God's Word Will Never Fail
- Standing on the Promises
- Every Promise in the Book is Mine
- Read Your Bible, Pray Every Day
- God Will Make A Way


## CHAPTER 17
## THE WAIST OF GOD
SONGS:
- Sound of Heaven—Terry MacAlmon #5 Righteous Ruler
- Great is Thy Faithfulness
- Only You are Holy
- Watch your lips, watch your lips what they speak
- The steadfast love of the LORD never ceases

- Your Steadfast Love extends to the heavens
- Fear thou not for I am with you…I will uphold you with the right hand of my righteousness
- Faithful is our God—Hezekiah Walker
- God is faithful (Brooklyn Tabernacle)

## CHAPTER 18
## THE HAIR OF GOD
SONGS:
- Give me a Clean Heart
- Create In Me A Clean Heart
- Create In Me A Clean Heart And Purify Me (Donnie McClurkin)
- Purify my heart
- Lord Jesus I Long to be Perfectly Whole
- O To Be Like Thee

CD
- Pure in Heart #7 "Pure in Heart"

## CHAPTER 19
## THE HEAD OF GOD
SONGS:
- Above All
- Lord You Reign
- Ancient Of Days
- Immortal, Invisible God Only Wise
- Hosanna in the Highest (Israel & New Breed)
- Crown Him With Many Crowns
- Now Unto the King Eternal
- I Worship You In The Beauty Of Holiness

- Majesty, Worship His Majesty
- Come Let us Worship & Bow Down
- Mighty is Our God, Mighty is Our King
- Take Me to The King
- Hosanna, Hosanna, Hosanna In The Highest
- Glory, Glory LORD
- All Hail King Jesus
- What A Mighty God We Serve
- You Are God Alone
- I See the LORD Seated On The Throne

CD
- Sound of Heaven—Terry MacAlmon #9 "My God & King"

## CHAPTER 20
## THE FOREHEAD OF GOD
SONGS:
- I Want To Know You, William McDowell
- I Wanna Know Your Ways, Fred Hammond
- No Secrets, Worship Outreach
- We Worship You Today, Darwin Hobbs
- Hungry, Jeremy Camp
- I Will Never Let God #15, The Bride, Terry MacAlmon

## CHAPTER 21
## THE THIGH OF GOD
El Elyon—God Most High
SONGS:
- King Of Kings Forever And Ever
- All Hail King Jesus
- He Is The King Of Kings
- You're Royalty
- Lead On O King Eternal

- Above All
- Our God is Greater
- Revelation Song
- Who Is Like Unto Thee?
- O LORD, O LORD How Majestic is Your Name
- Immortal, Invisible God Only Wise
- We Exalt Thee
- There is None Like You
- Holy (Donnie McClurkin)
- Bring Forth the Royal Robe
- How Great is our God
- How Great Thou Art
- Your Presence is Heaven to Me
- Hosanna
- Thank You For the Cross LORD
- Laad Yu Gud  JoAnn Richards
- You Are the Most High, You are the Most High God
- LORD God of Abraham, Isaac & Israel
- Exalt the LORD our God

CD
- Pure in Heart #1 "Worthy is the Lamb"; # 12 "Be Exalted"

Have a procession using I Chronicles 15:1-16:3; II Samuel 6:12-19 as a guide

- Prepare a purple banner with gold tassels that reads "KING OF KINGS; LORD OF LORDS"
- Priests to form a bugle corps/trumpets to march at the head of the procession
- Ministers—consecrate yourselves in preparation (the holiness of God demands the purity of God's people engaged in the service or worship of God).
- Singers/worship leaders & orchestra—the procession must be marked by:

Shouts of joy
Blowing of horns and trumpets
Crashing of cymbals
Loud playing on the harps
Loud and joyous playing on the instruments
- Pause at regular intervals to offer sacrifices of thanksgiving and praise to the King of kings and dance with all your might Readings Psalm 105:1-5; Psalm 96
- At the end, bless the people and the name of the LORD

Now unto the King eternal, immortal, invisible, the only wise God, be glory and honour forever and ever amen, amen, be glory and honor and power forever amen!!!

# SCRIPTURE INDEX

This Scripture Index is a quick reference guide to passages from the Word of God that
1. make direct reference to an aspect of the Anatomy of God;
2. are dealt with in this Study and relate indirectly to the Anatomy of God

**GENESIS**
1:3,6,9,11,14 ........ Mouth
1:30 ........................ Breath
2:7 .......................... Breath
3:8 .......................... Eye
3:9 .......................... Voice
14:19 ...................... Thigh
15:16 ...................... Eye
16:13 ...................... Face
18:12-15 ................ Ear
18:20-32 ................ Mind
19:29 ...................... Ear
32:30 ...................... Face

**EXODUS**
2:23 ........................ Ear
2:25 ........................ Eye
3:7-9,1 ................... Eye/Ear
7:20-21 .................. Thigh
8:3-4, 13-14,17 ........ Thigh

8:19 .......................... Finger
9:3,6 ....................... Thigh
9:20 .......................... Voice
10:7 .......................... Voice
10:21-23 ................. Thigh
11:4-6 ..................... Thigh
12:12 ....................... Thigh
13:3 .......................... Hand
13:9,16 ................... Forehead
14:21 ....................... Breath
15 .............................. Hand
15:3-18 ................... Thigh
15:8, 10 .................. Breath
15:16 ....................... Arm
15:26 ....................... Voice
16:3 .......................... Hand
17:1-7 ..................... Voice
17:15 ....................... Arm
18:9-11 ................... Thigh
19:19 ....................... Voice
22:26-27 ................. Ear
24:9-10 ................... Feet
28:36-38 ................. Forehead
31:18 ....................... Finger
32:15-16 ................. Finger
33:11,20 ................. Face
33:22-23 ................. Hand
33:23 ....................... Back
34:6 .......................... Waist
34:29 ....................... Face

**NUMBERS**
6:25 .......................... Face
12:8 .......................... Face
14:14 ....................... Face
22:21-31 ................. Eye
23:19 ....................... Mind
24:11 ....................... Voice
33:3-4 ..................... Thigh

**DEUTERONOMY**
1:45 .......................... Ear
2:14-15 ................... Hand
4:33-36 ................... Voice
4:34 .......................... Arm
5:4 ............................. Face
5:23-29 ................... Voice
5:28 .......................... Ear
5:29 .......................... Heart
6:8 ............................. Forehead
6:17 .......................... Eye
7:19 .......................... Arm
9:10 .......................... Finger
9:29 .......................... Arm
10:17 ....................... Thigh
11:12 ....................... Eye
12:25 ....................... Eye
30:20 ....................... Voice
31:17 ....................... Face
32:10 ....................... Eye
32:20 ....................... Face
33:3 .......................... Hand, Feet
34:10 ....................... Face

## JOSHUA
4:21-24 ................. Hand
10:24 ...................... Feet

## JUDGES
6:22-23 ................. Face
13:18 ...................... Forehead
13:22 ...................... Face

## I SAMUEL
1:10-20 ................. Ear
2:35 ........................ Mind
3:8-10 .................... Voice
13:14 ...................... Heart
15:29 ...................... Mind
15:22 ...................... Voice
16:7 ........................ Heart
17:48-49 ................ Forehead

## I KINGS
5:3 .......................... Feet
8:42 ........................ Hand
18:16-39 ................ Thigh
18:29 ...................... Voice
19:12-1 .................. Voice
19:14 ...................... Ear
20:35-36 ................ Voice

## II KINGS
5:15 ........................ Thigh
20:5 ........................ Ear

## I CHRONICLES
16:11 ...................... Face
16:25 ...................... Thigh
28:19 ...................... Finger
29:12,14,16 ........... Hand

## II CHRONICLES
2:5 .......................... Thigh
6:15 ........................ Hand
7:14 ........................ Face/Ear
7:16 ........................ Heart
9:18 ........................ Feet
16:9 ........................ Eye
32:1-23 .................. Arm

## EZRA
7:6,9,27-28 ............ Hand
8:18,22-23, 31 ....... Hand
9:6 .......................... Face

## NEHEMIAH
2:7-8, 18 ................ Hand

## ESTHER
6:1 .......................... Finger

## JOB
1:20 ........................ Feet
4:8-11 .................... Hand,
 Breath,
 Teeth
5:18 ........................ Hand

| Reference | Body Part |
|---|---|
| 7:17-20 | Eye |
| 9:13 | Feet |
| 10:8-9 | Hand |
| 11:7-8 | Mind |
| 11:11 | Eye |
| 12:10 | Hand |
| 15:30 | Breath |
| 16:7 | Eye |
| 16:9 | Teeth |
| 19:26-27 | Face |
| 22:22 | Mouth |
| 23:10 | Finger |
| 23:12 | Mouth, Lips |
| 24:23 | Eye |
| 26:13 | Breath |
| 27:3-4 | Breath |
| 27:13-23 | Hand |
| 29:17 | Teeth |
| 31:4 | Finger |
| 32:8 | Breath |
| 33:4 | Breath |
| 33:14-19 | Voice |
| 34:14-15 | Breath |
| 34:19 | Hand |
| 34:21 | Finger |
| 34:21-25 | Eye |
| 34:27-28 | Ear |
| 34:29 | Face |
| 36:5 | Mind |
| 36:26,32 | Hand |
| 37:2-5 | Voice, Mouth |
| 37:10 | Breath |
| 38:41 | Ear |
| 40:9 | Voice, Arm |
| 41:21 | Breath |

**PSALMS**

| Reference | Body Part |
|---|---|
| 2:4 | Mouth |
| 3:7 | Teeth |
| 4:1-3 | Ear |
| 4:6 | Face |
| 5:1-3 | Ear |
| 5:6 | Ear |
| 7:17 | Thigh |
| 8:3 | Finger |
| 9:4, 7 | Head |
| 9:12 | Ear |
| 11:4 | Eye, Head |
| 13:1 | Face |
| 16:8,9-11 | Hand |
| 17:1-2, 6 | Ear |
| 17:7,14 | Hand |
| 17:8 | Eye |
| 18:6 | Ear |
| 18:8 | Breath, Mouth |
| 18:9 | Feet |
| 18:13 | Voice |
| 18:15 | Breath |
| 18:19 | Heart |
| 18:24 | Eye |
| 18:25 | Waist |
| 18:30 | Mind |

| | | | |
|---|---|---|---|
| 18:35 | Hand | 48:7 | Breath |
| 18:49 | Face | 48:10 | Hand |
| 19:1 | Hand | 51:7 | Hair |
| 19:9 | Hair | 51:9 | Face |
| 21:7 | Thigh | 55:1-2, 17 | Ear |
| 21:8 | Hand | 57:2 | Thigh |
| 24:6 | Face | 57:4 | Teeth |
| 25:4-10 | Eye | 57:10 | Waist |
| 27:8 | Face | 59:8 | Mouth |
| 28:1-2 | Ear | 59:17 | Ear |
| 28:9 | Arm | 61:7 | Waist |
| 29 | Voice | 62:12 | Eye |
| 30:7 | Face | 63:8 | Hand |
| 31:15,20 | Hand | 66:7 | Eye |
| 31:16 | Face | 66:17-19 | Ear |
| 33:4, 6 | Mouth | 67:1 | Face |
| 33:11 | Heart, Mind | 68:33 | Voice |
| 33:13-18 | Eye | 69:1,13,33 | Ear |
| 34:15 | Eye, Ear | 71:2 | Ear |
| 34:16 | Face, Mind | 73:1 | Hair |
| 37:13 | Mouth | 73:13 | Hair |
| 37:18 | Eye | 74:11 | Fist |
| 37:23-24 | Hand, Finger | 74:17 | Hand |
| 39:10-11 | Hand | 75:8 | Hand |
| 39:12 | Ear | 77:13-18 | Thigh |
| 44:2-3 | Hand, Arm | 77:16-19 | Feet |
| 44:4,24 | Face | 77:15 | Arm |
| 45:5 | Feet | 77:18 | Voice |
| 46:6 | Voice | 78:1 | Mouth |
| 47:2 | Thigh | 78:35 | Thigh |
| 47:8 | Head | 79:11 | Arm |
| | | 80:3, 7,19 | Face |

| | | | |
|---|---|---|---|
| 80:14 | Eye | 108:4 | Waist |
| 81:11-14 | Hand | 110:1 | Feet |
| 83:18 | Thigh | 110:4 | Mind |
| 89:1, 8 | Waist | 113:4-5 | Head |
| 89:6 | Thigh | 115:1 | Waist |
| 89:10 | Arm | 115:4-6 | Voice |
| 89:13 | Hand, Arm | 118:10-16 | Arm |
| 89:14 | Head | 119:58,135 | Face |
| 89:15-16 | Face | 119:72,88,130 | Mouth |
| 89:19 | Mouth | 121:5-8 | Hand, Eye |
| 89:34 | Mind, Lips | 125:2 | Hand |
| 91:1 | Thigh | 132:9 | Hair |
| 91:4 | Waist | 135:5-7.15 | Thigh |
| 92:1 | Thigh | 135:15-17 | Voice |
| 93:1 | Head | 136:2-3 | Thigh |
| 95:2-3 | Thigh | 136:11-12 | Arm |
| 95:4-5 | Hand | 138:4 | Mouth |
| 95:7-9 | Voice | 138:7 | Hand, Fist |
| 96:4-5 | Thigh | 138:8 | Finger |
| 97:7-9 | Thigh | 139:9-10 | Hand |
| 98:1 | Arm | 139:7-12 | Eye |
| 99:1-5 | Thigh | 139:2-18 | Finger |
| 102:1,2 | Face, Ear | 143:7 | Face |
| 102:17, 19 | Ear | 144:1 | Finger |
| 102:27 | Mind | 145:8-9 | Heart |
| 103:6 | Ear | 145:16 | Hand |
| 103:15-16 | Breath | 147:15 | Mouth |
| 103:19 | Head | 147:16-27 | Breath |
| 104:28 | Hand | | |
| 104:29 | Face | **PROVERBS** | |
| 105:4 | Face | 2:6 | Mouth |
| 107:20,25 | Mouth | 3:6 | Voice |

15:3 .......................... Eye
15:26 ........................ Hair
16:31 ........................ Hair
20:11,29 .................... Hair
21:1 .......................... Hand
22:11 ........................ Hair
27:19 ........................ Heart
30:4 .......................... Hand
30:14 ........................ Teeth

**ECCLESIASTES**
2:24-26 ................... Hand

**SONG OF SOLOMON**
2:14 .......................... Voice, Face

**ISAIAH**
1:15-17 .................... Eye
1:18 .......................... Hair
1:19-20 .................... Mouth
5:25 .......................... Hand
6:1-5 ........................ Face
9:12 .......................... Fist
11:3 .......................... Ear
11:4 .......................... Breath, Mouth
11:5 .......................... Waist
14:13-14 .................. Thigh
14:26-27 .................. Hand
16:12 ........................ Thigh
17:1-2,8 ................... Thigh
19:1 .......................... Thigh

19:16 ........................ Hand
23:4, 8-9 .................. Thigh
26:11 ........................ Hand
30:1-4 ...................... Hand
30:21,30-31 ........... Voice
30:27,30 .................. Lips, Tongue
30:28, 33 ................. Breath
30:30,32 ................... Arm
31:2 .......................... Mind
31:2b-3 .................... Hand
31:3 .......................... Fist
32:1-2,4 ................... Hand
34:16 ........................ Mouth
34:17 ........................ Hand
40:5 .......................... Mouth
40:6-7 ...................... Breath
40:10 ........................ Arm
40:11 ........................ Heart, Arm
40:12 ........................ Hand
40:13 ........................ Mind
40:17 ........................ Breath
40:23-24 ................. Breath
40:28-31 ................. Thigh
41:10 ........................ Hand
43:13 ........................ Hand
44:6-20 ................... Voice
45:11-12 ................. Hand
45:19, 23 ................. Mouth
46:1-2,9 .................. Thigh
46:10-11 ................. Mouth
48:3-7 ...................... Mouth

| | | | |
|---|---|---|---|
| 48:13 | Hand | **JEREMIAH** | |
| 49:2, 15-16 | Hand | 1:9 | Hand |
| 50:2 | Arm | 3:15 | Heart |
| 51:5 | Arm | 7:31 | Mind |
| 51:9 | Arm | 10:3 | Voice |
| 51:16,17 | Hand | 14:17 | Eye |
| 52:1 | Face | 15:1 | Mind |
| 52:10 | Arm | 15:6 | Fist |
| 53:1 | Arm | 16:17 | Eye |
| 53:2-5 | Face | 17:5 | Arm |
| 53:7,9 | Mouth | 18:7-10 | Mind |
| 54:8 | Face | 18:17 | Face |
| 55:8-9 | Mind | 21:5 | Arm |
| 55:10-11 | Mouth | 23:20 | Heart |
| 56:1 | Thigh | 23:23-24 | Eye |
| 57:17 | Face | 25:12-17 | Hand |
| 58:3-4, 6-9 | Ear | 27:5 | Arm |
| 59:1 | Ear | 29:23 | Eye |
| 59:1, 16 | Arm | 30:24 | Heart |
| 59:2 | Face | 32:17, 21 | Arm |
| 59:15-21 | Breath | 32:19 | Eye |
| 62:2 | Mouth | 46:15, 25 | Thigh |
| 62:3 | Hand | 48:7, 12-13 | Thigh |
| 62:8 | Arm | 49:3 | Thigh |
| 63:5, 11b-12 | Arm | 50:2 | Thigh |
| 64:7 | Face | 51:44,52 | Thigh |
| 64:8 | Hand | | |
| 65:2 | Hand | **LAMENTATIONS** | |
| 65:3 | Face | 3:22-23 | Waist |
| 65:24 | Ear | | |
| 66:1 | Head | **EZEKIEL** | |
| 66:2 | Hand | 1:18 | Eye |
| 66:6 | Voice | | |

1:24 ..................... Voice
1:26-28 ................. Waist
3:14.22 ................. Hand
8:1 ......................... Hand
15:7-8 ................... Face
16:26-7 ................. Fist
22:13 ..................... Finger
25:12-13 ............... Fist
33:22 ..................... Hand
34 .......................... Heart
35:3-4 ................... Fist
37:1 ....................... Hand
37:4-10 ................. Breath
39:23 ..................... Face
40:1 ....................... Hand
44:12 ..................... Hand
47:14 ..................... Hand

## DANIEL
2:22 ....................... Eye
2:47 ....................... Thigh
3:26 ....................... Thigh
4:34 ....................... Thigh
6:25-26 ................. Thigh
7:6 ......................... Head
7:9 ......................... Hair
8:25 ....................... Hand
9:11-13 ................. Voice
9:17 ....................... Face
9:18 ....................... Eye
10:6 ....................... Voice, Face

## HOSEA
7:9 ......................... Thigh
12:4 ....................... Face
12:4-5 ................... Mouth
13:12 ..................... Eye

## AMOS
5:25-27 ................. Thigh
9:3-4,8 ................. Eye

## JONAH
1:16 ....................... Thigh

## MICAH
2:7 ......................... Mouth
3:4 ......................... Face, Ear
4:12 ....................... Mind

## NAHUM
1:2-3 ..................... Feet

## HABAKKUK
1:13 ....................... Hair
2:16 ....................... Hand
3:4 ......................... Hand
3:19 ....................... Thigh

## ZEPHANIAH
1:4 ......................... Fist
3:2 ......................... Voice
3:14-15 ................. Hand
3:17 ....................... Voice, Mouth

## HAGGAI
2:23 .......................... Finger

## ZECHARIAH
2:8 .............................. Eye
2:8-9 .......................... Fist
3:9 .............................. Eye
4:10 ............................ Eye
7:11-12 .................... Voice
10:12 ........................ Hand
12:11 ......................... Thigh

## MALACHI
2:15 ........................... Hair
3:16 ........................... Ear

## MATTHEW
3:17 ........................... Voice
4:4 .............................. Mouth
5:8 .............................. Hair
7:28 ............................ Head
11:29 ......................... Heart
17:1-3 ........................ Face
18:10 ......................... Face
23:12 ........................ Forehead
28:2-3 ....................... Hair
28:8-10 .................... Feet

## MARK
1:22 ........................... Head
7:32-35 .................. Finger, Mouth
8:22-25 .................... Mouth
14:60-61 .................. Mouth
15:3-5 ...................... Mouth
15:24 ........................ Feet
16:5 ............................ Hair

## LUKE
1:51 ........................... Arm
1:66 ........................... Hand
4:32 ............................ Head
4:38 ............................ Mouth
4:40 ............................ Hand
5:8 .............................. Feet
6:47-49 ................... Voice
7:13 ............................ Heart
7:16 ............................ Hand
8:28 ............................ Feet
10:38-39 ................. Feet
11:20 ......................... Finger
21:33 ......................... Voice
22:70-71 ................. Mouth
24 ............................... Hand
24:39-40 ................. Feet

## JOHN
5:25, 28-29 ............ Voice
8:6 .............................. Finger
9:31 ............................ Ear
10:3,27 .................... Voice
11:32 ......................... Feet
11:41 ......................... Ear
12:3 ............................ Feet

13:15 .................... Feet
19:34-37 ............... Side
20:20 .................... Side
20:22 .................... Breath

## ACTS
2:17 ...................... Voice
4:30 ...................... Hand
7:31-32 ................ Voice
7:49-50 ................ Hand
10:1-4 .................. Ear
13:9-11 ................ Hand
13:22 .................... Heart
15:9 ...................... Hair
22:2 ...................... Feet

## ROMANS
3:3-4 .................... Waist
11:33-34 .............. Mind

## I CORINTHIANS
2:16 ...................... Mind
13:12 .................... Face
15:25 .................... Feet

## II CORINTHIANS
1:8-10 .................. Hand
7:1 ........................ Hair

## GALATIANS
1:8-9 .................... Voice

## EPHESIANS
1:22 ...................... Feet
4:2, 11 .................. Heart
4:21 ...................... Voice
5:1 ........................ Heart
6:14 ...................... Waist
6:17 ...................... Mouth

## PHILIPPIANS
2:5 ........................ Mind
4:8 ........................ Hair

## II THESSALONIANS
2:8-10 .................. Breath

## I TIMOTHY
1:5 ........................ Hair
5:1-2, 22 .............. Hair
6:15-16 ................ Thigh

## TITUS
1:15 ...................... Hair
2:3-5 .................... Hair

## HEBREWS
1:1 ........................ Face
4:13 ...................... Eye
7:26 ...................... Hair
10:12-13 .............. Feet
10:30-31 .............. Hand
12:9 ...................... Head

## JAMES

| | |
|---|---|
| 1:2 | Teeth |
| 1:24 | Eye |
| 1:27 | Hair |
| 3:17 | Hair |
| 4:8 | Hair, Side |
| 5:4 | Ear |
| 13:4 | Hair |

## I PETER

| | |
|---|---|
| 2:23 | Hand |
| 3:2 | Hair |
| 3:7 | Ear |
| 3:12 | Eye, Face, Ear |

## I JOHN

| | |
|---|---|
| 1:7,9 | Hair |
| 4:1 | Voice |
| 5:6-8 | Voice |
| 5:14 | Ear |

## REVELATION

| | |
|---|---|
| 1:5 | Thigh |
| 1:14 | Eye, Hair, Head |
| 1:15 | Voice, Feet |
| 1:16 | Hand, Face, Mouth |
| 2:12, 16 | Mouth |
| 2:18 | Eye |
| 3:4 | Hair |
| 3:20 | Voice |
| 4:4 | Hair |
| 4:10 | Head |
| 5:6 | Eye |
| 6:11 | Hair |
| 7:9,13 | Hair |
| 7:15 | Head |
| 14:14 | Head |
| 14:18 | Eye |
| 17:14 | Thigh |
| 19:4 | Head |
| 19:12 | Eye, Head |
| 19:12 | Forehead |
| 19:14 | Hair |
| 19:15, 21 | Mouth |
| 19:16 | Thigh |
| 20:11 | Face |
| 21:5-6 | Head |
| 22:3-4 | Face |

# BIBLIOGRAPHY

Hickey, M. (2009). *The names of God.* New Kensington, PA, USA: Whitaker House.

Kapur, T. (2007, April 7). Jesus' suffering and crucifixion from a medical point of view [Transcription of an article given by Dr. Keith Maxwell]. *South Asian Connection.* Retrieved March 2012, from http://www.southasianconnection.com/articles/184/1/Jesus-Suffering-and-Crucifixion-From-a-Medical-Point-of-View

Kroll, W. *Lessons on living from Moses: Living in the valleys.* USA: Back to the Bible.

Kroll, W. (1997). *Lessons on living from Moses: The practice of God's presence.* USA: Back to the Bible.

Kroll, W. (2007). *Knowing God better.* Back to the Bible (Meet With God Series). USA: The Good News Broadcasting Association, Inc.

Meyer, J. (2006). *The battlefield of the mind for teens: Winning the battle in your mind.* USA: FaithWords.

Padfield, D. (2002). *Against all the gods of Egypt.* Retrieved October 2011, from http://www.padfield.com/acrobat/history/gods_of_egypt.pdf

Walker, J. (2011, March 8). *Why is it essential to hear God?* [Daily Hope With Rick Warren](Vol. Purpose Driven Connection).

Warren, R. (2002). *The purpose driven life: What on earth am I here for?* Grand Rapids, MI, USA: Zondervan.

Warren, R. (2011, March). *How to recognize God's voice* [Daily Hope With Rick Warren](Vol. Purpose Driven Connection).

Matthew Henry's Commentary on the Whole Bible. Retrieved October 2011, from www.biblestudytools.com/commentaries/matthew-henry-complete/1-samuel/5.html.

Matthew Henry's Commentary on the Whole Bible. Retrieved December 2011, from www.biblestudytools.com/commentaries/matthew-henry-complete/exodus/17.html.

www.ingramcontent.com/pod-product-compliance
Lightning Source LLC
Chambersburg PA
CBHW072002150426
43194CB00008B/971